T0320059

# CRITICAL RACE THEORY AND THE SEARCH FOR TRUTH

"Through the lens of Critical Race Theory, Rodney D. Coates has produced a powerful analysis of racism in the modern world. While this book focuses on the immense negative consequences of global racism for the oppressed, it does much more. It shines an illuminating light on the pivotal struggles launched by oppressed Black people to free themselves and liberate humanity. In so doing, *Critical Race Theory and the Search for Truth* is a must-read for all concerned about dismantling the current conflicts rocking the modern world."
**Aldon Morris, Northwestern University**

"Rodney D. Coates completely debunks the Critical Race Theory misrepresentations with resounding clarity, professional impartiality, and, above all else, authentic truths."
**Woodrow Keown Jr., National Underground Railroad Freedom Center**

"Just when we needed a clearheaded, analytical, and creative analysis of Critical Race Theory, Rodney D. Coates has given us just what we – and the public – need. Coates's book is a welcome antidote to public misconceptions about the origins and meaning of Critical Race Theory."
**Margaret L. Andersen, University of Delaware**

"For years, Rodney D. Coates has been a go-to public scholar whose interdisciplinary and encyclopedic knowledge has helped people around the nation understand a critical counter-narrative to racialized stories of 'western civilization's' triumph and what Du Bois called 'history as propaganda.' This book demonstrates Coates's coherent take on what Critical Race Theory is, why it's such an important intellectual tool, and how its success has placed it in the crosshairs of White nationalists and their political operatives. This book is a must-read for anyone hoping to stave off fascism and build a true multicultural democracy."
**Corey Dolgon, Stonehill College**

"Mindful of the deep historical and intellectual foundations of systemic racism theory and of what has aptly been referred to as 'the Black radical tradition' in African American social thought, Rodney D. Coates's *Critical Race Theory and the Search for Truth* makes its case that 'racism is systemic and that it is interconnected with other systems of oppression.' Viewing Critical Race Theory as 'just the most recent attempt' of the racially oppressed to conceptualize their oppression, he skilfully places its development and its opposition in their proper social and historical context. From there Professor Coates takes us on an insightful journey through time and space with his critical analysis of systemic racism in both the United States and in Haiti."

**Noel A. Cazenave, University of Connecticut and author of *Conceptualizing Racism***

# Sociology of Diversity

Series Editor: **David G. Embrick**, University of Connecticut, US

---

This series brings together the highest quality sociological and interdisciplinary research that critically engages with the broad topic of diversity and inclusion, including, but not limited to topics that cover racism, ethnic oppression, gender, sexuality(ies), class and immigration.

## Scan the code below to discover new and forthcoming titles in the series, or visit:

bristoluniversitypress.co.uk/
sociology-of-diversity

# CRITICAL RACE THEORY AND THE SEARCH FOR TRUTH

Rodney D. Coates

BRISTOL
UNIVERSITY
PRESS

First published in Great Britain in 2024 by

Bristol University Press
University of Bristol
1–9 Old Park Hill
Bristol
BS2 8BB
UK
t: +44 (0)117 374 6645
e: bup-info@bristol.ac.uk

Details of international sales and distribution partners are available at bristoluniversitypress.co.uk

© Bristol University Press 2024

British Library Cataloguing in Publication Data
A catalogue record for this book is available from the British Library

ISBN 978-1-5292-2833-5 hardcover
ISBN 978-1-5292-2834-2 paperback
ISBN 978-1-5292-2835-9 ePub
ISBN 978-1-5292-2836-6 ePdf

Cover design: blu inc
Front cover image: Stocksy/Matt Watson
Bristol University Press uses environmentally responsible print partners.
Printed and bound in Great Britain by CPI Group (UK) Ltd, Croydon, CR0 4YY

FSC
www.fsc.org
MIX
Paper | Supporting
responsible forestry
FSC® C013604

# Contents

# Series Editor Preface

The year 2023 was gut-wrenching for me and many of my colleagues, certainly a foul endcap to a series of years that began before the COVID-19 pandemic. In 2022, I asked just how many rights are we collectively willing to lose before enough is enough, that year marking the historical heartbreaking decision of the U.S. Supreme Court to reverse *Roe* v *Wade*. In the year to follow, we witnessed further attacks to academic freedom; the stifling of protests; whitelash against changes to the White supremacist status quo; anti-DEI/JB (diversity, equity, inclusion/justice, belonging), anti-CRT (Critical Race Theory), and anti-woke sentiments and legislature; increased antisemitic and anti-Muslim hate across the globe; and attempts (some failed yet some successful) at rewriting history(ies) in ways that further erase or render invisible U.S. racism and ethnic oppression. As I write this series preface, we are only a couple of weeks in to 2024 and it remains to be seen what further freedoms will be lost, and in what ways will whitelash continue to regain lost nostalgic White supremacist ground (forget about maintaining the status quo). The anti-CRT and anti-DEI/JB rhetoric that has spread across the United States, and in several states like Texas, Florida, and Oklahoma (33 states as of December 2023) that have passed anti-DEI legislation, is alarming although it was not a surprise to those of us who have been studying diversity in the U.S. for the past many years. Several scholars, me included, questioned diversity ideology in higher education and other institutions as empty rhetoric. So, attacks against DEI are political at best. However, it does allow for liberal diversity "champions" to make claims that were it not for right-wing politicians/politics, we would be better off in terms of racial and other forms of equity and equality. There is little evidence for many U.S. institutions that this is true. And I would suggest that many such organizations who claim this are more likely to be White sanctuaries than bastions of critical diversity. Yet here we are.

So how might we best understand the current moment? And more specifically, how can we critically examine what is going on throughout the U.S. regarding the attacks, politically and socially, against DEI/JB and CRT. Enter the latest book published in the *Sociology of Diversity* series titled *Critical Race Theory and the Search for Truth*, authored by Dr. Rodney D. Coates.

In this book, Dr. Coates provides a contextual and historical overview on CRT, tracing its roots to Dr. Derrick Bell and weaving its course through the U.S. legal apparatus, higher education, and other institutions. In doing so, Dr. Coates aims to provide the readers with various perspectives on not just the original intents of CRT as a critical lens from which to fully capture systemic and institutional racism, but also the myriad ways that CRT has been misunderstood, misused, and/or co-opted, and ultimately made out to be one of the tools of the anti-White boogeyman. *Critical Race Theory and the Search for Truth* goes deeper than many superficial books on CRT, with topics that cover covert racism, imperialism and the racial state, the process of othering, and resistance. Unfortunately, the book also serves as a reminder of just how much work we still need to do to get to the promised land. Fortunately, it also makes visible what is often rendered invisible, so we are reminded of what is, and what could be.

*David G. Embrick*
*University of Connecticut*
*Series Editor*

# Acknowledgements

I was blessed to be born into a supportive family. My mother and father taught me the value of being true to myself. My brothers, Kenneth and Kevin, always challenged me to do more than survive but to achieve at the highest levels. I grew up in what many call a ghetto, but I call home. Rather than a ghetto, East St. Louis was a rich community of history, love, and Blackness. I did not have to discover my Blackness, I grew up in Blackness. These experiences fostered a different reality, a different agenda, and a different perspective on life. To my children, Angela Renea, Christopher, and Avery – this one is for you. Thanks for allowing me to be your dad. And to the hundreds of people who have read various sections of this project over the past few years, your insight, encouragement, and critiques helped to make this volume come into being. To Anna Richardson, Emily Ross, and Gail Welsh from Bristol University Press, thanks for your confidence in this project. So while I have made every attempt to document every source, I recognize that over my career I have thousands of manuscripts, heard even more presentations. These going back decades have helped shape my thinking. I recognize that there is no such things as originality, just new ways of viewing old things. Past all this, I alone accept responsibility for errors of both omission and commission. Experience has taught me that I am not perfect but authentic. Herein lies my testimony to how blessed we, the Africans, are as a people.

Chapters 6 and 7, and the stereotypes that are described are indebted to the historical, and phenomenal pioneering work of David Pilgrim and the Jim Crow Museum.

# What's in a Name?

Africans in America have gone by several names, from Colored to Negro to People of Color, Black and African American. The changes reflect attempts by Blacks to control not only how they are viewed but how they view themselves. The term one uses reflects a particular historical period and a political stance. Hence, there are some from a previous era who preferred Negro or Colored, while since the civil rights movement, the terms Black and African American have held sway. One can even find some who use what might be considered inclusive language and the term People of Color. I am a product of the civil rights movement and have consistently used either Black or African American. It reflects my historical reality and my positionality.

# Introduction: Critical Race Theory

During the insanity of war, an unknown pregnant woman and her baby were killed as a massive missile attack destroyed the maternity ward where she and other expectant mothers were being treated. They join thousands who have died and millions who have been displaced as a result of what can only be called the egomaniacal desires of an autocrat.

As a paranoid dictator, Vladimir Putin joins not only his predecessor, Stalin, but a list of others, such as Hitler, Idi Amin, Papa Doc, and Ferdinand Marcos. Like these other dictators, Putin has no concern for what will happen once he leaves the scene. Putin frankly doesn't care, as he follows the script laid down by dictators who came before.

One such example comes from 1757 when King Louis XV of France dismissed the stunning defeat in the battle of Rossbach. According to one account, Madame de Pompadour, equally unfazed, declared "après nous le deluge," or "after us, the deluge" (Mould, 2011). Such dismal conditions are standard fare for failure among autocrats and dictators.

Similarly, Putin exhibits a nihilistic indifference to the consequences of his actions. The reality is that this insane war was premeditated, conspicuous, and deliberately conceived and executed by Vladimir Putin. The truth is that Vladimir Putin is waging this war, has been planning this war, and has no intentions of ending this war until Ukraine no longer exists and its people have been annihilated. And this will serve no political, economic, or sane reason other than the inflation of Putin's ego. These same truths are part and parcel of the history and reality of racial imperialism across time, space, and reality. These truths are the essence of this volume.

Let us begin.

There are many truths, as many as there are realities. What truths you subscribe to in many ways reflects the position you occupy. The truth of a child is different from that of their parents, and the truth of the victim is different from that of the victimizer. Which truth you choose to adhere to is the truth you will live by. But all truths, as with all realities, grant your insight. The more truths you can learn, the more understanding you will gain. And there is nothing worse than those who choose to be ignorant of multiple truths or believe that there is one truth.

The basic premise of this volume has been that for far too long, the truth has been externally provided to Blacks and others who do not occupy positions of power within the racial state. In our current political climate, the truth is dictated by those in power from the extreme right. Books are banned, teachers and professors are silenced or fired, and schools and institutions are sanctioned or defunded because they dare to present different "truths."

This is not the first time in our country or world that those in power have victimized truth claims. Typically, as this volume will document, it has been in those times when the "racial power elite" perceived existential threats that they used all power at their disposal to curtail, derail, or destroy alternative versions of the truth. Therefore, the first laws to control the enslaved Africans in this country followed the successful Haitian Revolution and the fear of similar revolutions. The slavocracy, gripped with the fear of similar slave rebellions, banned reading and writing for the African – slave and free. As the enslaved people gained freedom during Reconstruction, the first institutions that were constructed were the church and schools. The first things to be destroyed by the Ku Klux Klan and other anti-Black groups were the churches, followed by the businesses. To control the Native Americans, the U.S. government established boarding schools where the motto was "Kill the Injun, save the man." Consequently, we see Native American children forcibly removed from their homes, stripped of their names, hair, language, customs, and identities, and inculcated into the "whitened truths of imperial history." And the racial state came into full bloom.

It would take a hundred years and the various civil rights movements to finally challenge the racial truths embedded in every aspect of the U.S. educational apparatus. With these challenges, calls for more equitable and inclusive histories and pedagogies were heard. For a brief period, what may be called the "second reconstruction," racial and ethnic studies, women and gender studies, were presented and coexisted with the standard "racial imperialized" version. These programs, particularly at colleges and universities, never were intended to replace the dominant version, but at least they gave the "illusion of inclusion." Such programs in higher education, underfunded and overworked, have always existed on the periphery of the academy. But they existed, nonetheless. Strangely, they never had the numbers (regarding faculty or students) to represent a serious threat, but they have always been suspected. Now, Critical Race Theory (CRT) and its proponents are being targeted by the extreme right. But it is not the academic programs that are at stake but the truth itself.

The current battles in the United States, Israel, and Ukraine are part of an old script that has occurred across time, space, and circumstances. It takes on many names but is often draped in the flags/ideologies of nation and patriotism, religion and science, history and reality. Strangely, these are all fictions created and maintained to preserve a particular racial order at all costs. As these racial orders are challenged, as they approach existential moments, they respond with virulent tactics that confuse those who dare to challenge the system. At the core of these responses is to control the narrative and assert which "truths" will be adhered to. Countering these constructed truths are alternative viewpoints, experiences, and realities. Together, these alternatives constitute the essence of what CRT is and what I mean by TRUTH.

Within the United States, the far right is now targeting CRT. In the 2022–2023 school year, 3,362 books were banned. In most cases, the banned books were written by women, people of color, and LGBTQIA+ authors (Meehan and Friedman, 2023). Across 24 state legislatures, a total of 54 different bills have been introduced to restrict education and training in K-12, higher education, and state agencies and institutions. Most of these bills target CRT and gender studies. They explicitly want to dictate what, how, and when American history is taught. Clearly, these bans are aimed at dictating academic and educational discussions and imposing state rules on how teaching is done (Meehan and Friedman, 2023). But this targeting is not for what CRT is doing, but what it might do if it continues to provide anti-racist critiques of our institutions and society. It could be argued that White conservative attacks against CRT are a call for "Uncritical Race Theory." These challenges lay bare the existential fears that threaten the very core of the racial state. In this chapter, I will outline how CRT might offer us some hope moving forward.

Let me begin with a story because I love stories. Wars and other crises have historically been the impetus for technological innovation. World War I provided the platform by which aviation advanced to become the dominant instrument of destruction. But as radar and global positioning satellites had not been invented, pilots had to navigate by the stars. One of the things that alerted the pilots that they were over the target was they would begin to get heavy flack. This leads to the conclusion that the hue, cry, and all the flack now targeting CRT indicate it is over the target. Why else would the racist be so upset? If CRT were indeed inconsequential or such a waste or misguided approach, why so much anger, angst, and frustration to the point where conservative legislators in virtually every Republican-dominated state are trying to ban its teaching or even its discussion? Every aspect of education, from K-12 through higher education, has been targeted to ensure that presumed CRT is not present. The charge: CRT is indoctrinating our youth by fostering racial divisions, hatred, and anti-democratic values. The strange thing is that within these concerted attempts to ban CRT, there is limited, at best, understanding of what CRT is. Why are they so afraid of CRT? Perhaps it targets the core problem with our racist American history.

CRT, deriving from both legal and feminist scholarship, starts from a set of assumptions. These assumptions are that systems of oppression, such as race, gender, sex, and class, are all interrelated and intersectional. So, while one might discuss them separately, only by understanding this intersectionality and their interrelatedness can one truly begin to grapple with this monster. Intersectionality is interwoven throughout our social institutions and history (Coates et al, 2021). While we might prefer analyses of race, gender, sexuality, or class as we discuss one facet versus another, all of these are intertwined. Hence, as William J. Wilson (1980) explains, race dictates the outcomes of many within our society. Although women of all races and ethnicities face the highest rate of poverty, it is among American Indians, Blacks, and Latinas that we see the highest rates. While Latinas are only 18.1 percent of all women in the U.S. population, they comprise over a quarter of women in poverty.

Similarly, while Black women are only 12.8 percent of all women in the United States, they make up 22.3 percent of those in poverty. And nearly one in four American Indian or Alaska Native women are impoverished (Bleiweis et al, 2020). Life chances have gotten worse for minoritized individuals, particularly Black males from poor urban backgrounds, radically different from those from more affluent backgrounds. This means that dealing with one facet without understanding the interconnectedness and intersectionality tells only part of the story. Racism, as it was used in the 1960s, was a term that applied to individuals who were biased and used these biases to discriminate against individuals or groups. As we entered the modern era, racism has been applied more and more at the institutional and societal level. Thus, many confuse the two terms. Therefore, I and others have begun using intersectionality and systemic racism to address these societal and institutional levels of racism. Even more, while those occupying liberal/moderate/centrist positions may have no problem with these terms, they nevertheless adhere to policies and politics that reproduce racial stratification (and as they intersect with gender, class, and sexuality). Consequently, we have many who explore the terms or concepts but whose analysis and policy recommendations do little to address the problems associated with the matrix of race, class, and gender.

Central to this volume will be the voices of marginalized people. Many who look at this process concentrate on the objectification, victimization, and marginalization of the Indigenous, the colonized, and the enslaved. What is essential is to understand that they are active agents. This means that Indigenous, colonized, and enslaved peoples were more than blank templates on which were written the epithets of racism and racialism. Still, they were already contemplative, whole peoples from societies that had already spent hundreds of years writing their own stories. We shall explore some of the central myths of both liberal and conservative historians that the history of these peoples began at the junction where they entered history as victims and rarely as thinking, sentient peoples. Failure to see this lie means that we fail to understand how counter-narratives and alternative narratives existed and persisted even as the racial transformations deliberately attempted to wipe their existence from the face of history. CRT advocates the essential use of storytelling (Cooper, 1993), counter-stories (Delgado Bernal, 1998; Villenas et al, 1999), and counter-narratives (Lather, 1998) as not only correctives but necessary transformative processes in producing equitable and systemic anti-racism policies, practices, and policies (Miller et al, 2020).

What is CRT? Essentially, it's a theory of oppression. The basic idea is that instead of being an invisible force or a force of nature, systems of oppression are socially constructed. These systems are further complicated by the intersections of race, gender, sex, and class as they work together to warp groups' life chances and create identities. The more integrated these systems are into our institutions, the more normal they appear. The more normal they seem, the less likely we will see them as arbitrary constructs. Time and space do not allow for examining all racialized social institutions. One example is higher education, which has been viewed over the decades as an important pathway toward a higher quality of life.

Nonetheless, higher education has seen the racial gap in both access and graduation get worse over time, past all the attempts to level this playing field. Black enrollment in colleges and universities has dropped 22 percent between 2010 and 2020. This means more than 650,000 fewer Black students are enrolled than a decade ago (National Center for Education Statistics, 2021). As states across the nation challenge diversity programs at public universities and as the Supreme Court has ruled against affirmative action in college admissions, we must ask whether higher education provides a level playing field, especially between Black and White Americans.

## Othering

Recently, I came across an interesting story in which Robert Sapolsky, a professor of biology, neurosurgery, and neurology, explains how herd animals tend to stay in packs. Trying to understand this behavior, Sapolsky decided to tag one wildebeest he was studying with a red spot.

Sapolsky was surprised that animals so tagged were killed by predators repeatedly. Predators, often unable to distinguish individual animals in a herd, responded to this marking. Such markings also apply to what we call Othering and have the same effect (Sapolsky et al, 2003).

Strangely, the very reason for racial and ethnic markers is to make human groups stand out so they can be targeted. But even further, the targeting within groups serves to mark those whose actions serve to single them out for even crueler victimization. Hence, we note that during slavery, the favored enslaved people might be made to wear an earring, while those less favored might have been branded with hot irons. Selected enslaved people might wear distinctive, colorful garb (such as the butler, cook, or carriage driver), while field hands wore discorded, often badly torn, clothes. (Sidebar: The fact that Black people made such clothing into fashion statements remains a cultural innovation even today. Consider hip-hop clothing.)

As noted by Szasz (1970), there is a long history of marking those deemed outside the norm. These markings served to marginalize, dehumanize, delegitimize, humiliate, and often punish certain individuals for being different. We have used such terms as evil, heretic, subhuman, feral, and insane to justify what Szasz refers to as a "rhetoric of rejection."

This rhetoric, he demonstrates, can be traced to the so-called father of modern psychology, Samuel A. Cartwright, who used the term "drapetomania," or the willful manifestation of aggressiveness, arrogance, or rebellion among slaves, leading to their seeking to escape from their slave masters.

The masters were, therefore, justified in using excessive force to return the enslaved person to the normal state. Consequently, those enslaved people that chose to speak out were also more likely to be marked with physical scars, even gelding and the loss of fingers, ears, and so on, to serve as a pointed reminder to both free and enslaved persons what happens when one dares to violate the rules.

In later years, such things as lynching, imprisonment, expulsion from schools, and capital punishment were to continue marking those who choose to deviate from the norm – and be Others. But first, let us deal with how CRT came into being.

## The origin of Critical Race Theory

CRT originates in critical legal scholarship, which posited that legal doctrine, discourse, practice, and outcomes were intended to favor the economic elite. As such, the law has consistently benefited the affluent and people who are impoverished have been disadvantaged.

As pointed out over a half-century ago by Miller (1966), U.S. laws were created specifically to regulate and control the disadvantaged. A point brought home with sterling clarity by then-Attorney General Katzenbach, who asserted: "To us, laws and regulations are protections and guides, established for our benefit, and for us to use. But to the poor, they are a hostile maze, established as harassment, at all costs to be avoided."

Miller continues by observing that the "original Constitution condoned and permitted discrimination against Negroes and that there was a great leeway for racial discrimination under late 19th and early 20th century laws from the Civil War and Reconstruction, through Jim Crow Laws, Plessy V. Fergusson, redlining, up through the modern civil rights movement."

As observed by Justice John Marshal Harlan, in his dissent in the civil rights cases, the laws served the purpose of allowing "Whites (to) retain the power ... to dole out ... to the Negroes just such privileges as they may choose to grant." No wonder, when the High Court was finally forced to set aside *Plessy*, even then, it tried to delay doing so as long as possible through "all deliberate speed." Since then, we have observed the law differently applied to persons of color, such as in murder and rape cases, drug enforcement and sentencing, and the creation of what we term "the cradle-to-prison pipeline."

The story starts with observations by Marx, as he documented the barbarism that was attendant to the "discovery of gold and silver in America." Thus began the conquest, looting, enslavement, treason, bribery, massacres, and meanness that characterized this "system of stealing men," kidnapping children, debauchery, depravity, and "an exquisite refinement of cruelty" (Marx, 1867: 532).

Robinson (2019) first identified racial capitalism and demonstrated how racialism operates within specific layers of capitalism to produce stratified population groups. However, Robinson was traveling a road that started with scholars such as W.E.B. Du Bois and C.L.R. James, who linked colonialism and slavery with the origins of modern imperialism.

Merging these two, even from the Marxist perspective, as done by the critical legal scholars and the originators of CRT, Kimberlé Crenshaw and Derrick Bell, to name but two, takes us to a new space. A space that threatens the system built on race and privilege.

These scholars were followed by such Black radicals as St. Clair Drake, Horace Clayton, and Oliver Cox. Hence, as William J. Wilson (1980) demonstrated over four decades ago, the realities and life chances of Black males from poor urban backgrounds are radically different than those from more affluent backgrounds.

## The evolution of Critical Race Theory

The next evolution of CRT was to link race and class with other systems of oppression, such as gender and sexuality. The work of scholars such as Patricia Hill Collins (2009) points out that race does not operate alone but intersects with other systems, most notably gender.

So, while one might discuss them separately, only by understanding this intersectionality and their interrelatedness can one truly begin to grapple with this monster. This means that dealing with one facet without understanding the other only tells part of the story.

Scholars have more recently begun to look at things through an intersectional lens, called the matrix, and across multiple institutions and nations (Coates et al, 2021). That is, we look at how race, class, gender, sexuality, age, and so on interact and intersect to form our identities (Coates et al, 2021). But, such people do not merely react but act and engage these structures as true agents of social change and architects of social justice (Brubaker et al, 2004).

The evolution of CRT demonstrates that, for over a hundred years, we have been investigating oppression through multiple lenses of race, class, and gender. Consequently, the debate about CRT seems not only coincidental but also convenient. Conveniently, it allows some to forget this history, and few link this brutality to Whiteness and how it impacts us all, regardless of race.

Racial realities are not identical, and neither are realities similar within racial groups. It is not "one reality fits all", that is for sure! The "racial state," as experienced by so many Americans, is a reality that needs to be faced, and face it we shall.

It is important to do so for members of all races. In what follows, I will go through some common misperceptions regarding guilt, bias, fragility, and victimization. For now, let me assert that any common experience, belief, tendency, fear, or result is more than misleading; it is dangerous, and when used in conjunction with a racial group, it is racist.

One of the purposes of this volume is to realize that minoritized people are not merely victims. Counter-narratives from Indigenous, colonized, and minoritized peoples have consistently and critically assailed these illusions. Another purpose is to argue how both major perspectives – liberal and conservative – have not only served to keep the racial status quo stagnant but also to preserve the illusion of White supremacy, monolithic Whiteness, and White racial naivete.

As pointed out by Derrick Bell (1987), real change will not come about until White people themselves realize how they are negatively impacted by race. History is replete with examples where racial White minorities have been used to combat racial progress under the mistaken belief that they benefit from such.

## Critical Race Theory and its discontents: the attack on Critical Race Theory

There is much confusion, on both the right and left, in the Americas and throughout Europe, regarding what exactly CRT. This book will provide a clear, concise, and working definition of CRT, some of its major tenets, and how it can help former colonializing nations deal with the racial legacies they created.

People of color across the globe continue to be an integral part of the historical realities of Western nations. Unfortunately, as observed by W.E.B. Du Bois over a hundred years ago, the "problem of the 20th century is the problem of the color line" (Du Bois, 1903: 7) and "the question of how far differences of race ... will be made hereafter the basis of denying to over half the world the right to sharing to their utmost ability the opportunities and privileges as we continue to re(discover) the question of racial differences" (Du Bois, 1899: 5). But across the globe, we witness the enduring legacies of racial discrimination, acts of violence, and antagonism that continue to be visited upon Indigenous, former colonized, marginalized, and minoritized peoples and groups.

CRT is just the most recent attempt to capture these critical responses by people, research, and the continual debates on resolving this problem.

Transformative social movements sought to give voice to the marginalized, power to the powerless, and instruments to the agents of change. In many regards, post-modernism was a failed experiment. It failed because it centered critical thinking, existentialism, and protest toward disrupting the social order, not transforming that social order.

Let us consider these attacks and offer some critiques.

Ruffo raises four central problems associated with CRT and why he and conservatives think it is dangerous:

1. It is Marxist-inspired.
2. It defines race structurally and argues that it is systemically part of the American reality.
3. It defines White people as oppressors and all others as oppressed (White guilt); Whites have "internalized racial superiority" and their "complicity in the system of White supremacy."
4. It is a form of indoctrination found in our Diversity, Equity and Inclusion (DEI) efforts and throughout educational institutions, particularly within K–12 and college curriculum.

Let us deal with each of these.

1. *According to the myth, CRT is derived from Marxism.*

Critical race theory is derived from several critical legal scholars and writings, including Michel Foucault, Max Weber, and, yes, Karl Marx. But whereas critical legal scholars, from which CRT derives, believed laws primarily reflected and sustained class interests, CRT argues that laws, policies, and systems are constructed to maintain a racial power hierarchy (Clark, 2021).

It is also believed that CRT is being advocated by activists who view all Western values – including the nuclear family, religious freedom, and Judeo-Christian concepts of morality – as inherently oppressive (Hardin, 2021/2023).

As noted by scholars engaged in this work, the truth is that CRT encourages those working with families and young children (such as early childhood educators) to think about culturally relevant teaching focusing on family and community engagement in culturally meaningful and inclusive ways.

They specifically advise teachers and equity scholars to adopt the 4e framework (Durden, 2021). This guides childhood professionals to consider the following:

- Expect families and students to do their best.
- Educate families on how to support their children's optimal development.
- Explore ways to partner with families and value their strengths.
- Equip families to advocate on behalf of their child's education and wellbeing.

2. *CRT defines race structurally and argues that it is systemically part of the American reality.*

According to this view, CRT and its proponents reject the basic premise of the Declaration of Independence that "all men are created equal." Rather, according to this myth, CRT casts aside inherent rights and freedoms and declares all opposition as racist, leading to censorship, silencing, or canceling of critics on college campuses.

The reality is that CRT challenges the historical record by pointing out that when we were making the declaration, we were exterminating the Indigenous peoples, enslaving the Africans, and denying full citizenship to a vast assortment of Others, including women.

Further, as taught by several disciplines – sociology, for example – modern civilization created institutions and bureaucracies to facilitate the ordering of behavior, regulating activities and surety that society's mundane and essential activities were accomplished efficiently, deliberately, and consistently.

Our values, for good and evil, moral and immoral, just and unjust, are also embedded into these institutions. For this reason, the women's rights movement, the civil rights movement, the Indigenous rights movement, and all social justice movements target institutions as they attempt to transform society for the better.

3. *It defines White people as oppressors and all others as oppressed (White guilt); Whites have "internalized racial superiority" and their "complicity in the system of White supremacy."*

Attacks on CRT have been in the form of intentional misrepresentations of critical race theory to inflame and activate the Republican voting base. Conservative activist Christopher Ruffo appeared on Fox News in the summer of 2020 and said that CRT had permeated every institution in the federal government. Then President Trump responded by denouncing the 1619 project, initiating the 1776 project, and prohibiting DEI training in any federal program or agency. He argued these were "efforts to indoctrinate government employees with diverse and harmful sex- and race-based ideologies." This was followed by Russell Vought (Director of the Office of Management and Budget) ordering all federal agencies to identify any CRT and White privilege training taking place within their departments. In this memo, it stipulated that funding would be halted by any programs or practices that suggested that the "United States is an inherently racist or evil country or that any race or ethnicity is inherently racist or evil" (quoted in Cineas, 2020).

On the contrary, CRT argues that any simple division of society between oppressed and oppressors is simple. This applies to all terms that assume a universal experience to include White guilt/fragility/privilege or minority (Black, Indigenous, Hispanic) victimization.

4. *And finally, critics argue that CRT is a form of indoctrination found in our DEI efforts, and throughout educational institutions, particularly within K-12 and college curriculum.*

Across the United States, over 165 local and national groups are trying to cancel, disrupt, or block any lessons that deal with either race or gender issues in K-12 institutions (Gross, 2021). Fueled by conservative think tanks, law firms, and media outlets, we have witnessed school board meetings being disrupted, conservative school board members replacing those considered liberal, fist fights, and shouting by parents on either side of this issue. Currently, 18 states have banned it, and nine others prohibit teaching CRT. Although most of these states are in the southern states comprised of the old Confederacy, many are also in the Midwest. Alternatively, voters and legislators in 17 states have voted to veto or positively affirm the goals and intentions of teaching about racism and its negative impacts on various minoritized groups (World Population Review, 2023), passed Anti-CRT bans, and nine others have proposed bills affirming the utility of teaching CRT. The ultra-right conservative social movement that this has spawned is the actual indoctrination that is taking place as it serves to promote antisemitic conspiracy theories, distribute propaganda, and promote a radical political agenda. Such groups have consisted of neo-Nazis, the Proud Boys, and Aryan Nation. Major media personalities have used Fox News, the Telegram Channel, and Newsmax to foster these attacks (ADL, 2021).

CRT examines the historical and contemporary aspects of racism within America. It looks at this from the slave trade through Jim Crow, redlining, racial profiling, and police brutality, and how it has become enshrined within many of our institutions. CRT is not about guilt, blame, or privilege. It is about the mechanisms, practices, and policies that reproduce race and racism systemically within our country.

## "When lions tell their stories, they control the arc of history"

Achebe reminds us in the proverb that forms the title of this section that Western historians have continued to glorify imperialism, racial hierarchies, and the racial state. The dominant historical narrative produced promotes European institutions, values, and perspectives.

The racialized ideologies that are created reflect the centrality of Europeans and the marginalization of all others. These realities not only justify but serve to perpetuate the idea that racial Others (specifically Blacks and Indigenous peoples, but essentially all non-Europeans) occupy lower statuses biologically, socially, politically, and historically. But these are not fixed in stone; they are not scientifically but socially constructed.

To understand how to change these systems, we must understand how, why, and under what circumstances they came into being. These are the truths we must uncover; these are the truths we must understand. The process starts by understanding the current moment in which we find ourselves.

The political divide has never been so expansive, nor the choices so clear. On the one hand, there is the Make America Great Again (MAGA) movement, White existential fears, attacks against abortion, LGBTQIA+, voting rights, CRT ... and the list goes on.

On the other hand, there is the reality that one of the leading causes of death among White and Black youth is gun violence, that the cradle-to-prison pipeline is all too prevalent, and that the feminization of poverty, hopelessness, and frustration continues unabated. Across the United States, hospitals are closing (in rural and urban areas), and hundreds of schools are closing or restricting educational opportunities. There are severe shortages of medical, educational, and other critical professionals.

For these reasons, there is a critical need to understand what the truth is, why there is a concern with being "woke," and how we survive these existential crises without serious damage to our democracy.

However, social movements, civil rights activism, and the courage of countless individuals have challenged us to take charge of our realities, change the trajectory of our histories, and create new futures. Somewhere between the arc of history and the possibility of change rests that small area where I believe free will resides.

If indeed, as remarked by Martin Luther King, Jr. (1963), the "arc of history is long, but it bends toward justice," the question is who does the bending and how is that bending possible. If all is predetermined, the results will be the same no matter what we or anyone else does.

But, if indeed the path to social justice is paved with the blood, sweat, and tears of thousands of unsung heroes who stumble and fall, are frustrated and often denied, but continue to rise, continue to battle, and continue to push forward, then free will is a reality: a small, very small, reality. It is much like the drops of water that produce the trickle that becomes the stream that, over eons, erodes the boulder and makes the ravine until it finds the sea.

Is it idealism or realism? Is it myths or the substance of faith? I choose, I freely choose to believe that our efforts are indeed choices, much like that tiny drop of water. And as these drops join others, they become streams of possibilities that can and often do bend the arc of history toward justice.

My basic premise is that for far too long, the truth has been externally provided to Blacks and others who do not occupy positions of power within the racial state. I am reminded of Göring's remarks during the Nuremberg Trials: "Der Sieger wird immer der Richter und der Besiegte stets der Angeklagte sein," which may be translated as "The victor will always be the judge, and the vanquished the accused" (quoted in Phelan, 2019).

Such programs in higher education, underfunded and overworked, have always existed on the periphery of the academy. But they lived, nonetheless. Strangely, they never had the numbers (regarding faculty or students) to represent a serious threat, but they have always been suspected.

Now, these suspect academic programs and their proponents are being targeted by the extreme right. It is not the educational programs at stake but the truth itself.

CRT must provide critiques of both liberal and conservative perspectives. It looks at Western imperialism, not only in the United States and Europe but how these views are baked into the various societies (colonized and colonizer).

History is replete with examples where racialized individuals, such as poor whites, have been used to combat racial progress under the mistaken belief that they benefited from such. It takes but a moment to realize that the laws that not only permitted but enthusiastically encouraged the racially exploitative systems of colonialism, slavery, apartheid, genocide, rape, murder, and the theft of land, gold, silver, and life itself were passed by parliaments and congress, endorsed by kings/queens and presidents, and applauded by the church and merchants alike.

These systems, once given birth, only expanded and became incorporated as Western imperialism created racial capitalism, racial states, and a global racialization of peoples across the globe. These systems continue today and feed off past and present normative structures. From the beginning, these systems have reflected not only the consensus but the collaboration of both conservative and liberal forces.

## Outline of the book

*Critical Race Theory and the Search for Truth* is a comprehensive text integrating various issues regarding CRT. It is intended for classroom use (upper/graduate) and the public. It provides critiques of both liberal and conservative perspectives.

This book will explore the essentials of CRT and its relationship to oppression, survival, and social movements. We start from the basic assumption that racism is systemic and that it is interconnected with other systems of oppression.

Our journey into the truth will begin in Chapter 2, with the musings of W.E.B. Du Bois. In the process, we argue that the double consciousness he identifies can be used to discover the "truth." Specifically, it is argued that the history of America and Western imperialism is not one history but multiple histories. Further, these histories are best understood as parallel realities. So, concerning the Blacks, they found themselves creatures of two worlds. To be African and to be American, object and subject. Therefore, it is not a question of the European version of history or that of the African (or any other racialized group). Rather it is a question of understanding how both coexist and that what is truly "critical" about CRT is the ability to explore both roads, both realities.

Chapter 3 continues this dual process of examination by investigating "the bipolar construction of identity" that emerged because of racial imperialism, African agency, and their reactions to being othered. The chapter expands on these notions by highlighting how racial imperialism created racial hierarchies in the colonized countries based on the ideological and presumptive beliefs of the colonizers toward the colonized. This chapter will explain how racial imperialism constructed and externalized the other. But rather than being mere reactive objects, the Africans are demonstrated to be active agents in their struggle to fight colonialization.

Black agency and resistance are the central themes of Chapter 4. It will explore the Haitian Revolution, Black agency and how this challenged British, French, Spanish, and U.S. colonial systems. The most successful insurrection resulted in the Haitian Revolution, which resulted in the overthrow of European imperialism.

Chapter 5 demonstrates that Africans have been central to the shaping and the making of the Americas from its founding. The first antislavery societies were established the same year the Declaration of Independence was penned. From then to the present day, our nation has been consumed with the idea and the reality of race. This chapter will explore this shaping and making. More formally, this chapter will examine the system of racial triangulation created to keep the Africans in their places. Racial triangulation, the intended outcomes of racial imperialism, has been associated with centuries of forced servitude, followed by the Civil War and Jim Crow laws, forced segregation, racial intimidation, and terror, redlining, differential access to education and training, and finally, the cradle-to-prison pipeline. The Africans have repeatedly and consistently fought against each of these attempts to contain, restrain, and pervert their very being.

The next two chapters examine how Black women and men countered the proscribed and conscribed stereotypical identities created to keep them in their places. As pointed out in Chapter 6, Black women's identities have been prescribed and conscribed almost from the beginning of our nation. These representations of the African woman in America have rarely reflected the contributions to the American project. Even when there is an attempt to acknowledge their true histories grudgingly, it barely scratches the surface. Black women have blazed the trail, set the bar, and creatively constructed their identities and realities from the Revolutionary War to the Civil War, from the Industrial Revolution to the era of civil rights, and from "Hidden Figures" to "the Black Lives Matter movement." This chapter acknowledges the various ways Black women have been both sterilized and characterized, yet they remain resilient, resistant, and rebellious, unsung warriors. Explored, therefore, will be the classic stereotypes that have attempted to racialize and minimize her. But this chapter will also explore the responses and active engagement in creating, sustaining, and maintaining feminine identities that are uniquely African, Black, and proud.

Then, in Chapter 7, we discuss how Black men devised methods to counteract the Black male stereotypes created to convince him that he, not the system, was the problem. The vilest of these characterizations would be the ape, Coon, Jungle Bunny, Kaffir, monkey/porch monkey, zibabo, spade, spook, and of course n*****/n****(h). Attached to these words are such stereotypical characters as Zip Coon, Sambo/Uncle Tom (Remus), Jim Crow, and Buck/Mandingo. And for most of this same period, there has been a constant rejection of these images as Black men and women have fought for the very soul of our community. Tracing these stereotypes to their origins helps us understand how and why they came into being and how and in what ways Blacks continually recreated their identities.

The last chapter will explore how self-empowerment and self-identification originated with and by Black people. The truth, I suggest, is a song by James Brown in 1968 when he declared, "Say it loud: I'm Black and I'm proud." Go ahead, get your funk on, make that move, and repeat after me, "I'm Black and I'm proud." In this final chapter, we shall explore the rich music produced by Africans in America. In the process, we shall understand that this music was more than soul, gospel, hip-hop, or funk. African music was an assertion of being, a testament of faith, and a clarion call to the Universe – I am. These were songs of protest and process, anger and love, action and determination. They were songs that called out the racism faced by Blacks. But they were more than a complaint, as Brown asserted, "As Blacks, we demand a chance to do things for ourselves." Self-empowerment and self-identification originating with and by Black people are not externally rendered but internally endorsed.

As ambitious as this volume is, it nevertheless is limited. There is no way to cover all the periods, all the situations, and all the realities that were, are, and will continue to be experienced by the Africans in various racial states. Past that, it is recognized that racial states were not biracial but multiracial. To do justice, all racial and racialized people should be examined. This would mean looking at the various people who have been racialized and epitomized within the racial state. These projects are the true task of CRT as it moves forward. This would mean to continue to deconstruct the various racial categories. How and in what ways, for example, did the various pan-ethnic groups differ as they ultimately were merged into the racial categories within the different racial imperial states? Specifically, how did Europeans' racial trajectory into Whiteness impact their perceptions of realities? What stereotypes were needed to sustain and maintain the racial state to make this happen?

Similarly, what of the Asians, Hispanics, or Native Americans? Or how are religious groups such as Muslims and Jews racialized? How do these different groups preserve their agency within a racial structure that would deny such? And then, how do the different racial states and systems interact and intervene in shaping racial realities?

Perhaps we can construct realistic and sustainable solutions when we know these answers. Until then, the work and the search for truth continues.

## 2

# In Search of the Truth

One ever feels his twoness, —an American, a Negro; two souls, two thoughts, two unreconciled strivings; two warring ideals in one dark body, whose dogged strength alone keeps it from being torn asunder. The History of the American Negro is the history of this strive-this longing to attain self-conscious manhood, to merge his double self into a better and truer self. He simply wishes to make it possible for a man to be both a Negro and an American, without being cursed and spit upon by his fellows, without having the doors of Opportunity closed roughly in his face.

Du Bois, 1903/2009: 6–7

Our search for truth begins with the musings of W.E.B. Du Bois as he struggled to explain the contradictory place Blacks found themselves. They are at once at odds with themselves, creatures of two worlds. To be African and American, to be both object and subject. To exist in a "double consciousness" space of being and not being, of reacting and acting, of being the constant shadow always on the verge of becoming. Herein lies the truth of race as it is experienced and lived. It is both externally and internally defined, yet always problematized for those who have been minoritized, racialized, and scrutinized for the act of being and becoming. In the sections that follow, we shall travel on both roads. One charted by imperialist theorists whose primary job was to justify, explain, and buttress racial imperialism that came into being. The other charted by those subject populations that refused to be subjugated, sublimated, and subjected to externally defined identities. Their writings challenge the myth of otherness, inferiority, and racialized realities. We shall explore these as they are linked with imperialism and the creation of the racial state. But first, we must examine how othering came about in the ancient world.

## The beginning of othering in the ancient world

Scholars, media, and others have attempted to whiten Egypt for the last hundred years. According to this view, Egyptians were White and European. Afrocentric scholars such as Bernal (2002) have argued for Egypt's Black or Afroasiatic roots. D.N.A. analysis suggests that the ancient Egyptians were more likely related to peoples from the Near Eastern groups and the Levant (Schuenemann et al, 2017). The origins of race and racism are contemporary ideas that had no relevance in the ancient world (Whitmarsh, 2018). So, while ancient peoples, such as the Romans and Greeks, did acknowledge phenotypical differences, they did not systematically practice what we would term racism (Talbot, 2018). McCoskey (2002) argues that the form of racism in the ancient world was more in line with cultural racism. Greek identity, for example, reflected the centrality of Greek culture and the periphery of the Egyptian and barbarian. By excluding non-Greeks, Greek identity was reinforced and solidified (Erskine, 1995: 43). We will explore these in depth in later sections, but for now, it is essential to understand that cultural differences, associated with both political and economic power, were the key differentiating factors between the Greeks and colonized Egyptian subjects (McCoskey, 2002: 19). The continual misrepresentation of the ancient world reflect political and racist motivations, not scientifically arrived conclusions. As we know it today, race is directly associated with European imperialism and its various colonial projects (Christian, 2019). However, long before imperialism, othering, genocide, and ethnonationalism occurred. All major religious and philosophical systems, periods of history, and civilizations have participated in, created, and defined those considered the select and elect and those deemed to be other, the infidel, and the savage.

> One of the marvelous thynges that God useth in the composition of man is colored: which doubtless cannot be considered without great admiration in beholding one to be white and another black, being coloures utterly contrary. Sum likewise to be yelowe which is between Black and white: and other coloures as it were of dyvers lives. (Francisco Lopez de Gomara [1555], quoted in Jordan, 1968/2012: 7)

Race first appeared in English in the late 16th century and referred to ordinary people. It might have derived from Old French *rasse* or Italian *razza*. Its roots might stem from the Arabic *ras* (رأس) which means the head of someone or something. In this context, *ras* points to the selected species' root or head. Even earlier forms of the word might be traced to the Latin *gens* or Arabic *genat* (جينات), which refers to a clan, stock, or people and *genus* meaning birth, descent, origin, race, stock, or family, or the Greek word *genos* (γένος) and its attendant translation of "race, kind," and *gonos* "birth, offspring, stock."[1] Before Christopher Columbus and the advent of European imperialism, these terms reflected a bipolar and hierarchical characterization of self and others for most of human history. During this period, other terms reflected the same bipolar hierarchy, such as nation and tribe. After the advent of European imperialism, race and ethnicity replaced these terms. Human groups throughout history have created elaborate constructs to explain, normalize, and justify these hierarchical characterizations.

All forms of othering utilized a series of constructs to justify, legitimize, and normalize hegemonic cultural processes associated with exploitation, extermination, castigation, and enslavement. In addition, religious, philosophical, and other cultural myths provided the ideological basis for creating these systems. Over time, these systems became racial hegemonies and racial states. The journey of difference begins in the ancient world.

## The ancient world of difference

Every major cultural group has created a religious tradition addressing the unknown and the known. Our journey into difference in the ancient world must therefore start with religion. Looking at the various ancient peoples from Egypt, Ethiopia, Greece, Rome and China provides us unmistakable evidence of othering.

### Distortions and misrepresentations of the ancient world

In 2021, Princeton University discontinued offering Greek and Latin in its Classics majors to combat what it saw as "institutional racism." Many scholars, such as Dan-el Padilla Peralta, a Dominican Republic scholar at Princeton University, believe we must open the classical tradition to a broader group of scholars. The current concentration on Greece and Rome presents an overly White, overly male view that erases all other racial groups (Poser, 2021). Far-right groups throughout the Americas and Europe have co-opted classical Greece and Roman imagery, ideas, and histories to promote racial hatred. Search the internet, look for "alt-right," and find many sites that worship the ancient Greeks and Romans, whom they believe to be the basis of Western civilization and the testament to the superior accomplishments of White civilization and White men. The reality is far different from these perceptions. Rome, Greece, Egypt, and much of the ancient world were just as diverse as our modern realities (Bond, 2017).

The British novelist L.P. Hartley once remarked, "The past is a foreign country: they do things differently there" (Hartley, 1970: 5). Much of the past is ill-conceived, misrepresented, and poorly remembered. It is often hard for us to understand just how much of the past is unknown or how much of it we invented to serve our ends. Almost any portrayal of the ancient world in museums, art history books, or media (from films to news) depicts a White-skinned Greek or Roman, a Black-skinned African, and a universal oriental in Asia. Such homogeneity reflects a false narrative, often created to align with our modern-day biases concerning the ancient world.

Over a hundred years ago, various descriptions of the Chinese defined them as "an inferior race of malleable Orientals" (Clairmonte, 1970: 416–417). Said clarifies this perception by arguing that for nearly 4,000 years, Western scientific disciplines have negatively portrayed various cultures from the continent of Asia, including the Near East, Middle East, and the Far East. While comprising multiple cultural groups, the most extensive studies have been on the Chinese. (Other groups would include those from Japan, Korea, Taiwan, Indonesia, Malaysia, the Philippines, Myanmar, Singapore, Thailand, Vietnam, Cambodia, Mongolia, and Laos.) The development of scientific disciplines, such as anthropology, ethnology, and sociology, provided formal legitimacy for the othering of these peoples (Said, 1979; 1985).

The Blackening of Africa only parallels the Whitening of the ancient world. Nevertheless, Diamond (1994/2023) pointed out this is a European or Western fantasy. Indeed, for centuries, the continent of Africa, before European historiography, was home to "five of the six major divisions of humanity."

Several historical factors account for the current groups inhabiting this continent, such as the migrations of the Bantu and the Indonesian colonization of Madagascar several centuries ago. No other continent can match the diversity and complexity found in Africa regarding cultural, linguistic, religious, and physical diversity. How we classify people racially obscures much of the variability. Consider the differences between the Zulu, Masai, or the Ibo, all are Black. Or consider which Egyptians or Bergers are either White or Black. The racialization of Africa occurred as the Europeans began to colonize and thus racialize Africa. With 1,500 language groups, Africa demonstrates a complex history over seven million years. The reality is that all of humanity, our most remote ancestors, originated here close to seven million years ago.

Much of African history is an invention of contemporary archeological, ethnographical, or ethnohistorical theories of antiquity. We have argued over the ethnicity, race, and identities of the Bantu-speaking populations near the Niger-Benue region and how these point to different ethnicities, races, and identities of those in the Southern Bantu peoples. We have discovered the "tendency to project contemporary identities" upon ancient African peoples (Richard and MacDonald, 2015: 34).

According to this false narrative, the Romans, Greeks, and Egyptians are White. The reality is that Whiteness or race was not how the ancients characterized each other. These false narratives derive from much more recent history, such as the work of Winkelmann (1764), which became the foundation for modern art history. The celebrated figure displaying a White Apollo is the quintessential model of Whiteness, perfection, and beauty. Scholars, such as Painter (2011), point out that such views were Eurocentric and racist as other groups such as Chinese, Africans, or Middle Easterners are depreciated. The Roman Empire was multiracial, multicultural, polytheistic, and a pantheon of groups. How did the ancient people's views differ, and what does this say about race and otherness?

## In the beginning: Ethiopia, ethnoreligious groups, and the social construction of others

Ethiopia, where some of the earliest hominid remains can be found, might be the oldest human civilization on our planet. Here were found the remains of Lucy and Salem, 4.3-million-year-old remains that scientists labeled Australopithecus afarensis. More of our hominid ancestors have been found in Ethiopia than elsewhere. Furthermore, here, the first migration of humans might have originated out of Africa (Hellenthal et al, 2021). The nation of Ethiopia, a name assigned by the Greeks, is derived from the Greek word *ethio*, or burned, and *pia*, meaning face or the land of burned-faced peoples. Other Greeks, such as Aeschylus, described Ethiopia as a "land far off, a nation of black men."

Meanwhile, Homer depicted the Ethiopians as pious and favored by the gods (Levine, 2014). For most Greek observers, Ethiopia was less about a people or even a geographical location but a reflection of difference, or, as Levine puts it, "a state of mind." For the Greeks and Romans, the Ethiopians were dark-skinned people who lived south of Egypt and might include people from West Africa, Arabia, and India (Levine, 2014). The first Africans identified were located in the Kingdom of Aksum during the reign of the Aksumite king Ezana.

The oldest human tools, fossils, and advanced human behavior have all been associated with the Ethiopian highlands (Belcher, 2012). Prehistorical evidence, dating between 8000 and 5000 B.C.E., identifies Ethiopia as the first place where plants and animals were domesticated for food. Over this same period, the ancient languages of the peoples of East Africa came into being. This language family, spoken across Africa and the Middle East, includes Hebrew, Arabic, Aramaic, and Akkadian, as well as the modern languages of Egyptian, Berger, Hausa, Oromo, and Somali (Belcher, 2012). However, what did the Ethiopians think of themselves, and how did they view the world and others?

Ethiopia reflects the continual interactions of various regional groups, including Eritrea and the Horn of Africa. The oldest Indigenous peoples of Ethiopia reflect three distinct ethnolinguistic groups: the Semitic, Cushitic, and the Nilo-Saharan. Assuming that these ethnolinguistic groups reflect a static or fixed lens to interpret ethnicity would be oversimplified. The ethnic map of Ethiopia reflected a fluid, often heterogeneous, and, yes, contested set of categories. This ethnic map concentrated on groups in specific geographic regions like the Gojjam, Wallo, Shawa, and Gondar. Ethiopia's identities reflect a dynamic history of experiences (Yates, 2017).

Ethiopian identity formation was a product of religion and geography. For this reason, ethnoreligious identities have historically been the most salient. Ethiopian ethnoreligious identity formation is associated with four distinct periods: the establishing of a Jewish community around 587 B.C.E., the emergence of the Aksumite State and Christianity (8th to 12th century), and the Early Islamic Period (7th to 8th centuries). Historically, these influential ethnoreligious identity groups have been associated with various geographical areas that have also shifted over time. This complex history accounts for the varied and highly complex identities that continue today (Yates, 2017).

Many different theories account for establishing the first Jewish community in Ethiopia. While some cite the original Ethiopian Jews as descendants of King Solomon and Queen Sheba, others believe them to be the lost tribe of Dan. In contrast, others believe they are descendants of early Christians who converted to Judaism. Regardless of its origins, the community has a long history. There are also some clues concerning how they were received. For example, some Ethiopian Christians named them the "Falasha," meaning strangers. The name "Beta Israel," which means "house of Israel," represents their deep connection to the faith and the Torah from within the group (Friedman, 2018). When Ezana became the Emperor of Axum in 325 and declared Christianity as the religion of the Ethiopian empire, Beta Israel refused to convert to Christianity.

Beta Israel revolted, and a civil war ensued between the Jewish and Christian populations. As a result, an independent state in northwestern Ethiopia came into being. By the 13th century, Beta Israel controlled the more defensible mountain regions northwest of the Christianized region. Their central city was Gondar, and the first king crowned was Phineas. New conflicts ensued in the mid-9th century as the Aksum empire began to expand. This brought another round of armed conflict between the Empire and Beta Israel. Tensions, wars, and disputes would continue through the 15th century as Islamic and Christian forces converged, forcing Jews to align with Ethiopia. We shall pick up this story in the next chapter. For now, let us consider the other primary ethnoreligious origins (Friedman, 2018).

The Aksumite Empire, located in northern Ethiopia and Eritrea, was a significant trading network between Greece, Rome, India, and the Mediterranean. It dates as early as the 1st century and was an essential marketplace for ivory, incense, gold, and exotic animals. Ethiopia was believed to be the final resting place of the Ark of the Covenant and the home of the Queen of Sheba. The Aksumite people reflected the merging of several Semitic-speaking people – the Cushite and Nilo-Saharan. The major ethnic groups were the Proto-Tigrayans and Proto-Amharas, and were the basis of the early language form of the Ga'ez (Butzer, 1981).

With the arrival of Islam into Ethiopia, major identity shifts, conflicts, and assimilations appeared. The first *Hijra*, according to tradition, occurred in the year 615. Accordingly, the first converts of the new religion outside the close circle of the Prophet Muhammad, given the proximity of the Red Sea coast to the Arabian heartland, were Ethiopians. These converts resulted from Islam persecution by the dominant Quraysh authorities in Arabia (Mecca). Muhammad and his closest followers sought refuge in the empire of Aksum. Not only were they accorded protection, but when the Meccan authorities demanded that they be delivered, the Aksum refused. After Muhammad's death and in the following decades, there were several armed conflicts between Ethiopians and Arabians. The disputes continued, particularly in the highland areas under Christian control. Only gradually did the expansion of Islam occur in the lowland coastal regions occupied mainly by pastoral nomads. It was not until the 11th and 12th centuries that it spread to the Somali lands to the southeast (Abbink, 1998).

The tensions between these two groups outlined the basis of identities: those identifying with Ethiopian Christianity and those with Islam. Regardless, for many purposes of identity, regional and ethnic identities tended to vie with religious identities for dominance. During this period and much that followed, Ethiopian leaders consistently viewed Muslims as inferior in status and of secondary importance. War, conflicts, suppression, and religious bigotry, between Muslims and Christians, has been replicated throughout history (Abbink, 1998).

## Greeks, Romans, Egyptians, and the social construction of others

Throughout history and across all cultural groups, religion and philosophy developed to give meaning to existence and situate group identity. Typically, most groups use theology and philosophy to place their group at the center pre-eminently. In this way, either God or civilization favors one group, typically at the expense of others. Different groups interact, are absorbed into this existing identity, or are defined as others. The more mobile the group, the more complex, layered, and encompassing the ideological justifications in religion or philosophy. Several examples can exist across geographical and cultural groups.

As various cultural groups increasingly came into contact with groups different from themselves, there were consistent attempts to fit them into their religious or philosophical constructs. The simplest of these constructs were binary distinctions where they were defined as the people or humans juxtaposed to all others. As expected, differences in power (for example, whether one is dominant) often determine whose definitions of social constructs are deemed valid or prevail. These social constructs, describing the other, were also associated with conquest and domination, expansion and imperialism. Given the power of religious ideologies, it is often that these social constructs are legitimated and, for our purposes, preserved. While the terms differ by both religion, geography, and historical period, they all share a standard set of features – they define and legitimate: hierarchies; differential treatment and rewards/punishments; obfuscate responsibility and limit liability for damages; and marginalize, stigmatize, ostracize, and problematize the other. In the most extreme situations, subjugation, genocide, destruction, enslavement, forced imprisonment, or segregation have been the ultimate (if not planned) consequences of adopting these social constructions of others. Unfortunately, time does not allow for the complete examination of all these constructs. Therefore, we shall limit our analysis to pagans, heathens, infidels, barbarians, and savages.

The Greeks defined all others as "βάρβαρος" ("barbarian"), which means uncivilized. In many ways, the Greeks perceived themselves in opposition to the negatively characterized barbarians. Barbarians typically were depicted as coarse, unsophisticated, and sometimes ill-mannered. The Greeks alternatively defined themselves as civilized, sophisticated, and filled with social graces (Hall, 1989). Barbarians also reflected a biological component, as reflected in the adage that "no barbarian could share in Hellenic blood" (Hall, 1997). Barbarians were not limited to the Greeks. As Bonfante (2011: 22–24) points out, there were remarkable similarities with views held by the Chinese. Both referred to nomadic tribes that surrounded them, and they tended to stress their own superior culture. The entire western and central Asia region comprises what has come to be known as the "Great Wall of China." This wall effectively separated the "civilized" and the "barbarian." The division also reflected the debate between the sedentary urban civilizations, from China, India, and Iran to Mesopotamia, Egypt, Greece, and Rome (Stuurman, 2008). Whereas the Greeks, and later the Romans, would stress the simple lifestyles but essential honor of the barbarians, such was not the case among the Chinese and much of Asia (Bonfante, 2011). Although the frontiers were vital zones that symbolically and physically separated the civilized and the barbarian, this does not necessarily mean that the relationships were contentious. Both the Chinese and the Greek use of the term was remarkably neutral and unbiased (Stuurman, 2008: 13). Barbarian became a catch-all phrase for all foreigners. During the 6th century B.C.E., chattel slavery permeated Greek civilization. The Greeks also viewed the barbarians as lacking intelligence and as barbaric, savage, and lazy. Both barbarians and Persians dominated the enslaved people in Greece during this era (Hall, 1989).

Many would racialize Greeks, Romans, or Egyptians. McCoskey (2012) pointed out that racial designations do not align with historical realities and reflect our modern racial obsessions. She observes that scholars such as Bernal (2002), who focus on Cleopatra's skin color, ignore the fact that such distinctions are meaningless. Instead, the ancients focused on nation and culture, the Greek-ness or Egyptian-ness, to determine identities. McCoskey (2002) demonstrated that race within ancient Egypt and Greece reflected specific colonial derived and power differentials between particular identities. Therefore, she links Greek identity to the "political process of colonization" (McCoskey, 2002: 14).

For the Romans and Greeks, representations of the other, typically referred to as "barbarians," were a central component of how they distinguished Us from Them (McCoskey, 2012). This binary, among the Greeks, consistently dealt with the specific sovereignty threat since the Persian Wars. As a result, barbarian also refers to the form of government a group established. Accordingly, the Greeks described the barbarians as naturally inclined to subservience and tyranny. Furthermore, they define their form of government as more devoted to democratic rule and the equality of citizens (McCoskey, 2012: 54). Accordingly, within the ancient world, a biological basis of race, linking skin color, physical traits, or mental characteristics, was not presumed. Alternatively, they articulated a more nuanced one referring to cultural racism or proto-racism (Isaac, 2006).

Goldenberg (1999) points out that Hesiod, Herodotus, and Hippocrates considered the significant divisions of humanity linked to physical and nonphysical characteristics (such as courage, cowardice, and intelligence) to be attributed to specific environmental conditions transmitted through family lineage. These links, inherent in all the writers of antiquity, demonstrate ethnocentrism or "proto" racial accounting of differences among people. However, Isaac (2006) explains that proto-racism in the Greek and Roman conceptual processes did not lead to systematic persecution, marginalization, or structures in our modern era.

The Greeks and Romans traced their people's descent from mythical genealogies linked to the various gods. The physical and perceived differences of the respective peoples were related to descent, birth, environment, and culture. Further, Hippocrates defines the Scythians (a group that would refer to all northern European peoples in the 5th century B.C.E.) as being "red, flabby, unhealthy, and filled with water because they live in a cold, wet climate" (Kennedy, 2017).

The most challenging idea to reconcile as anything less than prejudice is Aristotle's claim that most human beings could be enslaved without being unjust because they were, by nature, enslaved people. Slavery was a principal institution throughout the ancient world. It was vital to ancient economies, cultures, customs, and status. Slavery, as Aristotle believed, was not only natural and normal but required. Aristotle provides an ideological rationale for slavery by insisting that the naturally enslaved person suffered from a human defect that made them incapable of being anything but an enslaved person. Coincidentally, this formally meant that all non-Greeks were brutes and naturally enslaved people (Harvey, 2001). Aristotle would conclude that among the barbarians, women and enslaved people were ostensibly equal and, by nature, subservient.

As movable property, much like an ox, their primary purpose was to serve the interests of a master (Millett, 2007). Lastly, Aristotle places Greeks at the top of a racial hierarchy and the natural rulers of all other peoples. Vitruvius and the Romans, Europeans, and all racial states would take this position later (McCoskey, 2006). What made the Roman system different was its attitude toward enslaved people. As pointed out by Isaac, a more straightforward route to freedom, manumission, was more prevalent within the Roman system. Consequently, slavery was less a fixed institution and more fluid for the enslaved (McCoskey, 2006).

## Confucius, China, and the social construction of others

When we discuss ethnicity, race, and difference, we ignore most of the world. By concentrating on the European or Western world, we fail to see how Eurocentric our ideas are and how limited our awareness of how different ways of viewing and coping with the other have been different. Such is the case when we consider how outsiders and ethnicity were navigated in ancient China. Many confuse the different periods of China, positing that there has always been a tendency toward homogeneity among various ethnic groups.

From some of the earliest periods, the historical reality demonstrates much of the heterogeneity and cultures in southern China today. In the late 6th century, dominant states and cultural groups such as the Chu, Wu, and Yue were infrequently in competition for dominance with other cultural states for power and supremacy. While the imperial Han dynasty profoundly influenced various groups, they created, maintained, and perpetuated distinct ethnic, historical, and cultural identities (Brindley, 2003).

The study of ethnicity in China poses a couple of problems. First, it covers an extremely long period. Much of what we know is derived from periods when geography was the most significant way people identified with each other. Second, when the Han Chinese scholars began consolidating their histories, they typically only considered those who were Chinese and non-Chinese in terms of lifestyle, language, or governance. In this way, those considered Chinese were civilized, while those non-Chinese were typically considered to be barbarians (West, 2008). The ancient Chinese created an ethnic map associated with the five regions or Wŭfāng. These comprised the Central, East, South, West, and North. The Huang Di resided at the center. This Central region or Central Land (Zhongyuan) or Zhongguo (or the Middle Kingdom) is where the term China is derived (Kwong, 2015).

Some 10,000 years ago, China's earliest historical records highlight a richly diverse, complex, multicultural, and multiethnic civilization. Philosophically, many thinkers from Confucius, Dao, and Tao represent it and emphasize universal harmony and cultural assimilation of diverse minorities (He, 2004). Nevertheless, this emphasis does not ignore how religion served as an important marker for Chinese identities (West, 2008).

Confucianism originated in the 6th–5th century B.C.E., the period at the end of the Zhou dynasty. Although many transformations have occurred, it has remained a primary philosophical system in China, Korea, Japan, and Vietnam. While East Asians may identify with specific religious affiliations such as Shintōists, Daoists, Buddhists, or Christians, their orientation continues to be Confucians (Weiming, 2021). While the Confucian ideal stresses unity and harmony, it vested the emperor as the ideal of moral perfection, peace, and benevolence (Li, 2006). Ethnic identities derive from the degree to which groups ascribed to these cultural norms.

The Han, defined as the most civilized, were typically distinguished from the barbarian. However, these were not physical features or based on language, but rather cultural differences based on values and norms of behavior (Fawad and Yu, 2016). These distinctions would carry over into other times and systems. For example, during the early medieval times, the Chinese saw the rapid growth of Buddhism. As the Daoist group expanded during the 5th century, it became highly critical of Buddhist ideas and practices. The conversations that were pursued served to marginalize those Buddhists within Daoist groups. The discourse became known as the "Conversion of the Barbarians" and represented secondary teaching and fit for barbarians. At the same time, Daoism is more appropriate for the Chinese or Han. The response to the barbarians and those Buddhist Daoists ranged from accommodation and contestation to outright rejection. At the height of the period, the 2nd through the 6th century resulted in a more substantial consolidation and relevance of the Daoist identity and a growing antipathy to Buddhism (Raz, 2014). Ethnic diversity continued to become more complex as China expanded its empire and interacted with more diverse peoples. However, these principles continued, even until today, to define the basis of Chinese identities and the others.

## The premodern world of difference

As we get to our premodern era, this process derives from turmoil associated with the so-called "Holy Wars." A form of ethnocentrism or what others have called proto-racism between Jews, Christians, and Muslims came into being as the Crusaders invaded Jerusalem in July of 1099 and decimated nearly 40,000 Jews and Muslim inhabitants. After this invasion, hostility, fear, and suspicion now defined relations between the Jews, Christians, and Muslims. Over time, hatred of Jews and Islam became part of the Western ethos (Asbridge, 2005). During this period, the Europeans discovered the "infidel," Mongols, Africans, Native Americans, and Romani. Caucasian slave women were imported to Islamic Spain by Italian human traffickers. Indian migrants, known the world over as the Romani (Gypsies), were forced into slavery by the church and elite in Wallachia and Moldova (Mellinkoff, 1993). The culmination of these various movements created our modern racial states. Let us begin.

## The Moors and the social construction of others

In 711 B.C.E., the Moors, comprising Berbers and Black African and Arab Muslims, stepped into the political and military vacuum left by the fall of the Roman Empire.[2] By the following year, the Muslim rule covered much of Spain. While Muslims dominated the political and economic structures, they did not enslave most Christians. By 750, they had conquered and controlled the Iberian Peninsula, primarily consisting of modern-day Spain and Portugal. At its peak, Moorish Iberia, formally known as Al-Andalus, stretched as far as Mauritania and Senegal (Segal, 2001). A series of Arab and Berber dynasties vied to control this flourishing empire from this period. By the 12th century, 5.7 million of the estimated seven million Iberians were Muslims. As a result, Al-Andalus became the focal point of constant war between Muslims and Christians. Frequent slave-raiding expeditions fueled the conflict. For example, in a raid on Lisbon in 1189, Yaqub al-Mansur, the Almohad caliph, captured 3,000 female and child captives. Two years later, his governor of Cordoba took another 3,000 enslaved Christians. Christian monarchs responded by grabbing a similar number of Muslims and enslaving them (Segal, 2001).

The constant war between Christian and Muslim contingents throughout Europe produced great uncertainty and chaos. Oddly enough, some of the rationales for encouraging feudalism might have been a deterrent to perceived Muslim expansion into Europe. Some commoners might have preferred serfdom, with its illusion of freedom, to the reality of slavery. Serfdom, starting as voluntary, soon became mandatory and was as harsh as slavery in many ways.

For many decades, the Muslim dominance of Southern Europe facilitated trade between the Northern Christians and Arab-controlled portions of Africa. During this period, Arab trade to Northern Europe consisted primarily of spices, silks, and enslaved Black Africans. Interestingly, while Islam and Christianity espoused the value of humans and their relationship to a deity, both sanctioned the trade and enslavement of Black Africans.

However, the presence of the Moors in Southern Europe altered the form of slavery. Whereas enslaved Black Africans dominated in Northern Europe, ethnic enslaved Europeans dominated in Southern Europe.

The contestation over land and enslaved people accounted for the continual conflict between the Northern Christian nations and the Moors. Finally, in 1085, the Christian King Alphons VI defeated the Moors to capture Toledo. This conquest led to the ultimate fragmentation and demise of Al-Andalus and precipitated the dawn of the Christian Crusades.

## Proselytizing religions and the social construction of others

The fall of the Roman Empire marks a significant period for religions and the social construction of others. This period, variously depicted as the Middle Ages, the Dark Ages, or the Islamic Golden Age, is remarkable. It also led to the massive development of proselytizing religions, specifically Islam and Christianity. Competition for converts, souls, and groups increasingly led to conflict, aggression, and war. Power was the goal; land, resources, and dominion were the outcome. The contestations reflected a complicated array of sects, denominations, and cults. Thus, there were major confrontations between the major religions, but there were also confrontations within significant religions for various human groups' hearts, minds, souls, and identities. It is difficult to determine if these religious confrontations caused the expansions of the period or if they were products of imperial expansion. What is clear is that whether one was called Shiite or Sunni, Catholic or Protestant, the wars between "true believers" invariably fought over non-believers as well. The following section will discuss how proselytizing religions affected the social construction of others. Our exploration will begin with the Moors and their conquest of Southern Europe.

## Pagans, heathens, infidels, barbarians, savages, and the social construction of others

All major religions developed otherness constructs that created exclusive cultural boundaries that defined self and simultaneously served to exclude non-believers culturally. Terms such as pagans, heretics, heathens, infidels, and gentiles designate the religious other. Alternatively, some philosophers utilized terms such as savages, brutes, and barbarians to accomplish the same purposes.

Pagans, derived from the Latin *paganus*, refer to those considered rustic or rural. *Paganus* connoted civilians or incompetent soldiers. Around 312 A.D., as Constantine embraced and instituted Christianity throughout Rome, the term initially described those who maintained connections to the old gods. Alternatively, thw term heathens from Old English has a similar meaning and refers to those who were uncivilized or rural. Within religious parlance, both terms have been used negatively by Christians, Muslims, and Jews to depict those who are non-believers (Bowersock et al, 1999). The words were soon layered with other meanings to suggest those who were hedonistic, materialistic, and self-indulgent. Such groups were associated with idolatry, child or human sacrifices, and sexual perversions. With the ascension of Christianity, pagans and heathens were directly linked to Satan and were subject to a range of sanctions from ostracism to execution. The now infamous Salem witch hunts in this country document the horrendous consequences of this form of othering (Petts, 2011). With time, the term pagan gradually gave way to heathen and became a pejorative term to refer to non-Christian people.

Nevertheless, unlike pagan, moral tones are also added to suggest uncultured, uncivilized, savage, immoral, and wild. These terms became racialized with time to justify colonialization, subjugation, and extreme genocide. Hence, the justifications for the extreme violence perpetrated against the Indigenous peoples of Africa (see, for example, Hubbard, 1931; Bar-on, 1999; Stanley, 2010), China (see, for instance, Liestman, 1993).

## The Christian Crusades and the social construction of others

During the Middle Ages, the first period of Christian resistance to Muslim occupation, known as the Reconquista or "the Recapturing," lasted almost 800 years, most of which occurred in Portugal.[3] Muslims, captured during the Reconquista, were enslaved. For example, the reconstruction of the Cathedral of Santiago de Compostela was performed by enslaved Muslims in the 12th century. The ideology of the Reconquista defined war against the Muslim states as a Christian duty. Formally, the Reconquista ended on January 2, 1492, when the Muslim ruler of Granada surrendered to the Catholic monarchies of Ferdinand II of Aragon and Isabella I of Castile. However, the Reconquista provided the overarching rationale for the more expansive Christian Crusades into the Holy Land between the 11th and 13th centuries.

The Crusades were military campaigns authorized by the Pope and orchestrated by Catholic monarchies. Nine Crusades, disconnected campaigns with varying degrees of success, occurred between 1095 and 1291. While Catholics primarily led these, other Christian groups (notably Orthodox Christians) participated. Although the official ideology of the Crusades was to reclaim the Holy Land and defeat the Muslims, other groups were also targeted, such as the Greek Orthodox Christians in Byzantium, as well as the Balts, Mongols, and smaller sets of Christians. The initial success of the Crusades led to the creation of the Kingdom of Jerusalem in 1099. Unfortunately, this period of conquest was immediately followed by the almost wholesale massacres or expulsions of Jews and Muslims.

While wars, crusades, and other forms of external conflict may serve as a unifying theme, religious factions, among Christians and Muslims, continuously preserved hostilities and fueled proselytizing wars between and among these significant religions.

Underlying the expansionism associated with the Muslim Golden Era and the Christian Crusades was an intense drive to proselytize. The campaign to convert fueled many conflicts between and among major religious factions. In the Middle Ages, wars of proselytism dominated much of Africa, Europe, and the Middle East.

Among Christians, even before the official start of the Great Crusades, the Catholic church splintered into Eastern Orthodox and Roman Catholic. This split between East and West produced a century-long bitter political battle over doctrine and governance. However, the division was more than doctrinal or theological; it included linguistic, political, and geographical distinctions. Under the guise of the Crusades, Christians massacred each other in the (1182) and Constantinople (1204). In the Sixth Crusade, Christians punished and partitioned Byzantium and attacked the independent Christian Kingdom of Cyprus.

Several religious scholars on either side of this divide have remarked on the East–West schisms. Warren Carroll (1993), a Catholic scholar, concludes that the sack of Constantinople reflected mutual distrust and atrocities from both sides of the East–West schism.

Horrible and utterly indefensible as the sack was, it was not unprovoked more than once (as in the massacre of 1182). Part of that provocation was the massacre of the Westerners in Constantinople in 1182. In this nighttime raid, about 2,000 Greeks died. Violence respected neither age, illness, gender, or religious standing. Of the survivors, over 4,000 were sold into slavery to the Turks (Carroll, 1993: 157, 131). No one was innocent, as each justified violence for past wrong (Ware, 2015). Violence notwithstanding, Christian domination through proselytizing efforts developed across much of Europe and significant portions of the Middle East and Africa.

## Islamic civil war, jihad, and the social construction of others

Many ethnic, religious, and cultural divisions within Islam arose from disputes over religious doctrine.[4] For example, the Shi'as believed that leadership should stay in the family of the Prophet. The Sunni, alternatively, believed that the community's elite should determine who should become the leader. The Sunnis prevailed in selecting the first Caliph, which only aggravated the tensions. Increasingly, from this point, the subsequent four Caliphs faced conflict. The assignation was a frequent response to these conflicts. Tensions peaked during revolts, culminating in the First Fitna or Civil War (556–661). This Fitna shattered the belief in a unified Muslim world and resulted in the first major division of Islam into Shi'a and Sunni sects. Over the centuries, the division between Shi'a and Sunni has alternated between extreme hostility and open cooperation. To some extent, these divisions led to increased proselytizing among other Arabs and Northern Africans.

While there is some evidence of Islamic proselytizing before the Crusades, most scholars date the more radical version of jihad between the fall of Jerusalem in 1099 and the Muslim Siege of Edessa in 1144. Specifically, before the Crusades, jihad was defined primarily as religious conversion. After the Crusades, jihad was also embraced by military conquest (Hillenbrand, 1999: 103–105). While some Muslims rejected the idea of forced conversions, others embraced it.

Military conquest expanded the reach of Islam over the next four centuries throughout India, the Middle East, and significant portions of Africa. Slavery was so widespread in Muslim-dominated Southeast Asia that enslaved people performed "almost every conceivable function." "Many members of the slave-owning merchant class had strong roots in the Islamic world, which had a clear body of law on slaves as property" (A. Reid, quoted in Khan, 2009: 299, 143). Throughout Islamic-controlled Northern Africa, close to a third of the populations were enslaved people in such places as western Sudan, including Ghana (750–1076), Mali (1235–1645), Segou (1712–1861), Songhai (1275–1591) and Senegambia (1300–1900).

In concluding this section, it is essential to observe that all major religions –including Judaism, Islam, and Christianity – developed nuanced and layered taxonomies and ideologies describing the other. At their core, these constructs linked identity to kinship, culture, and geography. It is also important to acknowledge that while these constructs of others included hierarchical, moral, and cultural valuations, these constructs were indicative of extrinsic, not intrinsic, differences. With the dawn of European imperialism, religious constructs of the other were well developed and provided a nuanced and layered taxonomy and ideology of differences. The religious terms and doctrines provided an umbrella subsuming all previous forms of othering. In the next section, we shall explore the story of European imperialism and examine how these terms of othering were transformed and became the ideological rationale for the subjugation, exploitation, extermination, enslavement, and colonization of non-Western others. Religious ideology in this period would also shift the extrinsic evaluative criteria of others to that which was explicitly intrinsic. Let us now turn to the dawn of European imperialism and the racial construction of the other.

*The racial construction of the other: liberalism, conservatism, and race*

How is it that we hear the loudest yelps for liberty among the drivers of negroes?

Samuel Johnson, 1775

Classical European philosophers were central to developing the concept of race and racial ideologies used in defining and characterizing human groups (Ward and Lott, 2002; Valls, 2005). Classical philosophers (from about 1600 to 1900), while in partial agreement regarding the origins, characteristics, types, or mutability associated with each race, were nevertheless consistent in their recognition of the existence of such groups (see, for example, Kant, 1796/2006; Boxill, 2005).

Racial categories originated in imperialism and became the justifications for colonial racial policies and practices. Colonies were controlled directly through settlements or indirectly through exploitative outposts under the authority of the military and merchants.

Each colonial form provided a different ideological justification for developing racial designations and constructions. These colonial models gave rise to two ideological justifications: classical liberalism and classical conservatism.

- *Classical liberalism* was a product of unique political and religious traditions that fostered specific institutional structures (Parry, 1996). Famous liberals included such intellectuals as Adam Smith, John Locke, and Thomas Jefferson.
- *Classical conservatism* was a product of multiple political traditions, religious patterns, or unique institutional structures. Foremost classical conservative intellectuals included Thomas Hobbes, Joseph de Maistre, and James Madison (Fawcett, 1952/2020). These three produced interesting alternative justifications for identifying people by race.

Consequently, the conservatism that developed in Britain focused on natural law, while French and German conservatism developed in opposition to natural law. Ironically, the United States represents a particular case and a blend of French liberalism and English conservatism.

But in each case, imperialism, colonialism, the genocide of Indigenous populations, forced slavery, and racial hierarchies were justified. More recently, conservative variants occurring in Germany, Italy, and later Japan were fundamental to the rise of fascism.

The next sections will discuss the origins of classical liberalism and conservatism. In the process, we shall discover how race, racial imperialism, and racial nations were created.

## The origins of classical liberalism

The ideas associated with liberalism date back to at least the Middle Ages, as various intellectuals began to consider the rights and responsibilities of being a citizen of a nation. For example, such requests during the Middle

Ages were derived from birth and determined one's place in the hierarchical social system.

In the 16th century, as commercialization, industrialization, and urbanization intensified across Europe, traditional power structures such as the church, the divine right of kings, and the fixed hierarchies determined at birth began to be challenged and gradually dissolved.

As the ruling elite tried to preserve and expand their power, more regressive policies were instituted, which resulted in ever-increasing wars among the European royal families.

During this same period, merchants and industrialists ascended as a newly emerging middle class. All of this led to the significant revolutions that radically transformed England and France in the 17th and 18th centuries, most notably, the English Civil Wars (1642–1651), the Glorious Revolution (1688), the American Revolution (1775–1783) and the French Revolution (1790). With the various "revolutions" taking place across Europe, existing proto-racial identities and biases were transformed as they became reinterpreted and imbued into the newly forming nation-states.

The conflict between these significant forces defined the new racial realities, starting with the "Jewish Question." Hostility toward Jews, prevalent in both major ideological streams, produced reactionary political elements. The results almost splintered the major ideological movements – with some embracing Jewish emancipation and others provoking opposition.

Strangely, the most contentious battles were within the so-called liberal movements. As we approached the end of the 18th century, political fractures had occurred, and a novel word and action came into being – antisemitism.

But unlike historical anti-Jewish hatred based primarily on religion, the modern version was political and targeted people. The new victims and conflicts were directly associated with Europe's transformation from a static agrarian world into an increasingly industrial and urban one. The release of peasants from feudal estates served to pit them against the Jews.

Nation-building, made possible by imperial expansion, intensified these conflicts, as diverse peoples from different regions were now racialized (Steinman, 2012). Classical liberalism and conservatism provided competing ideological frameworks that were both antecedents to and products of the various revolutions.

Every prominent classical liberal theorist, from John Locke and Adam Smith to Immanuel Kant and John Stuart Mill, was explicitly racist. Locke, often considered the father of liberalism, was a significant investor in the African slave trade (Buccus, 2020). One of the influential architects of English colonial policy, he proposed enacting legislation that would guarantee that "every freeman of Carolina shall have absolute power and authority over his negro slaves" (Locke, 1823: vol x, 196).

Liberalism provided sanctuary for the ideas of European imperialism and the ideological justification and lynchpin by which racism, genocide, and Western expansion found expression. The genocide was quick, as deliberate policies strove to eliminate Indigenous peoples and cultures from the Americas to the Pacific Islands, the Horn of Africa to the Pacific Rim, and the Middle East to Asia.

Charles Mill critiqued liberalism with racism in what he termed the "racial contract." Enlightenment, from which liberalism derives, also produced slavery, colonialism, the genocide of Indigenous peoples, and racial oppression targeting all non-Europeans. The racial contract that included racism, racial identities, racial ideas/ideologies, and systems was ironically part of the argument for European appropriation of the world (Mills, 1997: 122).

Locke was not alone in his sentiments. The racial "othering" and denigration of all those not European was also evident in the work of Adam Smith. Smith, famous for the *Wealth of Nations* (Smith, 1776/2000), explored what he theorized as the foundations of the modern capitalist state. He distinguished the current capitalist state as being "civilized" while all others are "savage."

From the beginning of his treatise, Smith notes:

Among the savage nations of hunters and anglers, every individual who can work is more or less employed in valuable labour and endeavours to provide, as well as he can, the necessaries and conveniences of life for himself and such of his family or tribe as are either too old, or too young, or too infirm, to go a-hunting and fishing.

Such nations, however, are so miserably poor that from mere want, they are frequently reduced, or at least think themselves reduced, to the necessity sometimes of directly destroying, and sometimes of abandoning their infants, their old people, and those afflicted with lingering diseases, to perish with hunger, or to be devoured by wild beasts.

Among civilized and thriving nations, on the contrary, though a significant number of people do not include labour at all, many of whom consume the produce of ten times, frequently of a hundred times, more sweat than the greater part of those who work; yet the produce of the whole labour of the society is so great, that all are often abundantly supplied; and a workman, even of the lowest and poorest order, if he is frugal and industrious, may enjoy a greater share of the necessaries and conveniencies of life than it is possible for any savage to acquire. (Smith, 1776/2000: 2)

Smith describes Peruvians and Mexicans as more ignorant than the lowest group in Europe, the Tartars of Ukraine. Added are those from Turkey, Indonesia, Egypt, Arabia, Africa, the West Indies, Persia, Bengal, Siam,

China, and all the Indigenous groups in North America. These groups were racialized and accorded the spot of the "lowest and rudest state of society." In sum, every country outside of Europe was brutal, savage, and, by implication, ripe for subjugation.

Immanuel Kant viewed "Whites," more specifically White men, as naturally superior to all other "races" and women. And as such, they should rule the rest of the world (Kleingeld, 2019). Kleingeld demonstrates that for most of Kant's writings, until the mid-1790s, he distinguished various racial groups as deficient.

These groups, such as the "yellows," "Negroes," and the "copper-red" races, when compared to Whites, were distinctively lacking in terms of self-government. Colonial rule in Northern Africa and much of Asia, and the enslavement and exploitation of non-Whites by White Europeans, were thus justified.

The Africans were only suited to be enslaved because they could not govern themselves, be educated, or be civilized. Although Indigenous peoples in India could be educated, they were still limited and had to be under the leadership of Europeans. In the middle of the 1790s, Kant recanted his more racist views.

Gone were racial hierarchies and White superiority; Native Americans ceased being weak and became courageous. Former savages became moral and civilized. Kant would also condemn both colonialism and slavery. All humans, covered by what he referred to as "cosmopolitan rights," were entitled to self-determination, autonomy, and sovereignty. Only through legitimate treaties could European powers inhabit and settle land owned by others. Slavery, the forced exploitation of people by Europeans, was thus morally indefensible (Kleingeld, 2019; see also Flikschuh and Ypi, 2014).

John Stuart Mill, a staunch supporter of toleration, liberty, and legal rights, was one of the fiercest apologists for British imperialism, colonialism, and racism. He believed that the civilized people of Europe had a moral obligation to "help" and govern the uncivilized societies. Looking at the colonization of India, he marveled at the improvements, specifically in education and health care, that the East India Company had introduced into the country (Tunick, 2006).

> It is, perhaps, hardly necessary to say that this doctrine Is meant to apply only to human beings in the maturity of their faculties. ... For the same reason, we may leave out of consideration those backward states of society in which the race itself may be considered in its nonage.
>
> The early difficulties in the way of spontaneous progress are so great, that there is seldom any choice of means for overcoming them; and a ruler full of the spirit of improvement is warranted in the use of any expedients that will attain an end, perhaps otherwise unattainable.

Despotism is a legitimate mode of government in dealing with barbarians, provided the end be their improvement, and the means justified by actually effecting that end. Liberty, as a principle, has no application to any state of things anterior to the time when mankind has become capable of being improved by free and equal discussion. Until then, there is nothing for them but implicit obedience to an Akbar or a Charlemagne, if they are so fortunate as to find one.

But as soon as mankind have attained the capacity of being guided to their own improvement by conviction or persuasion (a period long since reached in all nations with whom we need here concern ourselves), compulsion, either in the direct form or in that of pains and penalties for non-compliance, is no longer admissible as a means to their own good, and justifiable only for the security of others. (Mill, 1869: 4)

Mill believed that only by maintaining ethnically homogeneous states could representative democracy work. Freedom, he argued, could not be extended to the "uncivilized" and the "barbarians." Such groups had to be controlled and civilized by force, if necessary, by the civilized. Thus, truth and right were standards that only applied to the civilized. They alone can be free and enjoy the privileges attendant to their position. Racial hierarchies, racial imperialism, and the racial state were necessary while creating, reinforcing, and perpetuating status and power disparities favoring Europeans.

Classical liberalism served as a foundation for the English Revolution. In defining the "rights of men," it explicitly was referencing the rights of "White men", the oppression of non-Whites, and the creation of White supremacy.

These were the core principles in "The Rights of Men and Citizens" (Johnson and Koyama, 2018). The French Revolution, advocating liberal democracy and phrases such as *liberté*, *égalité*, and *fraternité*, also gave rise to Joseph-Arthur de Gobineau (1853). Gobineau, the architect of Social Darwinism, argued that human development was the outcome of the survival of the higher races.

Relying upon German archaeology, philology, and French anthropology, Gobineau argued that racial hierarchies, dominated by the White races, with lower Black and Asian ethnicities, were the driving force of human history. The dominance of the White or European race over all others resulted from this constant struggle. The battle would be eternal, with no clear victor.

But the White race had to be constantly vigilant as the lesser races continually tried to move up the human ladder by interbreeding with the dominant White races. Such interbreeding would produce a weaker version, as declared by Gobineau, as witnessed by the European peasantry and the urban working classes.

Social Darwinism, later biological racism, would become the lynchpin whereby the new positivist sciences of physical anthropology, psychology, and ethnology would come into being. These scientists' original research aims were to demonstrate the hypothesized biological link between racial hierarchies, intelligence, and civilization. Science, therefore, provided legitimacy to racial classification as it created the myth that head shapes, cranial capacity, and other measures demonstrated racial hierarchies among various human groups.

It is Gobineau who gives us the concept of Aryanism. Aryans were the source of ancient civilizations in Africa (Egypt and Ethiopia) and Asia (Elam, Mesopotamia, and the Indus Valley). The idea of Aryan superiority, genus, creativity, and blood all stem from the work of Gobineau (Moore, 1974). We shall return to this in the section on Hitler and Nazi Germany; for now, this also provided the impetus for European colonialism, imperialism, White supremacy, and the rise of racial nation-states.

Liberal thinkers such as Kant and Diderot, critical of the barbarity of colonialism, challenged the idea that Europeans had a right to "civilize" others. They believed the central use of violence, slavery, forced labor, and exploitation of land and resources was just the opposite of "Enlightenment."

Kant argued that "[t]he Negroes of Africa have by nature no feeling that rises above the trifling [Die Negers von Afrika haben von der Natur kein Geföhl, welches über das Läppische stiege]" (quoted in Judy, 1991: 1). Ultimately, for Kant, Hume, and other imperial theorists, not only Africans, but all Indigenous people, were reduced to a color, savagery, and stupidity. At least, this is what we conclude from the racialized lens of Whiteness. But let us consider another view, that from the subject.

Kant would stress an almost biological necessity for colonialism. From the liberal tradition, Kant argues that India was deserving and happier under European sovereignty. He identified three major racial groups, hierarchically arranged as follows:

1. Whites, a superior "non-deficient race ... with all the incentives and talents."
2. Black people were suitable to be bonded people but not freemen, incapable of leading themselves.
3. Hindus were superior to the Black people because they were at least educated, but only in the arts, not the sciences or anything requiring abstract thinking.

Kant, by 1795, would revise these views and begin arguing for the humanity and rights of all racial groups, along with the inhumanity of colonialism. Asserting these rights, termed cosmopolitan rights, he argued that informed consent of Indigenous peoples (including Native Americans, Africans, and Asians) was a fundamental right that should constrain the imperial ambitions of Europeans.

Kant went further by condemning slavery and paternalism (Kleingeld, 2014). Mahmud (1999) explains how these ideas inspired the enslaved Blacks of Haiti to challenge French sovereignty in articulated in "The Declaration of the Rights of Man and of the Citizen (1789)". Their pleas were not only rebuked but evoked the wrath of the colonizer. The rebels, both in Europe and after in the United States, were backward and dangerous, as they threatened the natural orders of private property, racial hierarchies, and civilization itself (Mahmud, 1999: 1219).

As we have seen, the contradictions were central to the "clarifications" by scholars such as Hegel and the creation of a dichotomy between human and subhuman. History and civilization belonged to mature nations, whereas, according to Hegel, immature nations, or "non-nations," could not make any claims to reason, progress, or science (Pradella, 2014).

The European colonization of Africa is instructive in its so-called "Civilizing Mission." As a civilizing force of modernity, the West was there to rescue the reluctant Africans from their tribal, brutal existence. African tribal units, with their common languages, culture, kinship, hereditary membership, and tribal laws, were detrimental to progress.

European imperialism disrupted, distorted, and destroyed these centuries-old systems, dismantling African cultural institutions and forcibly replacing "original" cultures with ones modeled on Europe. An educated and empowered African population was seen as a "threat to colonial rule." Race consciousness and adopting European values established and kept White political rule.

Therefore, the European model encouraged tribal and ethnic divisions by pitting various tribal groups against each other to ensure colonial control (see for example Nikuze, 2014). Similar conservative discourses in the 1820s and 1830s argued that colonial slavery in the West Indies had to be maintained, as the formerly enslaved people would not work. "Unless guided and directed by the intelligence and capital of White men, the Black people never would produce anything" (quoted in Taylor, 2014: 977).

Diderot, alternatively, questioned if the Indigenous people benefited from European civilization and whether the European colonists were the "civilized ones." He argued that culture, or a "national character" that served to socialize others into morality and norms of respect, tended to diminish the further the colonizer was from the country of origin. Therefore, according to Diderot, colonial empires became frequent sites for abuse, violence, and brutality because the colonists were far from the normative structures that would sanction (legally or informally) or otherwise restrain natural human instincts toward violence (Muthu, 2003).

The European history of race and others is considerably deficient. It presupposes that they alone had history and that history followed the imperial powers and their development of the racial state. Even among Europeans, this history is minimal at best. A more complete analysis must include the pre-colonial ancient world. It is here that we will venture to get a fuller understanding of how the other was constructed.

## Not object but subject: Black and Indigenous peoples

Indigeneity for far too many only comes through the racialized lens of imperialism. Questions abound regarding the actuality of such realities. Is there a place called Africa and people called Africans? Who are the original peoples of the Americas? How can they exist? Even granting such an existence, we are left with the racialized frame of asking, as Du Bois did, "What is it like to be a problem?" Countless scholars have challenged White America to identify the humanity of Blacks as asserted by Franz Fanon, Kwame Nkrumah, W.E.B. Du Bois or Marcus Garvey. Africa does not constitute a meaningful political or cultural unity throughout the diaspora in places like the Caribbean, Latin America, Asia, and the Middle East. They are regions and continents but not cohesive entities. How can there be an African, a Latin American, an Asian, and a Middle Easterner, much less diasporas? These questions go to the heart of what it means to exist, to have agency, and to have a reality that is not imposed but composed by the individual or group.

Our journey starts with a statement by Anna Julia Cooper, 21 years after the end of the Civil War and almost two centuries ago, declaring that Black people's plight, reality, and future depended upon the Black woman's success. For too long, the church, clergy, politicians, educators, and even the Black man thwarted these efforts by placing constraints upon the Black woman's hopes, dreams, and opportunities. Cooper's "Voice" provides a clarion call not to look back with inflated conceit but to glean wisdom from experiences, capture the spiritual essence of our being, and look to the future with hope and trust. This Voice shrugged condescension and victimhood yet shouted determination and "the radical amelioration," liberation, and regeneration of the Black woman and community. Cooper ends with hope, believing Black women shall arrive at the "promised land" (Cooper, 1892).

White America responded to the emergence of this new Black with lynchings and race riots. Again, targeted were Blacks, particularly males, who dared to assert their freedom. Ida B. Wells, taking up the challenge, led the anti-lynching campaign in the United States.

Wells rejected the negative image of the rapist and refused to be complacent.. One of the first to challenge segregated streetcars, she refused to stay in her place. It was she who argued that the South was dependent upon

Afro-American labor. Lynchings and segregation were means of keeping the Blacks in a humble position. She acknowledged that Jim Crow legalized racism and legitimated White racial hierarchies. Wells, anticipating Malcolm X and Carmichael, advised "that a Winchester rifle would have a place of honor in every Black home, and it should be used for that protection which the law refuses to give" (Wells–Barnett, 1892/2005).

Following in her footsteps, Du Bois questioned the "problematization of being Black." A problem complicated by prejudice, lawlessness, and ruthless competition. What is it like to be a Black and an American, two unreconciled selves, two paradoxes, two ends of a spectrum, in one body? Forty years after the promise of emancipation, freedom remained elusive to the freedman. Constantly vilified and condemned, overpoliced and undervalued, within just one generation, Blacks crafted institutions that provided escapes from the prison of poverty, mediocrity, and complacency. Yet, the soul of Black folks, the spiritual strivings of a people, was made manifest as they went from enslaved to free, from forced laborers to skilled artisans and farmers. They created thousands of businesspeople, clergy, teachers, and doctors (Du Bois, 1903/2009).

Du Bois asserted that a specific spirituality fundamentally characterizes Blacks and other distinct groups. Both historical and social factors causally construct this spirituality. These historical and social factors include laws, religions, habits of thought, and their conscious strivings that produce a cohesive, spiritually distinct subjective identity (Du Bois, 1897). The community and their humanity guided these stories based on economic, social, political, and educational freedom. The spiritual strivings, therefore, constituted a "self-consciousness, self-realization, self-respect." Thus emerged the "revelation of his power, of his mission." A truer, better self (Du Bois, 1903\2009: 8).

It is not coincidental; Kendi (2016) points out that Du Bois chose to call his book *The Souls of Black Folk*. The one thing that distinguishes humans from beasts is their souls. Being Black in America was often objectified and vilified by racist structures. Such an object only reacts, but Du Bois asserted the active agency of Blacks as he called for "The Talented Tenth" to forge a new path and create a "New Negro." *The Soul of Black Folks* is captured in their gift to America – "the spiritual heritage of the nation" found in the spirituals and folk songs that emerged from slavery.

Franz Fanon would describe this as a non-being, for the racialized, anti-Black world does not recognize it. But rather than a non-being, this is a being that reflects the subjective "yes" that vibrates to cosmic harmonies (Fanon, 1952/2008: 2). This existential reality is the cumulative essence of rejecting colonial objectivity, as Blacks in the Caribbean purposefully created Creole and pidgin. The racist structure would characterize these dictions as imperfect and conclude that the Caribbean Blacks were inferior. The creation of these imperfections was indeed a deliberate attempt to assert one's subjective control of their objective realities. Talking "properly" alienates and assigns a fundamental pathology to the speaker. We might today call this code-switching, where in one setting, the Black speaker demonstrates their ability to articulate perfect "English," yet among one's peers to perform "Black Speak" (see, for example, Luu, 2020).

The adoption of "Black Speak" parallels the civil rights and postcolonial discourses that challenged the imperial racial state. These voices were more than a reaction but also an act of creative agency as the struggle to define and reimagine the subjective realities of Blacks, Africans, and other Indigenous peoples.

Jamaican-born Marcus Garvey was the first major thinker on a massive scale to advocate for Black dignity, destinies, and pride. In the 1920s, living in Harlem, he unapologetically called for Black nationalism when Jim Crow, White supremacy, and segregation were the law of the land. It was a period when scientists and politicians deemed Blacks in the United States and Europe culturally, biologically, and socially inferior (Abdelfatah, 2021). Garvey rejected the notion that "[a] Black skin" was "a badge of shame, but rather a glorious symbol of national greatness" (Cronon, 1955, quoted in Abdelfatah, 2021). This journey begins by acknowledging that "[a] people without the knowledge of their history, origin, and culture is like a tree without roots" (History. com, 2009/2022). Only by reclaiming this past, these roots, could the Africans restore their dignity stolen by slavery and colonization. Garvey launched a United Negro Improvement Association (UNIA) between 1916 and 1927. This global movement, encompassing 40 countries and nearly 1,200 divisions in Africa, the Caribbean, Australia, and the United States, produced an international organization of Black resistance, self-determination, and affirmation (Lewis, 2009). The only way for Blacks to defeat universal prejudice and subjugation was to construct their systems of government, scholarship, and communities. Only then could they recover their identities and become free (Garvey, 1923/2009).

Garvey produced a unique voice that did not embrace oppression but spoke of liberation, did not embrace exploitation but articulated empowerment, and did not reflect objectification but the subjective articulation of Africa and the Africans. With these tools, the destructive forces of racialized ghettos and states were engaged. And thus, Garvey became "the greatest and most successful organizer for the Pan-African cause." He did this by "psychologically rehabilitating ... the colour 'Black,' instilling an awareness in black people of their African roots and creating a real feeling of international solidarity among Africans and persons of African Stock" (Adewale and Schepers, 2023: 110).

In Europe, an alternative fork emerged in the 1940s, originally known as the negritude movement. This movement challenged the notion that Africa was a figment of European imagination, with no agency or historical voice before its discovery by Western imperialism. This movement, centering around French-speaking Black intellectuals, began to show that Africa had a history and that civilization, mathematics, arts, and sciences derive from its people (Diop, 1954: 253). Soon, diasporic voices across the United States and Africa would make similar proclamations.

These ideas of Du Bois, Fanon, Garvey, and beyond inspired the modern civil rights and postcolonial movements. The most prominent voices of these movements were such activists as King, Stokely Carmichael, and Malcolm X in the United States. Often, we ignore the other voices of the Americas, but who can forget Che Guevara? Alternatively, the most potent postcolonial voice on the continent was that of Kwame Nkrumah.

The beginning of the modern civil rights movement is typically situated with the 1954 Supreme Court case, *Brown* v *Board of Education of Topeka*, which ended school segregation. Thurgood Marshall, chief counsel for the case, cited Pauli Murray's 1951 book, *States' Laws on Race and Color*, as the "bible" of the civil rights movement (Gavins, 2016). The case featured the work of Pauline "Pauli" Murray, yet her work was not acknowledged until decades later. Many point also to the 1963 March on Washington as seminal, yet, as pointed out by Pauli Murray, it had one fatal flaw: no women were featured in any of the major speeches or part of the delegation that met with the president. She wrote:

> I have been increasingly perturbed over the blatant disparity between the major role which Negro women have played and are playing in the crucial grassroots levels of our struggle and the minor part of leadership they have been assigned in the national policy-making decisions. It is indefensible to call a national march on Washington and send out a call that contains the name of not a single woman leader. (Quoted in Cole and Guy-Sheftall, 2003: 89)

One cannot talk about the modern civil rights movement in the United States without talking about Martin Luther King, Jr.'s (1963) focus on changing the structure of racism. Racial equality was not the job of Blacks but of Whites. These changes would not come "merely from court decisions nor from the fountains of political oratory … White America must recognize that justice for Black people cannot be achieved without radical changes in the structure of our society." And so, while much of King's activity was in organizing the Black community, much of it was directed at getting Whites to own the system they had created. As observed by Joe Feagin, "Whites created slavery, Jim Crow segregation and contemporary racial discrimination" (Feagin, quoted in Henton, 2022). But while King embraced America and pushed for changes to accommodate and ultimately free the

"Negro," others pushed for rejecting that America and called for creating a new identifying label: Black.

Although Martin Luther King, Jr. is viewed as the architect of the modern civil rights movement, he was part of a larger coalition of activists. One of the central features of this "movement" was the realization of what Stokely Carmichael would declare as "Black Power." In this regard, Carmichael remarked: "When you talk about Black Power, you talk about bringing this country to its knees any time it messes with Black men … any White man in this country knows about power. He knows what White power is and ought to know what Black power is" (Carmichael, 1966). Carmichael rejected American institutions, nonviolence, and King's accommodationist perspective. He appealed to Blacks to engage in an armed struggle as the only means of Black liberation.

"Black Power" was used by earlier race leaders such as Richard Wright, Paul Robeson, and Adam Clayton Powell. Their use of the term asserted the agency and reality of being unique in America. Therefore, they rejected assimilation (where Blacks were encouraged to blend into White America) and amalgamation (Blacks somehow coexisted within a White defined reality). For Carmichael and other Black Power advocates, the term was an attempt to control the narrative, instill pride, and redefine Black identity (Carmichael and Hamilton, 1967/1992).

Over time, and with the criticism of major civil rights leaders such as King and Whitney M. Young (National Urban League), advocates began to assert a transformed Black power that emphasized nonviolence, nonrevolutionary participatory democracy, self-empowerment, self-determination, pride, and control over one's destiny and community (Martin, 1991).

Malcolm X, following in the path of Garvey and representing his mentor Elijah Muhammad, asserted that Africans, Africa, and their history had been distorted by White "historians … (who) ignored the African roots of Western civilization" (Malcolm X, quoted in Martin, 1991: 6). With the founding of the Organization of Afro-American Unity in 1984, Malcolm X pushed for the elimination of racism and justice.

As the fight for freedom, justice, and empowerment was being waged in the United States, it was part of a much larger set of decolonial movements across the African continent. Africans were fighting to redefine their identities, independence, and paths forward. The struggles were interconnected as Africans worked to embrace each other by recognizing their shared histories of racial exploitation, oppression, and subjugation. In the process, the African diaspora shared a bond that transcended geography, language, and politics.

The voice of Ghana's Kwame Nkrumah loudly proclaimed the necessity to counteract the colonial legacies of illiteracy, ignorance, and self-hatred embodied in the ethnically based political and communal conflicts that seem to define African states. Nkrumah advocated a cultural revolution that would disrupt the Eurocentric perspectives by articulating an African ontological reconstruction of the political, economic, and cultural agenda.

At the core of Nkrumah's ontological reconstruction was a rejection of the dehumanized cultural personality of the colonized Africans. Nkrumah (1963) observed that African epistemologies, cultures, cosmologies, aesthetics, and realities were the first targets of colonial imperialism.

Che Guevara, in 1961, articulated the global struggle of the Africans. He asserted that all were in solidarity against racial imperialism. This struggle was not only in the Americas, "fighting for the independence of the Guianas and British Antilles," but also in Belize and "in Africa, in Asia, in any part of the world where the strong oppress the weak" (Guevara, 1961). This global liberation movement recognized that markets and financial institutions collaborated to create racially stratified systems. Victory could only come with intensive reform programs to counterbalance and produce a fundamental economic and social revolution (Guevara, 1964). The first successful challenge to European colonialism occurred in Ghana under the leadership of Kwame Nkrumah.

The voices of the Africans, both in the United States and abroad, sound the clarion call and are marked by progress, resilience, and perseverance; it is easy to ignore the trials, tribulations, and suffering endured by many Blacks over the ages. Maya Angelou's *I Know Why the Caged Bird Sings* reminds us that it is not always a bed of roses.

This is particularly true in this autobiographical work that traces a life often interrupted by tragedy, moving from kin to kin, grandparents to separated parents, and back to grandparents. Being the ugly duckling, battered and abused (sexually, mentally, and spiritually). But after being raped, pregnant, and disgraced, she continued onward. She did not allow these obstacles to drag her into hopelessness and despair. Head held high, she continued to pursue her path, gave birth to a marvelous son, graduated from high school, and the rest is history. So why can the caged bird sing? She dreams of freedom.

Time and space limitations preclude us from advancing; countless other voices that have surfaced to lift the African. But these brief glimpses provide the basis for how the African has been constructed (both objectively and subjectively) and how Crticial Race Theory (CRT) has evolved. Based on these observations, we can identify a set of theorems and postulates.

## Critical Race Theory: theorems and postulates

Central to CRT are the voices of marginalized peoples. Many who look at this process concentrate on the objectification, victimization, and marginalization of the Indigenous, colonized, and enslaved as they were minoritized and marginalized. And while there were obvious reactions by such people to the processes, they were nevertheless active agents. This means that Indigenous, colonized, and enslaved peoples were more than blank templates upon which were written the epithets of racism and racialism; they were already contemplative, whole peoples who had already spent hundreds of years writing their own stories. One of the principal lies and myths of liberal and conservative historians is that they began the history of these peoples at the junction where they entered history as victims and rarely as thinking, sentient peoples. Failure to recognize this important reality means that we fail to understand how counter-narratives and alternative narratives existed and persisted even as the racial transformations deliberately attempted to wipe their existence from the face of history. CRT advocates the essential use of storytelling (Cooper, 1994), counter-stories (Delgado, 1989; Villenas et al, 1999), and counter-narratives (Lather, 1998) as not only a corrective but necessary transformative process in producing equitable and systemic anti-racism policies, practices, remedies and solutions (Miller et al, 2020). Going further, I argue that the critical aspects of this perspective lead to an examination of the dual construction of race throughout history. This dual construction reflects what Du Bois referred to as double consciousness, or what I will call the bipolar construction of identity. This bipolar construction of identity reflects both the objective and the subjective construction of the identity of racialized individuals and groups. Each chapter will feature these bipolar constructions as a corrective to our histories and realities. From this analysis, several theorems will be derived. Summarized next are the most central theorems.

## Critical Race Theory theorems

- Minoritized, marginalized peoples/groups represented by Indigenous, colonized, and other ethnic/racial individuals and groups are not mere objects but subjects actively engaged as agents of social change and architects of social justice. What this means is that race is both objective and subjective. The objective aspects of race detail how the other(s) are constructed by racialized regimes. The ideological structures put into place by racial imperialism serve not only to objectify but to reify race. The subjective components of racial identities reflect how minoritized and majoritized individuals and groups construct cognitive maps, boundaries, and meanings (Brubaker and Cooper, 2000). Together, these create what Du Bois called double consciousness or what I will refer to as bipolar extremes in both historical narratives and racial realities.
- Racial triangulation refers to how institutional structures and racial designations intersect to "fix" the location of the lowest racial caste. This caste historically has been occupied by Indigenous, colonized, former enslaved, and colonial subjects. From the beginning of racial caste within the various Western racial states and their former colonies,

they have utilized three specific structural components to situate and trap Indigenous, colonized, minoritized, and marginalized people/groups in the lowest of castes. These structures – educational, economic, political, cultural, social and criminal justice – perpetuate race and the racial caste system. This is seen most recently in the reality that the majority of Blacks are trapped in ghettos that lack sufficient educational funding (we spend about US$26,000 less on Black education than White education), a decades-long war on drugs, and the militarization of police, and an economic system that has used such things as redlining, occupational segregation, and differential access to credit markets to keep Blacks in their place. These structures make up the system of racial triangulation that preserves and fixes Blacks in the lowest rungs in this Nations racial hierarchy. I would argue that racial triangulation has been a central component of the American racial state since its inception.

- Racial objectification leads to the development of racial tropes and other myths. The history of Indigenous, colonized, enslaved, and marginalized peoples has been distorted, denied, or perverted. In their place is taught the narrative that Whites are superior peoples, that Western nations were great, and that the destruction of other peoples, their nations, and theft of their lands either did not occur or was necessary to bring the savages into the modern world (Khatun, 2020). This whitewashing of history is reflected in national monuments, history books, street and building names, and much of our public discourse. In America, the founding of the Colonial National Monument in 1931 is one way in which African Americans and Native Americans were intentionally left out of American history. Co-conspirators included a balance of both conservatives and liberals, such as General John Pershing, France's Marshal Pétain, the Secretary of the Interior, and New York governor Franklin Delano Roosevelt, a year before his election to the presidency (Wills, 2019). We all agree that race is a social construction or a myth. We don't seem to understand that associated with this myth are components that help shape, preserve, and, at times, justify race. A few of these race components include, but are not limited to, systemic racism, racialized laws and differential enforcement, and covert and overt racial realities, codes, and cultures embedded and supported by our various institutions. Other aspects of race have to do with assumptions associated with racism. Racism, the ability and the power to enforce racial codes, sanctions, and rewards, operate at the system or institutional level. While individuals might be racially biased, they must be in positions of power or authority and willing to use them to enforce racial codes, sanctions, and rewards. But, racism is a form of discrimination that links bias with institutional power.

- Racial subjectification leads to racial dynamics and social movements. Like Newton's Third Law, the third theorem of CRT is that racial and racist

47

dynamics presuppose motion and a continuous set of opposite motions associated with racial social movements. More simply, racial and racist dynamics represent barriers, usually constructed or defined by the various policies, practices, and beliefs, that serve to protect or preserve racial and racist systems. Social movements aiming to disrupt these barriers often produce negligible or incremental changes. Consequently, the changes may appear to be insubstantial, particularly as the racial and racist dynamics re-emerge.

- Finally we must recognize that: Racial realities are social constructions; racial consequences are the consequences of believing that the results are normal and natural, and the victim is the cause, not the structures.
- Focus on systemic change rather than individual or even group behavior.
- Racial codes of conduct and norms are institutionalized and global in their prevalence, operationalization, and interconnectedness.
- Racial angst and fears of those Whites in power underlie racial constructions; thus, racial structures reflect a zero-sum mentality. Historically, this has limited the efforts to dismantle the racial state effectively.

3

# The Bipolar Construction of Identity: Racial Imperialism, African Agency, and Reactions of the Presumed Other

Racial imperialism created racial hierarchies in the colonized countries based upon the ideological and presumptive beliefs of the colonizers toward the colonized. In the previous chapter we examined how racial realities were created by ideologies developed by both conservative and liberal philosophers. We also examined the alternative construction of reality developed by the so-called racialized other. In this chapter we will examine how racial imperialism constructed and externalized the other. We shall also examine how the subjective realities constructed by the African and others served not only to react, but to actively engage those realities. In the process, we will see how history is the result of creating what Du Bois called double consciousness, or what I will refer to as bipolar extremes in both historical narratives and racial realities. We shall begin this chapter by exploring how the ideologies manifested in what has become known as racial imperialism, which created, maintained, and continually serves to perpetuate racial hierarchies. The colonial past, which included Indigenous genocide, slavery, racism, and colonial imperialism, cannot be ignored. But neither can we ignore the racial realities constructed by the African and various Indigenous groups. Their active agency not only denied racial imperialism total victory, but their subjective construction of self was both reaction and action. They were more than reacting to racial imperialism, but actively engaged in constructing/reconstructing their realities. The truth requires us to examine these bipolarities in an effort to understand the externalities produced by the racial state and the subjective awareness constructed by the various groups. We begin with an examination of racial imperialism and the racial construction of the other.

## The racial imperialism and the racial construction of the other

In 1914, only China, Japan, and the Ottoman Empire were free of European control. As Jared Diamond argues, three factors – guns, germs, and steel – account for the success of the Europeans. These germs (smallpox and other herd diseases) and gunpowder might be the primary culprits (Diamond, 1997/2017). However, while germs were quite effective in eradicating massive numbers of Indigenous peoples, the availability of gunpowder was tremendously important. Gunpowder allowed Europeans with a small military force to devastate a large population (Hoffman, 2017).[1]

## Spain and France: the dawn of colonial racial hierarchies

Racial imperialism created racial hierarchies in the colonized countries based upon the ideological and presumptive beliefs of the colonizers toward the colonized. Understanding these beliefs helps us understand the racial hierarchies created, maintained, and perpetuated. Understanding this racial reality is key to understanding how liberal and conservative practices supported the creation of the racial state, birthed racial imperialism, and created what Charles Mills called the racial contract. Specifically, as Charles Mills (1997/2020) pointed out, the social contract upon which "we the people derive" was and is fundamentally a racial contract. The racial contract serves to suppress, coerce, and dominate racial minorities through a complex interaction between privilege and disadvantage, where some are designated as insiders and others as outsiders. The colonial past, which included Indigenous genocide, slavery, racism, and colonial imperialism, cannot be ignored; these are the fundamental truths we must overcome.

Moreover, this is the truth that many White Americans refuse to accept (Lim, 2020). Mills asserts that much of our theories of justice and the social contract are absurd if we believe ours is "a cooperative venture for mutual advantage" where the rules are "designed to advance the good of those taking part in it" (Lim, 2020). As John Rawls (1971/1999) advocated, this myth was predicated on the idea that morally equal human beings were objectively and equally engaging in a mutually beneficial set of principles. The myth, citing Mills, resulted in which racial, gendered, Indigenous, and homophobic oppression are not only ignored but undermine any basis for any corrective social justice (racial, gendered, sexual) (Mills, in Rawls, 1971/1999; Lim, 2020).

Although colonialism dates to the Greeks, Turks, Arabs, and Phoenicians, the modern version, and what we refer to as imperialism, officially began in the 15th century and continued through the 17th century. Colonialism originated in Europe, primarily in Portugal, Spain, England, France, the Netherlands, Germany, Japan, and later the United States. The European drive toward discovery and colonialism in the late 15th century resulted from their inability to expand their trading opportunities.

Medieval Europe received most of its trade goods from the East–West trade routes known as the Silk Road. This route, originating during the 1st and 2nd centuries between China and Greece, was dominated by Muslim traders from Asia who sold spices to Genoa and Venice in the Old Roman Empire. This trade made city-states the dominant force in the region. Blocked from participation, European explorers began searching for new routes to Asia, and thus the age of discovery and exploration was born.

The Age of Discovery began as Europeans searched for new trading routes, wealth, and knowledge (Briney, 2020). The impact of this "Age" significantly and permanently changed the world, geopolitics, and economic systems that continue today.

Portugal and Spain were the first to challenge the Muslim merchants by searching for a direct sea route to Asia. Thus, Dom Henrique of Portugal, sailing east, began the exploration, conquest, and colonization along the Atlantic Ocean and the coast of Africa. Christopher Columbus stumbled into the Caribbean and Central and South America in search of India. Later, Amerigo Vespucci, an Italian merchant sponsored by Spain, then Portugal, would similarly stumble on a place named America. Thus, European explorers charted many areas within Africa and the Americas and generated profits from gold and other precious metals, trading goods, and spices. In addition, they led to significant navigational and nautical innovations. And in the process, the Portuguese and Spanish became the first global imperial empires to cross several continents and control multiple territories. From 1580 to 1640, these two imperial empires were under the Spanish monarchs. Later, in the 16th and 17th centuries, England, France, and the Dutch would join this exclusive club to compete for dominance.

The next period was one of uncertainty as the majority of the colonies in the Americas broke away from European rule. European colonial states, particularly Great Britain, France, Portugal, and the Netherlands, looked toward the Old World, particularly the previously secured coastal enclaves in South Africa, India, and Southeast Asia. As Europe entered the second industrial revolution in the 19th century, the second wave of imperial expansion began as they sought to control the vast resources across Africa. Belgium, Germany, and Italy would join in.

Two world wars, and dozens of minor battles, would pit the various colonial powers against each other. The world we know of today was forged during this period. In World War I, to the victors came the colonial spoils of war according to a set of mandates. But the issue was not settled; competition for these valuable colonies would be the leading edge of the conflagration that resulted in World War II and later fuel the battle for decolonization across the globe.

Furthermore, although Europe represented less than 10 percent of the land mass on the planet in 1492, it colonized and controlled more than 80 percent of the world by 1914. Colonial racial hierarchies reflected not only the colonizer's intellectual (liberal or conservative) nature but also the colonial ambitions of the specific nation. From these beliefs, two different racial hierarchies evolved. In one, known as settler colonialism, the object of the colonizer was to settle a geographical area and take the land. As a result, the Indigenous populations were exterminated, subjugated, assimilated, or displaced in this setting.

Alternatively, in exploitative colonialism, the colonizer's object was primarily geared toward gaining access and control over various resources (mineral, agricultural, or labor). Labor was supplied by forcing either the Indigenous populations or imported enslaved people that served as the cheapest source of work.

In both systems, racial regimes created European xenophobic traditions that supported antisemitism, Islamophobia, Negrophobia, and the genocide of Indigenous populations (Wolfe, 2006). Within these systems, racial, ethnic, and religious differences intersected to create and legitimize economically exploitative, socially stigmatizing, and politically exclusive structures that favored Europeans at the expense of subordinated groups (Spencer-Wood, 2016).

Hence, as Europe entered the Americas and the rest of the world, a long history of "racial othering" and systems of exploitation had been well-established. The American Revolution pitted the two ideals – English conservatism and French liberalism – against each other. Two key architects of what would become the United States, Thomas Jefferson, and James Madison, articulated the significant dimensions of the debate:

> When Alexis de Tocqueville first visited the United States in 1831, he was immediately impressed by what he coined American exceptionalism: the idea that nationality was not based on shared history or ethnicity but on common beliefs. (Martin, 2007: 111–113)

> Jean-Jacques Rousseau went so far as to classify this exceptionalism, or obsession, with a kind of American civil religion. Within this religion, "sacred American beliefs" provide the "sources of cohesion

and prophetic guidance through times of national crises." (Bellah, 1975, quoted in O'Brien, 1996)

American exceptionalism was a significant accomplishment of Thomas Jefferson. Jefferson, the American Minister to France from 1785 to late 1789, might have been one of the writers of the French Declaration of the Rights of Man and of the Citizen.

His ideas regarding liberty, as found in the Declaration of Independence, were central to his vision of civil religion and this new thing called the United States (O'Brien, 1996). Consequently, Jefferson envisioned that the United States would become an imperial power, destroy Europe's grip on North America, and destroy the last vestiges of a ruling class.

Jefferson had mixed views concerning slavery. So, on the one hand, he maintained a long-term relationship with Sally Hemings and fathered at least six children. He took Sally Hemings to France for two and a half years (1787–1989), where, as a domestic servant and maid to the Jefferson household, she was nevertheless free under French law. Interestingly, she agreed to return to Monticello if Jefferson would grant her "extraordinary privileges" and the freedom of her unborn children. It took decades, but Jefferson did free some of Sally Heming's children –Beverly and Harriet in the early 1820s and Madison and Easton through his will in 1826. Jefferson's other enslaved children were not freed. Jefferson remained ambiguous regarding slavery (Monticello, nd). In many public documents, we see a different Jefferson, as he viewed slavery as adherent to, and a continual form of, despotism. Slavery was a stain on the fabric of our country. Jefferson went so far as proposing, in the Declaration of Independence, that one of the crimes committed by British tyranny was the imposition of slavery and the creation of chattel slavery, thus depriving over one-fifth of the population of their "inalienable" rights (Williams, 2020).

Different views regarding slavery lay at the core of the conflict between the North and the South. Yet, strangely, we did not settle this but have been compromising since. Hence, while the United States of America came into being heralding "freedom, justice, and equality," it served to preserve the racial elite and the European systems and structures.

It also provided for the "gradual" abolition of slavery and the conversion of the enslaved person into a citizen. We are still in this process, and racialized groups are still waiting to become full-class citizens. The reasons for the continuance of the process have to do with the redefinition of conservatism and liberalism. We shall deal with these "neo" versions in the following sections.

This history guided the development of racial hierarchies in the Americas and later in the colonial empires stretching from Africa and India to the Middle East. Our modern ideas, from liberalism to post-modernism to neoliberalism and neoconservatism, all have been instrumental in supporting imperialism and reifying racism. The primary vehicles by which these instrumentalities manifested were our bureaucratic structures. Ray (2019) explains that these structures are not race-neutral; they encourage or discourage racial group agency, legitimize the racial distribution of resources, and secure racial hierarchies and the performance of Whiteness.

The framing of the U.S. Constitution and its political and legal institutions cast our nation as a democratic republic and a racial state (Mulcare, 2008). Racialized laws have historically, and often covertly, influenced American notions of deviance, crime, and justice in complex ways. The longevity of this influence, and its ability to impact laws and criminal justice institutions, demonstrates the pervasiveness of *racial consciousness* among some of the most important figures throughout our history.

This racial consciousness also perpetuated, legitimated, and normalized racial hierarchies by favoring Whiteness at the expense of people of color. Several critical race theorists have documented this process. Our first clue regarding this consciousness comes from one of the earliest debates concerning the founding of our country. In framing the set of offenses justifying why we as a nation would sever political bounds with Britain, Jefferson's original draft of the Declaration of Independence stated that:

> [King George III] … has waged cruel war against human nature itself, violating its most sacred rights of life & liberty in the persons of a distant people who never offended him, captivating & carrying them into slavery in another hemisphere, or to incur miserable death in their transportation thither. (Quoted in Helo and Onuf, 2003: 586)

Both South Carolina and Georgia threatened to abandon the revolutionary project if this "objectionable" language was not removed. The revolutionary project was subverted with this first of many racial compromises to the slave states. The deletion of the phrase "cruel war against human nature itself" in the edited draft implied an endorsement of both democracy and slavery in the Declaration of Independence.

Jefferson's dilemma was, in essence, one of morality, for he believed that the status of the enslaved prohibited them from exercising moral judgments. Within this framework, the redemption of the enslaved person could only come from the elimination of slavery. At least for Jefferson, the problem was that abolishing slavery would not overcome racial differences in education, self-direction, and acceptance of the other race, so nothing short of total separation of Blacks and Whites was feasible. Oddly enough, his fears were that only through such separation could we avoid "genocidal violence" (Helo and Onuf, 2003: 587).

We may never discover all the conversations Jefferson's ideas stimulated, but what we do know is that considerably divided congressional delegates hotly debated the issue. Looking at the loss of profits from a slave economy, Southern delegates were a driving force for removing the line. Ultimately, they won out. But they were not the only ones affected. From that moment to today, their racial consciousness and fears have shaped our views regarding morality, law, and deviance.[2]

So, while Jefferson was penning the Declaration of Independence and helping to write the U.S. Constitution, Native Americans, Blacks, and immigrants were racialized, decimated, and marginalized. But while Jefferson might have had misgivings regarding slavery, he was not so kind to Native Americans.

It is instructive to consider the message given at the time by George Rogers Clark regarding hostile Indians north of the Ohio river: "[T]he end proposed should be their extermination or their removal beyond the lakes or Illinois river. The same world will scarcely do for them and us" (quoted by Murrin, 2000).

Tocqueville, in the mid-19th century, argued that "culture and law were the primary sites where racial differences were constructed" (Tillery, 2009: 643). As a consequence, with the development of our democratic institutions, James Madison's ideas of "property in rights" quickly subsumed the category of Whiteness, investing it with rights, privileges, powers, and prerogatives.

Both colonial courts and legislatures socially constructed Whiteness as having access and entitled to the labor of Blacks. Whiteness as property was defended and expanded by both colonial courts and legislators, which supported the *"hyper-exploitation of Black labor,"* imbuing Whiteness "with the functions of the property" (Tillery, 2009: 643; original emphasis).

These colonial instructions differentially rewarded Whiteness at the expense of marginalized, racialized others (Higginbotham, 1978; Bell, 1989; Harris, 1993; Tillery, 2009: 644).

The genocide of millions of Native Americans in the Americas notwithstanding, we must also acknowledge the lynching of thousands of Black people. We must bear witness to the hundreds of thousands of Algerians slaughtered by the French between 1830 through 1871 and the Germans' destruction of over 200,000 Indigenous Africans. And the list goes on in India and the Middle East.

These horrors were legally sanctioned by implicit or even explicit laws, court actions of governments, police, courts, and other state institutions, and entailed all political and ideological stripes. At best, these genocides were tolerated; at the other extreme, they were encouraged.

When confronted by these atrocities by contemporary Indigenous peoples or their descendants, neoconservatives, neoliberals, and neo-imperialists become anxious, fearful, and even violent. But this has not silenced the marginalized, minoritized, and victimized voices or actions.

## Treatment of White and other women in the colonies

All too often, when we discuss colonialism, gender is excluded from the conversation. Such exclusion ignores a critical dynamic of how racialized structures were not only secured but how they endured over time. Feminist scholars have pointed out that different forms of colonialism can be identified by how women were included or excluded in various colonial situations.

One such type, "civilizing colonialism," explores how Christian European-bourgeois structures were fundamental to understanding colonizers' motives. Specifically, European/Western ideologies defined White women as "the primary civilizers of mankind" and therefore the "mothers of civilization" because of their moral superiority.

Because of this, as pointed out by Spencer-Wood (2016), White racial purity, cultural identity, and hegemony (both gender and race) were secured. In addition, English colonies differed from many of their European counterparts in that they tended to be formed by whole families and erected much more significant barriers to interracial marriage. As a result, comparatively simple racial hierarchies were constructed.

Such was not the case in either the Spanish or French colonies (see, for example, Coates, 2003). Instead, the Spanish and the French created exploitative colonial structures. Exploitative colonialism is when the colonizing power uses force to exploit land, labor, and natural resources. In such a system, the Indigenous or imported enslaved people serve as the cheapest source of work. Consequently, Indigenous women or enslaved Africans were pressured to become "respectable" mothers to the next generation of colonists in those colonies with a shortage of European women.

In these colonies, a multitude of racial mixtures was established and ranked according to the "racial purity" of the children. The Spanish and French colonies developed more complex racial hierarchies as creolization and pigmentocracies (see Figure 3.1).
Those European, Indigenous, or enslaved African/free women who refused to be "domesticated" were brandied as lascivious, dangerous, wanton, or witches (Hall, 2000, cited by Spencer-Wood, 2016). With time, colonized women of color were demonized, sexualized, and objectified.

In this process of othering, these women became the epitome of erotic objects with insatiable sexual appetites which were sexually accessible to White men. In a word, they were sex slaves, frequently sexually violated, often violently, as a public demonstration of domination of and to the colonized.

**Figure 3.1:** Latin American caste pyramid

Note: Casta painting shows 16 racial groupings.

Source: *Las castas*. Anonymous, 18th century, oil on canvas, 148×104 cm, Museo Nacional del Virreinato, Tepotzotlan, Mexico

An estimated 58 percent of the enslaved women between the ages of 15 and 30 were sexually abused by their enslavers and other White men in the Spanish and French colonies (Sommerville, 2004).

U.S. history provides multiple examples of intersecting racial, class, gender, and sexual abuse. Frontiers and borders were often the loci for the most contentious of these interactions to be staged. With the "conquest" of the West, sexualized encounters were glorified. At the same time, they were morally criticized. European explorers frequently described extreme levels of deviance such as cannibalism, excessive violence, and sexual indiscretions.

According to Agutierrez (1991), Franciscans repeatedly documented the sexual exploits of the Native Americans, often describing the Pueblo as lewd and sexually promiscuous (Nagel, 2000: 120). Lewis and Clark's exploration of the American Midwest appears to be one sexual encounter after another:

> Thursday, November 21, 1805: An old woman & Wife to a Cheif of the Chunnooks came and made a Camp near ours. She brought with her 6 young Squars I believe for the purpose of Gratifying the passions of the men of our party and receiving for those indulgiences Such Small [presents] as She (the old woman) thought proper to accept of. Those people appear to View Sensuality as a Necessary evel, and do not appear to abhor it as a Crime in the unmarried State. (Lewis and Clark, 1989: 324, quoted in Nagel, 2000: 121)

Sexual violence targeting Indigenous women has been demonstrated as a tool of settler colonial violence and conquest. Such targeting acknowledged that women within matriarchal Indigenous societies held great authority and were revered. Gender-based violence against women by settlers was used in many infamous episodes, including during the Trail of Tears and the Long Walk. Such attacks were not random or individual; they were an integral part of conquest and colonization (McKinley, 2023).

A long history of physical and sexual abuse is also associated with Native American youths forced to live in boarding schools (Morrissette, 1994; Braveheart-Jordan and DeBruyn, 1995). But far from being an exchange between equals, these encounters often were between grossly unequal participants and often were coerced (Nagel, 2000: 121).

Paul Gilroy (2004) explains that colonial and imperial structures continue to be transformed and reformed into a social pathology of neo-imperial politics. The result is continually direct hostility and violence toward Black people, immigrants, and various Indigenous publics. Portugal would take a different route but arrive at the same racial reality.

## Portugal: imperial empire and colonial racial hierarchies

In 2009, a mass grave was uncovered while excavating for an underground car park in Lagos at the Pro Putting Garden miniature golf course. Here the remains of both children and adults, all with their hands bound, were discovered. Forensic archaeologists have dated the remains and found that the deceased were of African descent from the 15th century. The discovery has forced Portugal to deal with its vicious past. Lagos was the first Portugese port enslaved Africans saw in 1444, and it was the beginning of the transatlantic slave trade. A history buried not only by mounds of dirt but history as well. Many, grappling with this history, are trying to fill the void, correct the myths, and confront the racial realities of Portugal's past (de Sousa, 2021).

Roque (2018) details the development of racial imperialism associated with the Portuguese Empire. She explains that the Portuguese Empire, lasting six centuries, was the first and most enduring European colonial power. The Portuguese colonial empire consisted of trading and military outposts, colonies, and occupied territories. The Portuguese, in 1415, searched for an alternative trade route to avoid those controlled by the Muslims. They ventured into and conquered Ceuta, a coastal town in Northern Africa. In East Africa, they continued to destroy and subjugate the small Islamic states such as Mozambique, Kilwa, Brava, Sofala, and Mombasa. The Portuguese Empire continued its road to conquest as it took control of Madeira and the Republic of Cabo Verde.

Portugal, at first, was more interested in trading than in colonizing. In fact, up until the 19th century, it primarily occupied coastal strips in territories with limited control of the interior. The Papal Bull of 1493 and the Treaty of Tordesillas of June 6, 1494 provided the Portuguese with almost exclusive rights to these territories. These offered exclusive rights to the two nations' land, peoples, and resources. The dividing line whereby all of Africa and most of Asia would belong to the Portuguese and all the Americas would belong to Spain.

With time, Portuguese control stretched from the Indian Ocean to the Persian Gulf as it challenged the authority of the spice trade of the Ottoman Empire. The Portuguese came to dominate much of the Southern Gulf through wars and forced diplomacy for the next few centuries. In addition, Portugal, with the consent of the Roman Catholic Pope, initiated and dominated the slave trade in the 15th century.

In the early 16th century, as the Portugese arrived in the Indian Ocean, they immediately began to engage in the various coastal ports in East Africa, India, and East Asia. With their links to inland African kingdoms and connected to the more elaborate Muslim network, these ports reflected trade and kinship and complex port-state complexes. Mastering this network allowed the Portuguese to control the African gold, spice, and other resources. The result was the establishment of Sofala port, through which flowed not only gold but also cotton, medicinal plants, enslaved people, pearls, ivory, and other African products in high demand in European markets. At this port, they would also enter its shipbuilding and mercantile center. With time, they established a fortified trading post, expanded their control of the inlands, and began politically, culturally, and economically controlling the region (Roque, 2021). They exploited the land and the peoples of West Africa, forcing them into slavery in the Americas. Through kidnapping, rape, murder, and genocide, they deported 5.8 million people from their lands. From 1715 to 1833, the Portuguese transatlantic slave trade generated gross estimated profits of £95,000,000 (today, this would equal about £12 million or US$15 million) (da Silva, 2021).

Portugal's colonial empire set new definitions for brutality and violence as they continued to invade, subjugate, and destroy Indigenous cultures and peoples on the west and east coasts of Africa, Indonesia, China, the Middle East, and South America. An absolute monarch ruled the empire. Appointed royal governors and viceroys represented the crown in the colonies. By establishing colonial legal and economic systems, the Portuguese were the first to articulate the racial imperialist idea that they were culturally, morally, and evolutionary superior to the "primitive" Indigenous populations. They constructed an image that glorified the Portuguese empire, purporting to be a humane, peaceful, and beneficial form of cooperative entrepreneurship and intercultural exchange. The romantic myth notwithstanding, the "colonial project" produced unspeakable violence, genocide, and destruction. In this way, the Portuguese pictured themselves as embodying "luso-tropicalism," a self-described "multi-racial, pluri-continental nation" that fostered peace, friendship, and a "liberal" attitude toward interracial marriages. Racism, and brutal colonialism, were submerged through centuries of state propaganda and stylized into statues, monuments, and history books that produced an alternative racial reality that they called history. As pointed out by Grada Kilomba, a Portuguese writer, artist, and psychologist, "we continue to feed on a romantic past, without associating it with guilt, shame, genocide, exclusion, marginalization, exploitation, (or) dehumanization" (quoted by Braga, 2020). At the dawn of the 16th century, Portugal was the wealthiest nation in the world (Pruitt, 2021). Portuguese colonial imperialism utilized education, science, culture, and information to cement its control over the colonized. At its peak, Portugal controlled 50 countries as colonies. The empire ended with the transfer of power over Macau to China in 1999. We shall return to this in the later section, but for now, we shall explore the new world order made possible by the racial blueprint provided by Portugal.

Portugal's dominance, particularly in the Indian Ocean and Southeast Asia, was destroyed by the Dutch in 1648. With the end of the conflict between the Netherlands and Spain, more money and soldiers were available. This allowed the Dutch East India Company to shift the balance of power from Ceylon on the Malabar coasts and the East Indies. By the late 17th century, the Dutch dominated the spice trade routes. The disruption led to a sharp decline in trade and the formal end of the Age of Commerce in Southeast Asia. Britain used this as the excuse to create the East India Company and embark on its path toward colonization and racial imperialism. They took over the entire subcontinent, and in 1857 India became part of the British Empire (O'Rourke et al, 2010).

## The United Kingdom and colonial racial hierarchies

Although the Portuguese were the first to establish trading posts in India, by 1619, the Dutch and the English would secure their own along the west coast of Surat. The European imperialists expanded their political and military control over the entire continent because of internal conflicts among the various Indian states. With time, Britain would be the dominant player in India. But that expansion was, as William Bagshaw Stevens observed, "cemented with the blood and sweat of Negro slaves" (quoted in Longmore, 2007: 225).

The killing of George Floyd in the United States on May 25, 2020, fostered protests that rippled across the world as people chanted Black Lives Matter (BLM). On June 7 the BLM protest took to the streets in Bristol, England. They gathered around the statue of Edward Colston, a 17th-century slave trader, who was part of the system that trafficked more than 80,000 Africans. As the crowd chanted "pull it down," some slung a rope around its neck and toppled the statue to the ground. Then they rolled it to the harbour and pushed it into the water (Jasanoff, 2020).

During the peak years of the African slave trade, between 1690 and 1807, approximately six million Africans were enslaved in the Americas. Of these, nearly half were sold by ships protected by the British crown or parliament. It was one of Britain's most profitable industries (Newman, 2020). Queen Elizabeth I initiated slave trading in Britain in the 1560s. She, along with other government officials and merchants, backed three different slave expeditions of John Hawkins. Hawkins was a pirate who raided Portuguese settlements and ships to seize hundreds of enslaved captives on these occasions. Hawkins sold the African captives to the Spanish in the Caribbean. Hawkins, for his efforts, was knighted and received a coat of arms featuring a nude African bound with a rope. Then under King Charles II, from 1660 to 1685, the royal family's chief investment was in the African slave trade. The profits were so significant that ultimately Charles set up a private joint-stock venture granting the Royal Adventurers a 1,000-year monopoly over trade, land, and adjacent islands along the west coast of Africa (Newman, 2020). Ultimately, the Royal African Company of England would ship more African enslaved women, men, and children to the Americas than any other institution during the entire period of the slave trade (Pettigrew, 2016).

Profits generated from the Atlantic slave trade created important trading centers in cities such as London, Birmingham, and Manchester from its beginning through much of the 18th century. They also provided for the expansion of ports in places like Glasgow, Liverpool, and Bristol. The tremendous overseas trade produced a massive shipbuilding industry, allowing Britain to become a colonial empire and marshal into the second industrial revolution (Tapalaga, 2023).

The British colonies outside the Americas were tied to the East India Company from the 17th century. The first trading posts were in India, followed by the Straits Settlements (Penang, Singapore, Malacca, and Labuan). James Island, in the Gambia River, became the first British settlement on the African continent in 1661. And in 1806, it controlled the Cape of Good Hope (South Africa) and opened the South African interior to the Boer and British pioneers. By the 19th century, Britain's most expansive power base was in Africa, and by 1882 it controlled Egypt and, later, in 1899, Sudan (Encyclopedia Britannica, 2023). Within a few short decades, the British extended their control over what today is known as Nigeria, Ghana, Kenya, Uganda, Zimbabwe, Zambia, and Malawi. And by the end of the 19th century, Britain had become the largest colonial empire in the world (Khilnani, 2022).

As the British Empire expanded, disparities in power, wealth, and might easily circumvented the liberal philosophies (suggesting moral, spiritual, and equality among all humans). The colonial governors and the White settlers realized that "Her Majesty's Government lacked both the will and the power to inhibit them" so long as they maintained the "veil of decency" (Huttenback, 1973: 111). The non-British were defined as heathens, anti-Christian, morally degraded, diseased, and as undermining British democratic government, with their willingness to work for significantly less undercutting the White working man. Soon, as the 19th century unfolded, a new term evolved, the "British race." Accordingly, the British race epitomized human civilization, and their Creator uniquely endowed them with the abilities and character so missing in other peoples, such as Africans, Asians, and even Europeans (Huttenback, 1973). Britain's racial hierarchies were designed to frustrate resistance by exploiting the tribal, religious, and other distinctions. The unique racial hierarchies that the British Empire crafted assured that White people would rule over people of color across six continents. Even the poorest White had higher status and could challenge anyone of color. The system was maintained by strict rules governing which jobs, typically domestic, persons of color could occupy and the frequency of corporal punishment. Pigmentocracies are defined as where individual ethnicities or skin color were part of the racial reality that governed access to occupations, education, legal and political rights, where one could live, and even where one had to sit on public transportation (Lester, 2022).

The concentration on racial hierarchies often obscures the differences experienced by gendered racial groups. The intersection of race and gender played a significant role in the construction of British attitudes toward non-White others. No better example of this is the story of Sarah Baartman, the "Hottentot Venus" kidnapped from her homeland in South Africa and forced to satisfy British sexual fixations and obsessions with non-White imperial subjects. Oddly, these obsessions are conveniently derived from the liberal attitudes of British masculinity and femininity during the Victorian era. British males, within this framework, were characterized as noble, brave, loyal, moral, and Christian imperial subjects. At the same time, the ideal British female was a domestic caretaker, virtuous, and pure. The degenerated fixation on women of color became the justification for their views. In many ways, they served to reinforce the racial hierarchies, as well as the savage administration of colonial subjects. Over the following decades, from 1870 through 1914, European control over Africa increased from 10 percent to 90 percent. The period, known as the Scramble for Africa, pitted the seven Western European powers as they partitioned Africa through annexation, division, and invasion (Linsley, 2013).

## The Scramble for Africa and World War I

Long-standing issues, problems, and frustrations across the African continent are rooted in European colonization and centuries of slavery, where an estimated 20 million Africans were forcibly exported. For example, Acemoglu et al (2002) demonstrated that the "reversal of fortune" was evidenced as some of the wealthiest colonies in 1500 were among the poorest by the end of the 20th century. This was primarily a consequence of the institutions created by the Europeans. Alternatively, scholars such as Nunn (2017) explain that the 400 years of slave raiding was "detrimental to economic development" and that those countries that lost the most enslaved people are some of the poorest in Africa today. The slave trade also aggravated ethnic fractionalization (Green, 2013). The high levels of African ethnic diversity, at the heart of many current-day conflicts, derive from the slave trade (Boxell et al, 2019). An examination of the period between these two events, the end of slavery and the beginning of colonization, constitutes another set of circumstances that must be considered. This period, the "Scramble for Africa," began with the Berlin Conference of 1884–1885 and lasted until the beginning of the 20th century, when Europe maliciously carved up Africa to accommodate European designs to maximize profits and control. In the process, Africa was partitioned into various protectorates, colonies, and territories. These partitions, although arbitrary, demonstrated limited knowledge of African ethnicities and tribal, religious, and cultural boundaries. The lines drawn were to benefit the Europeans, not the Africans. They reflected different European spheres of influence. With short lines at right angles to the coasts, East Africa was carved to distinguish the German sphere from the British to the North and the Portuguese in the South. Similarly, the Luso-German Treaty established the boundaries between Southwest Africa and Angola. The French drew a line in equatorial Africa separating the Congo Free State from the Spanish sphere. And in West Africa, the British Gold Coasts were separated from the French Ivory Coasts. Sierra Leone was juxtaposed to Liberia, and the two colonies of the Gambia and Portuguese Guinea were separated from the adjacent French territory (Griffiths, 1986).

In the 1860s, France and Britain began exploring West Africa earnestly. They were the first to sign a bilateral agreement designating their respective spheres of influence. From this start, European nations would sign hundreds of treaties, dividing the continent into territories, trade posts, and colonies. The most significant set of treaties would occur because of the Berlin Conference arranged by Otto von Bismarck from November 1884 to February 1885. The primary purpose of this conference was to preserve the "status quo" and minimize conflict between the European powers (Michalopoulos and Papaioannou, 2011). African leaders were not even invited to the "conference" (Asiwaju, 1985).

European imperial dominance of Africa was severely challenged on March 1, 1896, as Ethiopian defeated the Italians as it attempted to expand its empire by taking the Horn of Africa. Ethiopia and Liberia were the only African countries to resist the Scramble for Africa (Woldeyes, 2020).

European competition over its imperial territories was one of the most significant factors leading to World War I. Imperial dominance was the prize.

Africa was central to the ambitions of the European nations in their quest for natural resources. The Europeans looked to Africa for various minerals, metals, oil, and raw materials. It also pitted the most powerful European empires against each other in what we have seen as the Scramble for Africa. The expansion of the European empires was a significant cause of World War I, as countries like Germany, Austria-Hungary, and the Ottoman Empire challenged the expanding realm of Britain and France.

Ironically, the prospects of a major war between European countries were predicted as early as the mid-1890s. But this war would occur in Africa, not Europe. Joseph Chamberlain, the British Secretary of State of the Colonies, in May of 1896, warned that such a war would be "one of the most serious wars that could be waged. ... It would be a long war, a bitter war, and a costly war ... it would leave behind the embers of a strive which I believe generations would hardly be enough to extinguish" (quoted in Paice, 2019). Britain attempted to avoid the significant conflict by offering African colonial possessions to Germany. England declared war on Germany on August 4, 1914. But the first acts of the war took place in the small West African country of Togoland. Here the French, on August 6, began to invade Togoland, one of the four German colonies in Africa. The British joined forces there. And on August 7, the first shot was fired by Alhaji Grunshi of the Gold Coast Regiment (Sherwood, 2015). On August 6, the French invaded Togoland, one of the four German colonies in Africa. It was indeed the shot that was heard around the globe.

Often, we assume the progression of history as linear. But such an assumption rarely occurs in the real world. Things happen in conjunction with, antecedent to, or precipitated by specific events. As explored in other sections, philosophy was often used to justify national actions. The next period would challenge the world powers, colonial imperialism, and what we understand as truth. Not only has philosophy been used to distort the realities of the past, particularly as it has to do with Africans, but historians, politicians, and others. What has gone for history has denied the realities and the agencies of the African and other Indigenous peoples. Philosophical treatise have been invented to justify, often after the fact, these historical and imperialist pursuits. Only by looking the African, their agency and their reactions to being othered can we truly understand what the truth is.

## The African, agency, and reactions

*How Africa developed Europe*

While many point to the impoverishment of Africa, its multiple problems, corruption, crime, poverty, and so on, we cannot ignore the reality that Africa is one of the richest (in raw resources) of any continent in the world. In the 15th century it was Africans, Indians, Chinese, and Arabs that dominated the trade routes, not the Europeans (Blaut, 1989). As explained earlier, the Berlin Treaty of 1885 created the blueprint which allowed France, England, Germany, Italy, and King Leopold to initiate the Scramble for Africa. It was essential in this process to deny any agency or history to the African people, thus justifying European imperialism as a means of elevating the people (Fonchingong, 2006). Within a short number of years, Africa, except for Liberia and Ethiopia, were under the control of European powers. Over 100 million Africans and ten million square miles of African territory were now under European dominance (Tetzlaff, 2022). Rodney (1982) explained that African underdevelopment was directly linked to European development. The underdevelopment, both real and myth, serve to maintain the imperialist notion that Africa needed saving, as in the White man's burden, from itself. The European slave traders, operating between 1519 to 1867, forced an estimated 12.5 million African men, women and children aboard ships destined for the New World. Untold millions died either before boarding the slave ships or before the ships reached their destination (Harris, 2023). African resources, specifically gold, copper, petroleum, chromium, and palm oil, were critical for becoming an imperial power. Centuries of violence, theft, and plunder has resulted in 180,000 artifacts in Belgium's

Royal Museum for Central Africa, 75,000 in Germany's Ethnological Museum, almost 70,000 in France's Quai Branly Museum, and 66,000 in the Netherlands' National Museum of World Cultures, and 50,000 across museums in the United States (Gbadamosi, 2022).

## In the beginning there was Africa

All of humanity owes its origins to Africa (Hublin et al, 2017). And long before Europeans discovered Africa, Africans had developed rich civilizations, histories, and cultures. African kingdoms, city-states, and empires existed with complex political, social, and cultural systems encompassing hundreds of thousands of people. Africans were therefore skilled in medicine, mathematics, astronomy, agriculture, and the domestication of animals. They had extensive market systems that marketed these items as well as jewelery and artwork made of bronze, ivory, gold, and terracotta. For centuries, European merchants from France, Britain, Scandinavia, and the Netherlands exchanged goods in the elaborate markets created by North Africans. Thus, Africa was not unknown territory.

It would be an error to assume that the Europeans just walked into Africa as imperial lords. As the colonial imperialists approached the continent, they were met with fierce opposition across most of the Indigenous nations. There was never a time when such resistance was not present. But for the purposes of this section, we can identify two distinct periods which highlight the continual resistance with which Africans asserted not only their agency, but also their determination to be free and independent. These two periods are characterized by resistance to slavery and colonialism, and postcolonial resistance movements.

## What did America and the world gain from the African?

The state of Florida ignited a controversy when it released a set of 2023 academic standards that require fifth graders to be taught that enslaved Black people in the United States "developed skills which, in some instances, could be applied for their benefit" (Zhang, 2023). Such is the flawed and misleading assessment of those with either a limited understanding of Africa, its people and their history, or the purposeful misrepresentation of such.

Whereas Florida would have students believe that enslaved Black people "benefited" by developing skills during slavery, the reality is that enslaved Africans contributed to the nation's social, cultural, and economic wellbeing by using skills they had already developed before captivity. What follows are examples of the skills the Africans brought with them as they entered the Americas as enslaved.

## As farmers

During the period between 1750 and 1775, most of the enslaved Africans that landed in the Carolinas came from the traditional rice-growing regions in Africa known as the Rice Coast. Subsequently, rice joined cotton as one of the most profitable agricultural products, not only in North Carolina and South Carolina but in Virginia and Georgia as well (Twitty, 2021).

Other African food staples, such as black rice, okra, black-eyed peas, yams, peanuts, and watermelon, made their way into North America via slave ship cargoes (Harris, 2011).

Ship captains relied on African agricultural products to feed the 12 million enslaved Africans transported to the Americas through a brutal voyage known as the Middle Passage. In some cases, the Africans stowed away food as they boarded the ships. These foods were essential for the enslaved to survive the harsh conditions of their trans-Atlantic trip in the hulls of ships (Carney and Rosomoff, 2011).

Once on plantations in the land now known as the United States, enslaved people occasionally were able to cultivate small gardens. In these gardens, reflecting a small amount of freedom, enslaved men and women grew their own food (Mondragon, 2022). Some of the crops consisted of produce originating in Africa. From these they added unique ingredients, such as hot peppers, peanuts, okra, and greens, to adapt West African stews into gumbo or jambalaya, which took rice, spices, and heavily seasoned vegetables and meat. These dishes soon became staples in what would become known as down-home cooking (Deetz, 2018). Crop surpluses from the communal gardens were sometimes sold in local markets, thus providing income that some enslaved people used to purchase freedom. Some of these African-derived crops became central to Southern cuisine.

## As cooks and chefs

The culinary skills that the West Africans brought with them served to enhance, transform, and produce unique eating habits and culinary practices in the South. Although enslaved Africans were forced to cook for families that held them as property, they also cooked for themselves, typically using a large pot that they had been given for the purpose.

Using skills from various West African cultures, these cooks often worked together to prepare communal meals for their fellow enslaved people. The different cooking styles produced a range of popular meals centering on one-pot cooking to include stews or gumbos or layering meat with greens. The meals comprised a high proportion of corn meal, animal fat, and bits of meat or vegetables (Emmanuel, 2015). Communal gardens, maintained by the enslaved, might supplement the meager supplies and what was available from hunting or fishing. Some of the cooks who emerged from these conditions became some of the highest regarded and valued among the enslaved in the regions (Barton, 1997).

Enslaved chefs blended African, Native American, and European traditions to create unique Southern cuisines that featured roasted beef, veal, turkey, duck, fowl, and ham. Desserts and puddings featured jellies, oranges, apples, nuts, figs, and raisins. Stews and soups changed, given the season, sometimes featuring oysters or fish (Ganeshram, 2022).

### As artisans and builders

Slave ship manifests reveal that enslaved Africans included some who were woodcarvers and metalworkers (Trotter, 2019). Others were skilled in various traditional crafts, including pottery making, weaving, basketry, and wood carving. These crafts were instrumental in filling the perpetual scarcity of skilled labor on plantations (Stavisky, 1949).

When planters and traders considered purchasing an enslaved Black person, one of the key factors influencing their decision and the price was their skills. Slave auction sales included carpenters, blacksmiths, and shoemakers (Doesticks and Butler, 1859).

Architectural designs showing West African influences have been identified in structures excavated from some colonial plantations in various areas of the South Carolina Lowcountry (Wheaton, 2001). These buildings, with clay-walled architecture, demonstrate that the West Africans came with building skills. Excavated clay pipes in the Chesapeake region reveal West African pottery decorative techniques (James, 2004).

Across the nation, multiple landmarks were built by the enslaved. These include the White House, the U.S. Capitol, and the Smithsonian Castle in Washington, Fraunces Tavern and Wall Street in New York, and Fort Sumter in South Carolina (Pasley, 2019).

### As midwives, herbalists, and healers

As Africans entered the Americas, they brought knowledge of medicinal plants. Some enslaved women were midwives who used medical practices and skills from their native lands. In many cases, while many of these plants were unavailable in the Americas, enslaved Africans' knowledge, and that gleaned from Native Americans, helped them to identify a range of plants that could be beneficial to treat a wide range of illnesses among both the enslaved and the enslavers. Enslaved midwives delivered babies and, in some cases, provided the means for either avoiding pregnancies or performing abortions. They also treated respiratory illnesses (Mutter Edu Staff, 2022).

These practices and knowledge grew as they began incorporating techniques from Native American and European sources (Fitzgerald, 2016). They employed an interesting array of these practices to identify herbs, produce devices, and to facilitate childbirth and maternal health and wellbeing. They utilized several herbal remedies such as cedar berries, tansy, and cotton seeds to end pregnancies (NMAAHC, nd).

In 1721, of the 5,880 Bostonians who contracted smallpox, 844 died. Even more would have died had it not been for a radical technique introduced by an enslaved person named Onesimus, who is credited with helping a small portion of the population survive (Norton, 2022). Onesimus, purchased by Cotton Mather in 1706, was being groomed to be a domestic servant. In 1716, Onesimus informed Mather that he had survived smallpox and no longer feared contagion. He described a practice known as variolation derived by West Africans to fight various infections (Flemming, 2020). This was a method of intentionally infecting an individual by rubbing pus from an infected person into an open wound. Onesimus explained how this treatment resulted in significantly milder symptoms, eliminating the likelihood of contracting the disease. As physicians began to wonder about this mysterious method to prevent smallpox, they developed the technique known as vaccinations. Smallpox today has been eradicated worldwide primarily because of the medical advice rendered by Onesimus.

Regardless of how Florida's education standards misrepresent history, the reality is that the Africans forced to come to America brought an enormous range of skills. They were farmers, cooks, chefs, artisans, builders, midwives, herbalists, and healers. Our country is richer because of their skills, techniques, and knowledge.

## Resistance to slavery and colonialism: acts of agency and self-determination

Military confrontations, acts of sabotage, and other forms of resistance characterized the African resistance to European colonialism. While hundreds of examples can be identified, I shall explore a small handful as they demonstrate the African people's determination and ingenuity.

Africa, before 1500, was already exhibiting major empires in West Africa, Ghana, Mali, and Songhay. Their economic surpluses provided the gold necessary for Europe to develop in the 13th and 14th centuries (Adi, 2022).

As early as the 11th century, long before France, England, or Portugal were prominent nations, there was the Ille-Ife (Ife) Empire. From this empire, the Yoruba homeland, consisting of present-day southwest Nigeria, Benin Republic, and Togo in West Africa, came into existence. These people and their rich culture, philosophy, arts, and histories demonstrate the precolonial realities of African indigenous people. The Oyo Empire (southwestern Nigeria) was the most notable Yoruba state, which peaked from 1660 to 1750. Oya became dominant by establishing trade and building a formable cavalry and trained army. Coastal trade with European merchants during the mid-1700s allowed territorial expansion. With time, the Oya used its military to take control of the trade routes and engage directly with the European trading posts being established along the coasts. The central trading goods were African slaves for European guns. This led to increasing conflicts between various African nations, as Oya began to dominate the slave trade and exerted royal control in the Dahomey port of Whydah. European trading nations competed for slaves by offering more and more guns as an essential article of commerce (Fage and McCaskie, 2023).

Slavery in Africa was unlike that in Europe during this same period. Thus, Africans could become enslaved as captives in war, as punishment for crimes, or due to poverty and debt (Adi, 2012).

Yoruba became the second most important slave-exporting region in Africa during the 19th century. Only Central Africa produced more slaves. Enslaved Yoruba were found throughout the Atlantic, with the largest numbers going to Sierra Leone, Cuba, Brazil, and Trinidad. Other slave trading systems were in the Windward Coast, Asante, Igbo, Dahomey, Niger Delta, and Central Africa (Ojo, 2008).

Several African kingdoms refused to take part in slavery. Here are a few African domains that declined to participate and actively resisted slavery.

Of the numerous African-led attempts to resist colonial imperialism, the Fante Confederation stands out. Caseley argues that the Confederation also envisioned the creation of an infrastructure to include political, educational, and a system of roads, all paid for by taxes. As early as the 15th century, the Fanta, found in Ghana, actively prevented the Portuguese from coming on shore. King Ansah waged continuous battles and skirmishes, ultimately expelling the Portuguese from the region. The Fante Confederacy was formed in the early 18th century to provide a collective force to fight against European imperialism (Casely, 1903/2007).

Also in the 15th century, the Balanta, in present-day Guinea-Bissau, unable to thwart the slave-raiding armies, changed their ways. They established settlements in the mosquito-infested, marshy land between West Africa's Saloum River and northern Liberia. The Balanta and other ethnic groups benefited from a decentralized, stateless society in an area where the Kaabu decimated the region in slave raids. As the attacks increased, the Balanta relocated to more isolated regions within the swamps. In the process, they became highly efficient in developing paddy-rice production techniques. Thus, they were able to maintain political independence, as well as resist the slave trade (Hawthorne, 2001).

One of the first African opponents to the transatlantic slave trade was the Kongo ruler Nzinga Mbemba (also known as Alonso, 1446–1543). In a 1526 letter, he wrote to João III, the Portuguese king, objecting to the kidnapping and forced enslavement of their people.

The first armed resistance occurred in 1630. Queen Nzinga Mbandi of the Abundu Kingdoms of Ndongo and Matamba (now Angola), for close to 40 years, waged a war against the Portuguese and European colonization in Southwest Africa out of her realm. Described as a brilliant military tactician, she restricted the Portuguese colony to just a few square miles (Akinbode, 2021).

During this same period, Muslim state organizing among the Berber tribes began to formally reject slave raiding. Nasr al-Din, with the title of imam, refused to take any share or participate in the slave traditions of earlier Islamic states (Robinson, 1975). Under Nasr's leadership, a 30-year war took place. This war, known as the Char Bouba war, 1644–1677, started with al-Din declaring jihad and targeted the French trade in Senegal. Nasr's movement, aiming to abolish the slave-trading dynasties of the local kingdoms, was a populist movement. Many local peasants flocked to him to overthrow the traditional leaders embroiled in the slave trade (Barry, 1998).

By 1885, only Ethiopia and Liberia remained free during the European Scramble for Africa. Only Italy was without colonies, as France, the United Kingdom, Germany, Belgium, Spain, and Portugal had controlled the bulk of the continent. Italy, determined to make its mark, initiated a colony in Eritrea along the Horn of Africa. It was here, in a fierce battle in 1887, that 500 Italian soldiers died in a well-orchestrated ambush. Two years later, Italy signed a treaty with Ethiopia's emperor, Menelik II. Confusion over the terms of this treaty led to an all-out war, as Menelik mobilized an estimated 80,000 to 120,000 soldiers from across most of the Ethiopian region and ethnic groups (Woldeyes, 2020).

As Italian troops neared the Ethiopian capital of Addis, the Battle of Adwa began. Within two months, the Ethiopian army had vanquished the Italian column and had encircled the Italian fort at Mekel. Menelik declared victory in March of 1886 with the Italian military in full retreat and with the Ethiopians claiming 3,000 prisoners. And thus began the long road to African liberation. One of the remarkable military tacticians and strategies, leading a 6,000-person cavalry, was Etege Tayitu Bitul, wife of Emperor Menelik. Other protracted rebellions occurred in Somaliland from 1895 to 1920, the Egba revolt in Nigeria in 1918, and peasant uprisings in the Sudan from 1900 to 1904. These rebellions, revolts, and wars would sound the bells of liberation and redemption for leaders such as Nkrumah in Ghana and across the continent and the Black diaspora, including Marcus Garvey and W.E.B. Du Bois (Woldeyes, 2020). The next section will look at these colonial resistance movements of the 20th century.

## Anti-colonial movements of the 20th century
*World War I anti-colonial movements*

As the 20th century dawned, it was greeted by Africans across the continent in a continual battle to resist the colonial imposed systems. Resistance took many forms, from escaping and work stoppages to full-blown military engagements.

Perhaps the most popular movement of the early 20th century was the Dervish movement in Somalia. This movement, occurring between 1896 and 1925, was led by a poet named Mohammad Abdullah Hassan. Calling for the liberation of the Somali people, he waged a war to reclaim the region from British and Italian incursions and to restore self-government. They also targeted the Ethiopians who facilitated and collaborated with the British and Italians during this period (Hassan and Robleh, 2004). The movement attracted as many as 26,000 armed youths from different clans. Their first battle was an unequivocal success as the Ethiopians retreated. Next, the Dervish movement targeted the British administration in Somaliland. In response, the British armed several competing Somali clans with weapons and supplies. This resulted in several successful attacks against Dervish positions. From 1904, the Dervish resorted to guerrilla warfare, targeting Italian-controlled territories. By 1906, the Italians had signed the Illig Treaty in which the Dervish were ceded the Nugaal valley and granted protected status (Samatar, 1988). Increasing victories in 1908 saw the British retreating to the coastal regions as they suffered major losses in the interior areas of the Horn of Africa. For most of World War I, things were at a stalemate. But as the war ended in 1920, the British launched a massive offensive against the Dervish strongholds (Mohamoud, 2006).

From 1905 to 1907, the Jaji Maji Rebellion was orchestrated by the collaboration of Muslim and Animist Africans to challenge German colonial rule in East Africa. Between 75,000 to 300,000 died, mostly because of famine (Iliffe, 1967). Although unsuccessful, it nevertheless served as a model for future rebellions that would ultimately lead to the liberation of Tanzania (Sunseri, 2003).

As Europe entered World War I, Africans in countries such as Nigeria, Guinea, Dahomey, and Mozambique realized that there would be an exponential increase in labor demands, taxes, and other resources. Consequently, potential military inductees fled the colony and took refuge in other territories. Others escaped into different villages, clans, or other means to avoid compliance. Ultimately, they responded with rebellions, sabotage, and open warfare. European military threats and reprisals did little to gain full compliance (Moyd, 2017).

One particularly significant armed rebellion occurred in 1906 in Natal, a former province of South Africa. Although the smallest of the four traditional areas, it was integral in the struggle for independence. It was here, the Zulu chief by the name of Mbata Bhambatha, organized a major uprising. In many ways, Bhambatha might be considered a reluctant rebel. As chief, it was his duty to collect the poll taxes. He found himself not unlike other leaders across the colony, many of whom bitterly resented and chose to defy the tax. One such group, the Mpanza faction, decided to speak out and armed themselves to violently oppose the new tax levy. They were marching to the capital and confronted by Bhambatha, who successfully talked them out of open warfare and returned home. Frightened, the White settler community sought to punish the group and summoned Bhambatha to report on the rebellion. Fearing reprisals from the police and militia, he chose to escape instead. After a few weeks, he returned and organized an armed uprising in 1906 to oppose the poll tax and increasing hardships imposed by the United Kingdom. With 10,000 Zulu warriors, he began his mission to force the Brits out of South Africa. Although Bhambatha was ultimately defeated, he inspired the South African anti-apartheid movement that would follow (Thompson, 2008).

Increasing resistance among Africans and reprisals ultimately led to open and armed conflict between the colonizer and the colonized. One such incident, Chilembwe's rebellion, occurred in January 1915 in Nyasaland (Malawi). In this rebellion, John Chilembwe (1871–1915), a Baptist pastor, incited his congregation – consisting of teachers and the African middle class – to attack the British settlers and their properties. Raiding British estates, they acquired weapons and ammunition and continued for about two weeks until the insurgents were captured. The rebellion, although suppressed, nevertheless served notice to the colonial managers that the Africans were not docile and could be mobilized to fight back for liberty and justice. Islamic areas of Africa, particularly in the French West Africa and North African states, became the leading edges of anti-colonial movements of the period (SAHO, 2011/2019).

Muslim doctrine, recognizing Euro-Christianity as the antithesis of Islam, increased the militancy, vigor, and duration of these anti-colonial movements. The first of these rebellions occurred during World War I. Rebels, influenced by Islam, built campaigns across diverse populations and produced the wider sociopolitical activities necessary for a successful outcome. Reaching a peak in 1916, almost every major French colony in Africa and Asia witnessed anti-colonial rebellions during World War I. These activities engulfed Algeria, Burkina Faso, Mali, Niger, Chad, and Benin (Krause, 2021).

Although rarely successful, these rebellions, insurrections, and protests demonstrated Africans' unquenchable desire for freedom across the continent, the various religions, clans, and regions. These also fueled the next phase of liberation struggles across Africa as Europe and other Western nations were again engulfed in war, which was World War II.

## World War II and the modern anti-colonial movement

In many ways, Africa was at the center of World War II, if not the cause. Europe never settled World War I, as several states, notably Germany and Italy, attempted to reassert their control over their lost colonial territories. It might have started with the 1935 attempt by Mussolini and his unprovoked attack against Ethiopia. As the world watched on in silence, invading forces forced Haile Selassie, Ethiopia's ruler, into exile, and Mussolini proclaimed Ethiopia as a vassal state. Although the League of Nations responded with economic sanctions against the Italians, lack of support made it ineffective. What it did was reignite the various African nationalist movements across the continent. Wary of further Italian incursions, the Egyptians granted Britain and France military access and naval control of the Mediterranean. The real issue was control over the Suez Canal and access to the oil from the Middle East and other raw resources from Asia. In December of 1940, the Italian and British armies would face off at the Libyan–Egyptian border in the so-called Western Desert campaign. Facing massive defeats, the Italians called upon Hitler and the Germans for support. Ultimately, the English were victorious, and on January 15, 1943, the German and Italian forces were defeated, and Britain took over Tripoli (Zabecki, 2006). As the war concluded, Africans' struggle for freedom and autonomy reached new levels.

Even before World War II ended, President Franklin D. Roosevelt and Prime Minister Winston Churchill began discussing the future. Their conversations culminated in the Atlantic Charter, which declared that each country would "respect the right of all peoples to choose the form of government which they will live; and they wish to see sovereign rights and self-government restored to those who have been forcibly deprived of them" (Atlantic Charter, 1941). This agreement would become the catalyst for decolonization movements across Africa.

African nationalists were able to take advantage of the immense postwar debts facing many European powers. These debts meant that many could no longer maintain their control over their African colonies. The first step came when delegates from across the globe gathered in Manchester to participate in the Fifth Pan-African Congress in 1945. Three future African presidents would attend this historic meeting: Hastings Banda of Malawi, Jomo Kenyatta of Kenya, and Kwame Nkrumah of Ghana. At this Congress, Kwame Nkrumah, writing the preamble to the Congress, declared their vision: "[W]e believe in the rights of all peoples to govern themselves. We affirm the right of all colonial peoples to control their own destiny. All colonies must be free from foreign imperialist political or economic control"

(Nkrumah, 1945). As the clarion call for liberty and justice was heard across the continent, liberation movements surfaced across Africa.

By 1948, Ghanaians were rioting in response to three Ghanaian veterans being killed by colonial police as they protested colonial rule. Nkrumah and other leaders were imprisoned, and the independence movement was launched. Upon release from prison, Nkrumah founded the Convention People's Party, which began to push for "Self-Government Now!" The slogan gained momentum, and with the February 1951 election, the Convention People's Party gained 34 of the 38 elected seats. On March 6, 1957, the Ghanaians became the first sub-Saharan African country to gain independence from European powers (Esseks, 1971).

Also, in the early 1950s, the Kikuyu people of Kenya launched the Mau Mau nationalist movement. This movement, advocating violent resistance to British rule, was immediately banned by the British rulers in Kenya. After a four-year military engagement, and with over 11,000 rebels killed, 20,000 placed in detention camps, and an estimated 5,228 Kenyans tortured or abused, the battle waged on. Amnesty for the Mau Mau activists was ordered on January 18, 1955, by Evelyn Baring, the Governor-General of Kenya. Although later revoked due to a lack of response, a land reform program increasing Kikuyu's land holdings was granted in June 1956. Other land reforms followed, the most significant of which was that native Kenyans were finally allowed to reap cash crops for the most considerable import – coffee (Pinckney and Kimuyu, 1994). Formal direct elections took place in 1957 in which Kenyans were finally elected to the Council. Then, after the ban on national political movements was lifted, several Indigenous political parties came into being. These political parties, contesting the 1961 general election, gained a plurality of the popular vote and seats in the legislature. Following this victory, they rewrote the national constitution, leading to the formal independence of Kenya on December 12, 1963. Adding to the success, Jomo Kenyatta, a Mau Mau leader jailed in 1953, became the first prime minister of an independent Kenya (Perry, 2016).

A parallel path toward independence was occurring in Algeria. The movement for Algerian independence started during World War I but gained momentum after World War II. The National Liberation Front, from 1954 to 1962, was the vehicle by which Algerians fought for their independence. The National Liberation Front waged a diplomatic war (in the United Nations) and a guerrilla war against the French. Urban guerrilla fighting around Algiers forced several violent urban attacks formally known as the Battle of Algiers (1956–1957). Even with 500,000 troops, France had difficulty regaining control, and this was only with a level of brutality that caused the French people to lose their political will. The movement was so popular that it caused major ripples in France with the demise of the Fourth Republic (in 1956). Sensing defeat, Charles de Gaulle 1959 declared

Algerians had the right to determine their future. On July 5, 1962, after 132 years of occupation, France signed an agreement leading to Algerian independence (Rahal, 2022).

From 1975 to 2002, Angolan rebels fought the bloodiest and longest liberation war since World War II. At stake were abundant natural resources, including oil, iron, copper, bauxite, diamonds, and uranium. The rebellion was preceded by multiple complaints by workers regarding violations. As discontent mounted, the workers decided to go on strike and demand better working conditions and higher wages. Over time, these complaints were utilized by the Congolese PSA (African Solidarity Party) to bolster a riot by the Indigenous population. As violence escalated, rebels attacked security forces, which resulted in nine deaths on February 2, 1961, because of a dispute regarding labor conditions faced by the workers. The Angolan War of Independence was launched on March 15, 1961, as Holden Roberto led between 4,000 and 5,000 armed rebels. They attacked farms, government outposts, and trading centers. Further attacks over the next few months resulted in the Angolan forces taking several towns and villages. After several attempts, the Portuguese military regained control of several of these areas by mid-September. Still, a resolution of the United Nations Security Council on June 9 declared that Angola was a "non-self-governing territory" and called for Portugal to halt its repression against the Angolan people. During this period, the Angolan Independence Movement had control of a large portion of the colony. Portugal retaliated, forcing the rebels into a guerrilla war. A military stalemate had been reached by the early 1970s. A military coup overthrowing the dictator in 1974 opened the floodgates toward Angolan political liberalization. The period, rocked with violence targeting native Angolans, only intensified the call for independence. Open combat by Angolan forces re-emerged in Luanda in July of 1975. Portugal began ceding control to the militants. In 1974, rebel forces formally forced the Portuguese governor, Estado Novo, to leave the country. A coalition government was established, merging the various African liberation movements. Portugal, within a year, had ceded the colony and agreed to withdraw all troops from its African territories, including Sao Tome and Principe, Cape Verde, Mozambique, East Timor, and Angola (Samson, 2021).

Time precludes discussing all the African nations that declared their independence. In 1960 alone, called the Year of Africa, 17 African nations gained independence. The last African countries to achieve their autonomy were Guinea-Bissau (1974), Mozambique (1975), Djibouti (1977), Zimbabwe (1980) and Namibia (1990) (Wilson, 1994). Because of the sacrifices, courage, and vision of so many Africans who looked forward and not backward, Africa was liberated. As we shall explore in the chapters that follow, liberation for the African was filled with both promises and problems, possibilities and probabilities.

# Black Agency, Racial Imperialism, and the Creation of a Racial State: The Case of Haiti

In a scene reminiscent of the infamous Stanford Prison Experiment, Haitian migrants were run down by U.S. border guards for just trying to seek asylum. But this tragedy did not start here, nor is it confined to the Haitians. This particularly militarized zone along our southern border and these Black people have long been part of our tortured racial story.

It's a story that begins with European imperialism and runs through slavocracy; that matures during deliberate and strategic periods of disinvestment, disempowerment, and denial; and finally, it jettisons into our complicated, racialized universe. Tracing that story helps us to understand how we got here, how other racialized stories were constructed, and how we might get beyond the point of merely blaming or commiserating with the victims but confronting, repairing the damage, and remedying the problems.

## The first slave and Indigenous rebellion

Haiti is part of the island originally known as Hispaniola. The original inhabitants of the island were the Taino people, an Arawak tribe that originated in what is now Venezuela. The island formally came under Spanish control when Columbus claimed it in 1492. A year later Columbus returned with 1,300 men and African slaves to establish the permanent settlement. The Tiano population declined precipitously as they succumbed to excessive labor demands, military conflicts, and disease (Altman, 2007). This resulted in the Spanish needing a more durable labor source. Ferdinand and Isabel, in the charter of 1501, allowed for the importation of slaves. What the Spanish did not foresee was the Enriquillo Revolt, from 1519 to 1533, in which the African slaves and the Taino rebelled.

Enriquillo, a Taino chief, in 1519 orchestrated the one of the most remarkable rebellions against the Spanish empire in the Caribbean period. To this day, the Enriquillo Rebellion is celebrated across the island, in both Haiti and the Dominican Republic, as the most remarkable rebellion against the Spanish Empire in the Caribbean. The rebellion, following several during the first half of the 16th century, started as several Tainos in the mountain region of Bahoruco rebelled. The rebels utilized guerrilla tactics, taking advantage of their knowledge of the mountainous terrain (Altman, 2007). Two years later they were joined by a group of African escaped slaves. Not only was this the first known slave revolt in the Americas, but it was also the first instance in which Africans and Indigenous people united to fight against Spanish imperialism. The Spanish feared the slaves and their rebellion more, as within just 13 days they passed new laws which proscribed mutilation for any slave who dared to escape and rebel. Further, these ordinances made it illegal for them to carry weapons and restricted their movement while not in the presence of their masters (Stone, 2013). For another 15 years the two groups fought, then in 1534 Enriquillo surrendered. But the Africans and other Natives continued to rebel and terrorize the Spanish. Shortly before his death, Enriquillo struck a deal for immunity, full pardon, and the position of don. In return, he agreed to help the Spaniards find and capture future runaway slaves, and any allied groups. The Spanish, using divide and conquer, blocked any significant alliances between the Tiano and Africans from that point onward (Stone, 2013). It would be a hundred years before another rebel, this time an African, would challenge colonial rule.

## Black agency

Our journey continues in a racially fragmented settlement in what was known as Hispaniola. Here, in 1789, on the eve of the French Revolution, some 500,000 enslaved Africans and 24,000 *affranchis* (free mulattoes) banded together and began challenging the continual brutality of slave owners. The first real challenge occurred in late 1790 as an uprising was precipitated by Vincent Ogé.

Although the rebellion was unsuccessful, with Ogé captured, tortured, and ultimately executed, the French government attempted to split the opposition by granting citizenship to the wealthier *affranchis*. However, the acts of appeasement were disregarded as most of the Europeans within Haiti's population violated the law.

Slave colonies were only successful to the extent that the enslaved were compliant. Such compliance was rarely, if ever, achieved, as rebellions and insurrections were frequent. Rebellions such as the Stono Rebellion in 1739, Prosser's in 1880, Denmark Vesey's plot in 1822, and Nat Turner's Rebellion in 1831 are some of the most notable. But the one that struck fear in the

French, Spanish, and British enslavers' hearts, and those within the United States, was the one that began in 1791, known as the Haitian Revolution. The revolution, lasting 13 years, was the only successful insurrection led by self-liberated enslaved participants. The story, one of the largest slave rebellions in history, challenged European imperialism regarding the inferiority and docility of the Africans. We must examine these historical moments as they resulted in the French giving up their colonial possessions and ending slavery in the former colonies.

Saint-Domingue, a French colony since 1697, with a vast enslaved labor force, thrived as the wealthiest colony in America. It produced sugar, coffee, indigo, and cotton. The total population consisted of 500,000 enslaved persons, 32,000 Europeans, and 28,000 *affranchis* (freedmen, which mostly consisted of mulattos or mixed African and European descent) (*Encyclopedia Britannica*, 2023). The White planter elite often used torture and other forms of violence to control and prevent rebellions. Enslaved persons who rebelled, refused to work, or tried to escape could be beaten, maimed, or even killed to force them back into subjection. Saint-Domingue was also the center of Black resistance and power in the slaveholding Atlantic world (Fick, 2007).

In 1685, the French established the Code Noir to regulate the treatment of slaves. But even after its passage, the White planter elite often ignored these codes. By the 18th century, local legislation formally nullified many of these codes. Escaped slaves, called maroons, often lived on the margins of the plantations and frequently raided, stole, and perpetuated violence. This continual disruption only increased the cost of slavery. The whip, hard labor, and severe treatment meant that the enslaved had a high death rate. But profits continued the system. Saint-Domingue provided 33 percent of the French foreign trade. The French granted the colony nearly complete autonomy in 1790. As a result, the newly formed French National Assembly, in March of 1790, approved the Declaration of the Rights of Man. In so doing, they granted the *affranchis* (free people of color) full rights as citizens, but the White planter elite refused to recognize them. Therefore, the status of the *affranchis* was left unsettled. In October 1790, this ambiguity led to the first armed revolt against the White colonial authorities by the *affranchis* (Bradshaw, 2023). The enslaved took advantage of this conflict and, in 1791, began their own revolts. Seeing the chaos, the French National Assembly revoked the limited rights decreed to the *affranchis* in September 1791, only to provoke even more rebellions. One of the colonists' major fears was that as the revolution began, free men of color comprised close to half of the militia in Saint-Domingue (Geggus, 2006). One month later, fighting between the various factions led to the destruction of Port-au-Prince (Bodenheimer, 2019).

Born a slave, Toussaint L'Ouverture gained his freedom. As a free man for over 15 years, L'Ouverture continued to farm his land in the northern portion of the island. Seeing the conflict spread, L'Ouverture helped his wife and family find safety in the Spanish-controlled eastern side of the island. He then secured passage for his former master's family on a boat headed to the United States. Then, he joined the rebels that had allied with the Spanish against the French. He distinguished himself with his knowledge of both African and Creole medicinal techniques. With these skills, he joined the rebellion as a doctor and soldier. Soon, he demonstrated his ability in combat and leadership. Starting with an initial command of just 600 former slaves, he was commanding over 4,000 men within a few short months (Willis, 2023).

As 1793 approached, the significant military and political potential of the rebellion initiated by slaves in August 1791 was demonstrated. The leaders of the rebellion, having joined forces with the Spanish forces controlling the eastern of the island, essentially allowed Spain to control those areas of Saint-Domingue's northern provinces under rebel control. As the threat of a British invasion intensified, the ramifications of the rebellion became more severe. As the slave rebellions intensified and spread to the Western and Southern provinces, the situation became more volatile. The French, responding with more force, only intensified the crises as rioting and arson destroyed large portions of the northern capital city of Le Cap. Backed into a corner, the National Convention turned to the thousands of urban slaves to defend the colony as they acknowledged that "it is with the natives of the country, that it the Africans, that we will save Saint Domingue for France" (quoted in Fick, 2007: 405). Therefore, the French civil commissioner to the colony of Saint-Domingue declared all slaves in the Northern province legally free.

The British, fearing a spread of the slave revolt to their colony in Jamaica and to gain military advantage, decided to send troops to suppress the slave rebellion. The French colonial authorities, fearful of defeat, quickly, in 1794, acted to grant freedom and citizenship to all Blacks within the Empire. England continued to wage its war. L'Ouverture, mindful of the shift in political forces, aligned with the French against Spain. Their first battle, with newly freed soldiers, attacked the eastern, Spanish-controlled Santa Domingo. In a stunning victory, L'Ouverture's troops captured Santa Domingo, ending hostilities between France and Spain and signing the 1795 Treaty of Basel. L'Ouverture, by 1796, was one of the most influential military and political individuals in the colonies. The former slaves, whom he had helped to free, admired him, while the French officials respected him (Lawless and MacLeod, 2023).

L'Ouverture (1799) declared:

The first successes obtained in Europe by the partisans of liberty over the agents of despotism were not slow to ignite the sacred fire of patriotism in the souls of all Frenchmen in St. Domingue. At that time, men's hopes turned to France, whose first steps toward her regeneration promised them a happier future. ... [The Whites in St. Domingue] wanted to escape from their arbitrary government, but they did not intend the revolution to destroy either the prejudices that debased the men of color I or the slavery of the blacks, whom they held in dependency by the strongest law. In their opinion, the benefits of the French regeneration were only for them. They proved it by their obstinate refusal to allow the people of color to enjoy their political rights and the slaves to enjoy the liberty that they claimed. Thus, while whites were erecting another form of government upon the rubble of despotism, the men of color and the blacks united themselves in order to claim their political existence; the resistance of the former having become stronger, it was necessary for the latter to rise up in order to obtain [political recognition] by force of arms. The whites, fearing that this legitimate resistance would bring general liberty to St. Domingue, sought to separate the men of color from the cause of the blacks in accordance with Machiavelli's principle of divide and rule. Renouncing their claims over the men of color, they accepted the April Decree [1792]. ... As they had anticipated, the men of color, many of whom are slave holders, had only been using the blacks to gain on political commands. Fearing the enfranchisement of the blacks, the men of color deserted their comrades in arms, their companions in misfortune, and aligned themselves with the whites to subdue them. (L'Ouverture, 1799)

After a series of decisive victories, L'Ouverture ordered the military invasion of the Spanish part of the island in 1801. From this, L'Ouverture was virtually the supreme commander-in-chief and governor of a unified Saint-Domingue. Distrustful of the French authorities, he redefined the political structure, solidified the emancipation of the formerly enslaved, and directly challenged Bonaparte's coup. For the system to work, L'Ouverture realized, the economic prosperity of the colony must be established. And what was L'Ouverture's vision of freedom?

I never believed freedom to be license, or that men who have become free should be able to give themselves over to disorder and idleness: my formal intention is that workers remain bound to their respective plantations; that they receive one-quarter of the revenues; that they not be mistreated with impunity. But at the same time, I want them to work harder than they have ever worked before, and that they be subordinate and fulfill their duties correctly. I am resolved to punish severely he who strays. (Quoted in Fick, 2007: 410)

L'Ouverture was not trying to destroy the economy or the vitality of Saint-Domingue. Instead, he wanted the enslaved to be free and on an equal footing with the masters in the Atlantic world. By challenging the objectification of their identities and their status as slaves, the rebellion also demonstrated the futility of colonial empires based on slavery. Specifically, the rebellious slaves demonstrated the truth of Adam Smith's claim that slavery was both wasteful and uneconomical in that it cost more than free laborers (Knight, 2000). The constant vigil to keep the system from collapsing onto itself, the perpetual military, and police necessary to maintain control, and the continual problems of keeping the enslaved in captivity and productive eliminated any potential for real profits (Lucien, 2023). With L'Ouverture as their leader, the rebels, in ten short years, overthrew their colonial masters, transformed the economic system, and created a new political state consisting of the newly freed and empowered. They became the second group to declare their independence in the Americas. Xenophobic fears of slave rebellions were the European's worst nightmare. As the Haitians embraced their "Black" identity, they also challenged the racial hierarchy of European and North American imperialism (Knight, 2000).

Often, when we discuss history, we ignore the role of women. Doing this not only marginalizes women but also reifies patriarchy. Haitian women played a decisive role in the Revolution. These women, much like the males, provided a wide range of skills. First and foremost, Haitian women served as combatants. Such skills they had been taught in various West African societies, which allowed women to participate in war actively (Boisvert, 2001). Some Haitian women were trained in a variety of herbs and medicinal products. These women, who formally served as midwives, rejected the colonial-imposed Catholicism and again practiced Vodou. As priestesses, they weaponized their medicinal training and created poisons against the French enslavers (Boisvert. 2001).

Here are just a few of the legendary women who fought in the Haitian Revolution (source: https://guides.loc.gov/women-in-the-french-revolut ion/women-haitian-revolution):

- *Suzanne Bélair*, known as Sanité Bélair, was a Haitian revolutionary leader and served in Toussaint L'Ouverture's army. She and her husband, another lieutenant in L'Ouverture's army, were eventually found and executed at Napoleon's command.
- *Marie Sainte Dédée Bazile* was an important figure in the Revolution and is known for having gathered the remaining parts of Haiti's first Emperor, Jean-Jacques Dessalines, after his brutal assassination.
- *Marie-Louise Coidavid* was the first and only queen of an independent Haiti. She and her husband, Henri I of Haiti, endured the difficulties of

military life, and she was forced to witness the assassination of her firstborn child. After she lost her husband, she settled in exile in Italy.

- *Catherine Flon* was a seamstress who famously sewed the first Haitian flag at the request of Dessalines, but she is also known for having nursed the sick and wounded after nearby battles.
- *Cécile Fatiman* was a mambo (a Vodou priestess) who is believed to have formed networks on the island of Haiti that would transfer information from plantation to plantation.
- *Marie-Claire Heureuse Félicité* was an educator who shared her knowledge of French to free Blacks. She was married to a French painter who died shortly after. Eventually, she became the first Empress of Haiti after her marriage to General Jean-Jacques Dessalines, who crowned himself emperor of Haiti on October 8, 1804. Emperor Jacques I was assassinated on October 17, 1806.
- *Marie-Jeanne Lamartinière* was a Haitian soldier known for her courage and skills in battle and strategy. She was a leading figure in the pivotal Battle of Crête-á-Pierrot in 1802. She fought in a male uniform and was well-respected by her male compatriots.
- *Suzanne Simone Baptiste L'Ouverture* was the dedicated wife and caretaker of Toussaint L'Ouverture. Reports about her life contradict one another but she certainly underwent horrific torture when captured by Napoleon. They demanded information about her husband's whereabouts, which she never divulged. The details surrounding her death are unclear.
- *Victoria Montou*, known as "Toya," was a fighter in Jean-Jacques Dessaline's army during the Haitian Revolution. She had served as a warrior for the Empire of Dahomey in Africa before she was shipped as a slave to Haiti. She soon escaped the plantation and some report that she agreed to rescue a newborn baby and train him in battle skills she learned as a warrior in Africa. This young boy allegedly became the future leader, Dessalines.

It is strange, that as the enslaved challenged racial imperialism, slavery, and the colonial structure, they were also asserting the American notion of "life, liberty and the pursuit of happiness" and the French idea of "liberty, property, security, and resistance to oppression." Both declared the absolute right to rebel against any government that did not guarantee the "self-evident" and "inalienable rights" of all humans to live free. Alternatively, given the reality that two-thirds of the enslaved had been born in Africa, they would have been informed by African political philosophies, particularly Congolese. The principal interpretation of the meaning of a metropolitan revolution derived from this foundation. Here it would have been observed the connection between political freedom and the limitations placed on kings. Personal autonomy and communal rights codified through the Vodou religion derive from this. We also must observe the military, medical, and other skills that were part and parcel of African existence. While the American and French revolutions might have informed the rebellion, ignoring the African philosophies that undergirded it would be misleading. Again, let us remember that two-thirds were born in Africa, and therefore, the majority of the enslaved were from Africa (Shilliam, 2008).

The Haitian Revolution actualized these universal rights and ultimately fulfilled their actualization for all people. Black agency was not self-evident; it was constructed through 13 years of warfare, rebellion, and revolution. It came into being as a revolutionary construct of the Haitian masses and their leadership. It represented the opposite of the contradictory concepts that had materially constructed them as mere objects. In so doing, they asserted their dignity, separate identities, and humanity. Thus, Black agency challenged the hypocrisy of these racial tenants and asserted the right of the Africans to be and live free. They asserted that Black agency, the power of their will, could challenge the will of French masters and liberate them from a world of bondage.

The Haitian Revolution sparked enthusiasm among the enslaved in America, who began thinking of their own liberation. The inspiration of the enslaved brought terror to the Southern planter aristocracy. But while they feared, they grudgingly admired L'Ouverture as a competent leader. Southern newspapers even depicted him as a Black Napoleon, someone who was successful in battle, fierce and consequently a dangerous opponent. Jefferson, terrified of the rebellion in Saint-Domingue, castigated L'Ouverture and his army as cannibals (Scherr, 2011). His biggest fear was that the Blacks in America would be inspired and revolt. Jefferson began the process, described in the next chapter, of restricting and denying the Caribbean island of its hard-won liberty. He, therefore, initiated the U.S. policies that led to the creation of the "racial state" known as Haiti.

## The creation of a racial state

Although L'Ouverture was successful in January 1801 as he conquered Saint-Domingue, the war was not over. In 1802, Napoléon Bonaparte, to restore order, sent his brother-in-law, General Charles Leclerc.

Along with Leclerc were an estimated 23,000 seasoned French troops (*Encyclopedia Britannica*, 2022). They were able to overpower the rebel leaders, placing L'Ouverture and several of his lieutenants in prison. Although a truce was declared, no conditions were honored as L'Ouverture languished and died in prison. Several of L'Ouverture's lieutenants, such as Jean-Jacques Dessalines and Henri Christopher, took up arms again.

Seeing the writing on the wall, Napoleon quickly sought an escape route. He found one in the Louisiana Purchase in May 1803 and formally withdrew from North America. In three weeks, France and Britain fought to gain control over Haiti. Taking advantage of this conflict, Haitian rebels, under the leadership of Dessalines, defeated the French. On January 1, 1804, the island was declared independent. Ironically, most European powers, including the United States, fearing slave revolts, ostracized the newly liberated Haiti.

Two decades later, France sent an armada consisting of 14 warships equipped with 558 cannons, demanding reparations to compensate for its loss of property, including enslaved people, land, and other property. The French demanded 150 million francs to be paid in five equal installments. The first payment alone, at 30 million francs, was six times the gross domestic product (GDP) of the new nation. The continual payments on the debt were only possible through exorbitant loans, high import taxes, and, ultimately, a second revolution. And on this day, Haitians made history by becoming the first and only former slaves forced to pay reparations to their former enslavers (Porter et al, 2022). Haiti went from being the crown jewel of the French empire, one of the most successful colonies in the world, to one of the poorest in the world. The country that had produced massive amounts of sugar, coffee, and other cash crops was reduced to a pariah state by world powers (Rosalsky, 2021).

The presence of a nation of formerly enslaved Black people was an existential threat to European imperialism and the existing racial world order. Jefferson, who espoused the tenets of the French Revolution, was nevertheless a Virginia slaveholder. Jefferson feared the revolt of slaves would spread to the United States. He, therefore, provided federal aid to help suppress the rebellion. He also worked to isolate Haiti both diplomatically and economically (Rosalsky, 2021). Even Federalist rivals, such as Alexander Hamilton, supported Jefferson's Haitian policy.

The most immediate response was the formal silence of the United States. Responding to the fear and pressure of Southern slaveholding states, the U.S. government refused to recognize Haitian independence. Ironically, it was not until 1852, with the civil war, that Haitian independence was finally realized (Blackburn, 2006).

The United States continued to isolate, intimidate, and problematize the newly independent Haiti through much of the early 19th century. It, through force, occupied the nation and remained there for 19 years in the early 20th century. Even after the United States withdrew its troops in 1934, it continued to control Haiti's finances until 1947.

According to estimates, the United States stole approximately 40 percent of Haiti's GDP to repay the debt to the United States and France. The Marine Corps General in command of the joint occupation of Haiti and the Dominican Republic, Smedley Butler, confessed that he had been essentially a "high class muscle man for Big Business," and that he was "a gangster for capitalism" as he had "helped make Haiti ... a decent place for the National

**Figure 4.1:** The Baron de Mackau of France presents demands to Jean-Pierre Boyer, President of Haiti, in 1825

Source: Victor Duruy, *Histoire populaire contemporaine de la France*, Tome premier, Paris, Lahure, 1864, p 185 via Bibliothèque du Musée National de la Marine, https://gallica.bnf.fr/ark:/12148/bpt6k9616305h/f193.item

City Bank Boys" (Danticat, 2015). Perhaps to clean up its image, National City Bank's board of directors changed its name to Citigroup in 1967.

Foreign intervention served to destabilize the fragile state continually. Extreme poverty, high crime, and political instability resulted in thousands killed, massive human rights violations, and repeated revolutions. U.S. involvement continued through the 20th century, as Aristide and then Martelly were forced to step down. And then, on July 7, 2021, U.S.-trained mercenaries assassinated Jovenel Moïse.

## The tale of two nations: the social creation of a racial state

Often when discussing Haiti, it is easy to forget that it shares an island with another nation, now known as the Dominican Republic. In 1802, when Leclerc was sent to re-establish French rule, he was partially successful, as L'Ouverture was forced to flee the Dominican Republic. J.J. Dessalines led a Haitian force to expel the remaining French occupiers in the Dominican Republic.

Attempts to remove the Europeans resulted in a bloody trail of destruction as hundreds of residents were slaughtered and dozens of towns destroyed. When Haiti finally gained independence in 1804, it took control and ruled over the Dominican Republic for 22 years. The Dominican Republic was formed in 1844, but it was not until 1865 that it finally gained independence from Spain.

Coincidently, it was Haiti that helped the Dominican Republic defeat Spain (Bishop and Fernandez, 2017). From the beginning, the Dominican Republic was primarily made up of a light-skinned population that espoused Eurocentric ideologies, whereas Haiti was a nation of formerly enslaved people and considered Black.

Dominican leaders, who often presented the Haitians as racially inferior, institutionalized Whiteness. Anti-Haitian sentiments resulted in "ethnic cleansing" as thousands of Haitians were slaughtered under the dictator Rafael Trujillo in the 1930s.

In what would be known as the Parsley Massacre, persons who mispronounced the word "perjil" (meaning parsley) or did not have the proper Spanish inflection were marked for death. Under Trujillo, a government plan to "lighten" the Dominican population was instituted, as Jewish exiles from the Spanish civil war were encouraged to immigrate.

Dominicans were encouraged to marry only White persons to lighten the population further. These policies are ironic, given that the first enslaved Africans imported into America were destined to land in the Dominican Republic, and over 85 percent of the population had some African ancestry.

To be Dominican was to be anything but Black and certainly not Haitian. Consequently, as espoused by the elites, Dominicans viewed themselves as a mixture of Indigenous and Spanish. Haitians were viewed as morally inferior, while the Dominicans represented a more cosmopolitan, superior group akin to the White Europeans (San Miguel, 1997/2005).

From these myths, a whole set of realities were created. The Haitians spoke a broken French known as Creole, practiced Vodou and witchcraft and their failures "were a consequence of their actions." The Dominicans, alternatively speaking proper Spanish, were Roman Catholics, and their failures resulted from tragic victimization (Shaw, 2021).

## Monroe Doctrine and the White man's burden: the case of Santo Domingo

Whereas a slave rebellion precipitated the Haitian revolution, the one in Santo Domingo resulted from three revolutions orchestrated by White planters, mulattoes, and enslaved people. Although separate, they nevertheless fed upon each other as the call for liberation was paved through massacres, atrocities, and violence (Hazard, 1873).

Strangely enough, the catalyst of these revolutions was another – the French Revolution of 1789. The French National Assembly ratified the Declaration of the Rights of Man and granted the Dominican Republic's free people of color full citizenship rights. This immediately created a conflict, as the White planters refused to acknowledge these rights and instead decided to seek independence from France. As these tensions led to conflict, first by Whites, then between Whites and free people of color, the slaves of the Dominican Republic rebelled on August 22, 1791.

Civil war enveloped the country, as the enslaved people occupied the northern province of the country. The rebellion was led by three Black leaders, Toussaint L'Ouverture, Jean-Jacques Dessalines and Henri Christopher. Their connection to the White planter elite varied from being a slave to serving as an officer in the French Army.

Attempts by the French to stabilize the situation were ineffectual, as freedmen rebels continued to control the northern provinces, and the southern regions were a virtual lawless territory. The final straw came as France declared war on England; as the White planters supported England, slave-backed Spain (who was also at war with France over the control of the rest of Hispaniola). L'Ouverture, in May of 1794, and his army of formerly enslaved people, took the side of the French.

It was more than ironic that President Ulysses S. Grant, in 1869, attempted to annex the Dominican Republic as a U.S. territory. His promise of statehood was partly fueled by his fears that European nations would violate the Monroe Doctrine and attempt to retake the island nation (Hidalgo, 1997).

Oddly, it was a strange mix of climate and geographical determination of races that determined the outcome. Sumner, taking this notion from Alexis de Tocqueville, was the chief opponent of the annexation. Accordingly, he argued that this idea, first articulated by Alexis de Tocqueville, prophesying that the English race was destined to occupy the North American continent "between the polar ice and the tropics." This race would "[b]elong to the same family, who will have the same point of departure, the same civilization, the same language, the same religion, the same habits, the same manners and over which thought will circulate in the same form and paint itself in the same colors" (Sumner, 1874: 163, 164, quoted in Hidalgo, 1997: 65). The leading racialized arguments favored the race and geographical determination argument and the idea that the Anglo race could never operate and prosper in hotter climates (Hidalgo, 1997). Racial determinism aside, this did not stop several other attempts by the U.S. presidents to annex the Dominican Republic.

And if annexation was not feasible, special rights and concessions were frequently proposed, particularly regarding Samaná Bay (Lowenthal, 1970). Over the next decades, U.S. interests, guided by strategic interests in the region and economic interests, expanded. Both these interests merged with the creation of the San Domingo Improvement Company. This establishment represented a two-decades interest in commercial and financial domination of the Dominican Republic by U.S. commercial entities. The U.S. complicity in this signaled the formal beginning of U.S. active involvement in the Dominican Republic through closer control of the country's economic and political institutions (Duin, 1955, quoted in Lowenthal, 1970: 32).

President Theodore Roosevelt, fearing European intervention, utilized the Monroe Doctrine to justify his intervention into the Dominican Republic. Consequently, he negotiated with the Dominican Republic a protocol in which the United States would guarantee the republic's territorial integrity, take control of its customs houses, administer its finances, and become responsible for foreign debts. Although the Senate Democrats blocked ratification for two years, Roosevelt implemented the plan through executive order (Blassingame, 1969).

Formally, the United States' Road to Imperialism started here and was fully implemented by the beginning of the 20th century. From this point until 1915, the United States would exert its influence on several nations from the Caribbean to the Pacific. The United States ignored the national sovereignty of these people, who coincidentially were exclusively people of color, second-class citizens and considered inferior to White Americans.

Events reached a climax as the United States pressured the Dominicans to disband their armies and allow the United States to establish and control a civil, non-military police force. Dominican factions were also pressured to allow the United States to supervise and declare the outcomes of the elections. When the Dominican authorities said "hell no" in 1916, President Woodrow Wilson sent in the Marines.

## The social creation of a racially failed state: the case of Haiti

Walter Rodney's 1972 seminal text, *How Europe Underdeveloped Africa*, explores how European colonial powers' deliberate policies, strategies and practices undermined, exploited, and underdeveloped Africa. The poor African states that resulted were intentional and served to justify and condemn the Africans for conditions created by their adversaries. Oddly enough, while many have criticized the book and its author, the conditions he articulated were part of the duplicitous ways the imperial state penalizes racialized others for being different, and then shifts the blame onto the victims.

Let us consider how these policies, strategies, and practices served to underdevelop Haiti while simultaneously developing the Dominican Republic.

Before 1960, the Dominican Republic and Haiti were almost equal in terms of GDP and capital incomes. But now, the Dominican Republic's GDP is nearly 800 percent higher. And so today, Haiti, once the jewel of the

Caribbean, is now the pariah, as the United States and other world powers orchestrated the demise of this Black-led nation. As we have seen, over the last two centuries, continuing up to this day, Haiti has been targeted, occupied, marginalized, ostracized, and exploited.

As a result, Haiti is the poorest nation in our hemisphere. Moreover, the same policies, practices, and intentional strategies that created such a nation would be duplicated, refined, and reinvented as our nation discovered Jim Crow, redlining, the cradle-to-prison pipeline, and the resulting ghettos. The next chapter will continue this discussion but let us continue our exploration of Haiti.

## U.S. duplicity in the twisted tale of a failed state

Earlier, it was noted that the U.S. official policy toward Haiti was not indifferent, but duplicitous. So, while the United States refused to recognize the newly independent nation diplomatically, it continued to import Haitian agricultural products and export its goods to Haiti.

This commerce was a decidedly one-sided trade agreement that benefited the countries of the north at the expense of Haiti (Farmer, 2006). Much of the blame for Haiti's poverty in our modern era is attributed to what has been termed Haiti's Vodou dynasty – François Duvalier, aka Papa Doc, and Jean-Claude Duvalier, aka Baby Doc.

The dynasty, consisting of the Duvalier family, controlled the country between 1957 and 1986 through a reign of terror, totalitarianism, and barbarism that can only be called "cruel and inhumane." But, and there is always a "but," their rule would not have been possible except through major political ripples generated by the U.S. occupation from 1915 to 1934.

It was as a direct consequence of this occupation that the Duvaliers first gained power. The earliest member of this family, Duval Duvalier, an immigrant from the French Caribbean colony of Martinique, was a direct recipient of the professional and political opportunities the occupation provided.

Of things, U.S. imperialism targeted a Haitian medical school. They then established their own, in which François Duvalier would be trained. He later spent a year at the University of Michigan. During this period, he was deeply struck by the exploitation of U.S. occupation and the teachings of Haitian philosopher Jean Price-Mars. Price-Mars, a major Haitian figure during the initial years of the U.S. occupation of Haiti, challenged collective *Bovarysme*, which celebrated European culture, often at the expense of Africans.

As one of the leading proponents of Nigritude, Price-Mars articulated Haiti's African traditions and roots. He, therefore, joined other leading Black intellectuals and writers of the movement, such as W.E.B. Du Bois and those of the Harlem Renaissance.

François Duvalier, thus influenced, became elected president of Haiti in 1957. No one doubts, even from the start, that Duvalier was both cynical and aimed to produce a despotic African nation. But even knowing this, our State Department in 1967 determined that while Duvalier was psychotic, he was an appropriate president for the Haitians, who were generally perceived as being a "paranoid" group, often harboring a generalized belief in "animism" (quoted in Dubois, 2014).

Duvalier presented himself as a man of the people (the masses and Black middle class) who reflected the popular sentiment that the country had suffered because of the Roman Catholic hierarchy and the United States. Duvalier took advantage of the growing resentment in Haiti and other parts of the Caribbean toward these colonial powers. And then there came our fear of the spread of communism (Nicholls, 1986).

Two years into Duvalier's presidency, communist guerilla Fidel Castro overthrew the Cuban dictator Fulgencio Bautista (Dollar, 2008). Policy makers ignored Haiti and Duvalier because of increasing fears over communist uprisings in the Caribbean and Central America. The focus of this was the armed uprising of Castro against Fulgencio Batista. Oddly enough, the US backed Batista, even knowing he was corrupt.

The situation shifted when Batista fled, and Castro entered Havana on January 1, 1959. Castro, seeking help from the Soviet Union, was greeted by hostility in Washington. A colossal failure of the C.I.A. came during the Bay of Pigs, as the plot to assassinate Castro only made him stronger and an American president weaker. The installation of Soviet missiles brought us dangerously close to a nuclear disaster. Khrushchev backed down, and U.S. intervention in Cuba became primarily economic, as an almost total trade ban was instituted. And then, John F. Kennedy was assassinated (Smith, 1995).

From this point onward, president after president supported Duvalier, even as the humanitarian crises escalated, as waves of immigrants fleeing poverty and oppression came to our borders. Haiti became a haven for U.S. foreign policy, even to the extent that after the death of Papa Doc in 1971, we continued the insanity. Jean-Claude, bolstered by U.S. support, bragged that "the United States will always find Haiti on its side against communism." So, U.S. monies were funneled into the country, which Duvalier embezzled into offshore accounts. Poverty, climate and environmental disasters, and disease were endemic. All who opposed Baby Doc disappeared, were imprisoned, tortured, or forced to leave the country.

Corruption continued unabated, and Haitians began questioning the public disclosures of the millions embezzled by Jean-Claude Duvalier. Duvalier and his allies sought temporary asylum in France, staying at a luxury hotel on Lake Annecy. In the late 1970s, the United States had had enough, and President Carter pressed the government to democratize its political system, allow opposition groups to organize and publicly criticize the leaders. By the time Ronald Reagan was elected no U.S. support was forthcoming as Baby Doc arrested and tortured ferociously those who opposed him and refused to leave the country (Nicholls, 1986).

But in 1981, Reagan blinked and signed into law what has been labeled a repatriation policy with Jean-Claude Duvalier. This law, creating so-called boat people, requires the Coast Guard to "screen" refugees and return those considered unworthy of asylum. In the first eight years of the law, between 1981 to 1989, 21,369 Haitians were intercepted, and only six were deemed worthy of asylum.

Duvalier followed up with a Haitian law declaring any "irregular voyage destined for abroad" be punished with up to three years of jail time. These laws continue to this day (Doyle, 1994). Even amidst public tortures and the killing of opponents, by 1985, the U.S. government had begun distributing US$34 million in annual aid to Haiti (Dollar, 2008).

In 1987, a U.S.-supported coalition of Haitian military leaders adopted a new constitution. Accordingly, a Provisional Electoral Council would consist of one member from various sectors of Haitian civil society. One of the chief objectors to this Constitution, and particularly this clause, was the Catholic priest Jean-Bertrand Aristide, who stated that it was "a trap that would lead [Haiti] into sham elections directed by the US government and the Haitian army, and into a continuation of the downward political spiral begun when the United States supported François Duvalier's rise to power" (Dollar, 2008: 649).

Three years later, Aristide would become the first democratically elected president in the history of Haiti, with a two-thirds majority vote (Jones, 1993). Aristide began almost immediately with a program to improve and protect human rights and improve fundamental freedoms for all. Aristide appointed Lt. General Joseph Raoul Cédras as Commander-in-Chief of the Armed Forces. Cédras was educated in the United States and became a U.S.-trained Leopard Corps member. The United States and France chose him to oversee security during 1990–1991. He "was one important source for the CIA, providing reports critical of President Aristide" (Whitney, 1996). In 1991, Cédras initiated a military coup that removed Aristide from power.

Further U.S. involvement was detailed in declassified reports from the C.I.A. The Defense Intelligence Agency demonstrated they helped fund and create a paramilitary group called "The Front for the Advancement and Progress of Haiti (FRAPH)." In the first few days of the coup, an estimated 250 to 600 Haitians were killed (Dollar, 2008).

With the 1991 military coup against Aristide, the United States had another chance to effect change in Haiti. The Organization of American States almost immediately called for an economic embargo until the duly elected president was restored. President George Bush agreed. The then-Secretary of State James Baker declared that the "junta" would be treated as a pariah throughout the hemisphere.

But such strong words lasted less than a year, as U.S. companies began to lobby the State Department to allow them to resume their operations. Bush agreed, and the sanctions were lifted. Without U.S. support, the embargo failed. The United States formally embraced the military coup.

A year later, now-President Clinton attempted to reinstate Aristide. Another failure only underscored the increasing inability of the United States to negotiate or impose its will on the nation of Haiti or its leaders (Doyle, 1994).

Aristide would not return until 1994, as the US military again occupied Haiti, this time until 1997 to "establish peace and restore democracy" (Ballard, 1998). In an unprecedented move, the Clinton administration provided amnesty for the coup leaders and gave transportation and support for Cédras and over 23 staff members. U.S. bank accounts under the name of hundreds of Haitian army members, totaling US$79 million, were unfrozen (Dollar, 2008).

In 2000, Aristide was elected yet again to the presidency. The election was marred from the outset; all the opposition parties withdrew their candidates, handing over an overwhelming victory to the Fanmi Lavalas party led by Aristide. The Organization of American States, which monitored the election, refused to ratify the election, and declined to oversee the presidential race.

Again, opposition from the very beginning came from the U.S. government, which challenged the election result. By 2000, having lost much of its external support, Haiti's economic system was plunged into chaos as widespread poverty became commonplace. And on December 17, 2001, armed commandos stormed the presidential palace in Port-au-Prince in an attempted *coup d'état*. Although the attempt failed, the problems only escalated again in February 2004.

Rebels taking control of many of the towns were moving toward the capital. Aristide, with limited alternatives, resigned his presidency and was escorted out of the country by Haitian and American militaries and flown to South Africa (Farmer, 2006). In an interview just 13 days after his departure, Aristide charged the United States with orchestrating the coup and having "duped him into leaving Haiti and his presidency" (cited by Wines, 2004).

In 2004, the United Nations dispatched the United Nations Stabilization Mission to Haiti (MINUSTAH). From 2004 to 2006, MINUSTAH, in coordination with the Haiti military coup, launched "search and destroy operations to root out Lavalas rebel bases" in Port-au-Prince and surrounding areas, causing over 8,000 deaths and 35,000 rapes (many by security forces) (Roth, 2011). The 2006 election of Rene Préval also demonstrated

U.S. intervention, as millions of votes for the opposing candidate were declared null and void. And the 2010 election was ultimately determined by U.S. intervention and openly acknowledged as defective (Palsson, 2021).

On January 12, 2010, Haiti was battered by a 7.0 magnitude earthquake, lasting just 35 seconds with several aftershocks, leaving over 300,000 dead, 1.5 million injured, and another 1.5 million homeless. More than 100,000 buildings in metropolitan Port-au-Prince, Jacmel, and Léogâne were leveled. The UN post-assessment estimated that the destruction was at US$7.9 billion.

Although an estimated US$10.7 billion was pledged by donors, less than US$5 billion has been realized. Most of this has gone to economic and physical damage recovery. Virtually none has gone to the tens of thousands of people living in makeshift settlements with no running water, restrooms, electricity, or security (Charles and Iglesias, 2020).

Over 100 years ago, James Weldon Johnson concluded that "the forcible intervention on the part of the United States ... (was an attempt) to compel Haiti to submit" (Johnson, 1920: 5). But still, they rise.

## Follow the money: trade

What accounts for the meteoric rise to superstardom of the Dominican Republic and the dreadful fall and failure of Haiti? In this section, I will explore this fork in the road. We shall discover how this fork, and the access to significant resources, enhanced policies, and a whole range of choices structured success for one and failure for another racial state.

The fork in the road consisted of becoming a "most favored nation" and enhanced trade, investments, and liberal immigration, which provided easy access to education and training. In the end, we have a trading partner, a major tourist hub, and billions of dollars flooding the Dominican Republic.

In Haiti, freedom was significantly curtailed, and failure was assured. Broader choices and access availed a wider range of options for the Dominican residents, hence freedom. What this access will demonstrate is that freedom is not free. Let us begin.

A few examples demonstrate how differently the United States and other Western nations have engaged the Dominican Republic and Haiti. If we follow the money, particularly the separate trade treaties, the tale of these two nations becomes obvious. One set of treaties led to success, another to disaster. Consider how the Dominican Republic, with the aid of the United States, was able to establish one of the first free zones in the Western Hemisphere.

This program, allowing for diversification and massive growth, was fueled by the offshore U.S. textile and garment industry. Preferential trade agreements with extremely favorable exchange rates were established that shifted the Dominican Republic from a commodity-oriented economy to one whose manufacturing sector was the fastest growing in the Western Hemisphere.

The sector went from a GDP of just 18 percent in the 1970s to 30 percent by the 2000s. In 2003, it peaked and accounted for 75 percent of the country's total GDP and 90 percent of exports (Burgaud and Farole, 2011). However, all of this changed due to a recession caused by economic instability between 1999 and 2003 (Park, 2016).

This instability was associated with the rise in oil prices, the significant decline in tourism after 9/11, the failure of the second-largest Dominican bank, Baniter, and intense competition from China. The 2004 Dominican Republic-Central America-United States Free Trade Agreement (CAFTA-DR) provided preferential access to agricultural and manufactured goods. The GDP, which had been gradually growing over the previous decades, leaped from US$22.51 billion to US$35.95 billion in the first year of implementation. Each year, with few exceptions, it has continued to soar. It sits at slightly over US$112 billion; future predictions suggest this will continue (Park, 2016).

Now consider the case of Haiti and the Caribbean Basin Initiative (CBI), a trade initiative of the United States intended to bring about economic recovery. The act, coming into effect on January 1, 1984, aimed to provide tariff and trade benefits to many Central American and Caribbean countries. This agreement prevented the United States from extending preferences to certain countries judged to be contrary to the interests of American businesses, farmers, and other entities. Before this act, Haiti was almost self-sufficient due to its rice production. But the CBI, liberalizing Haiti's economy and forcing it to reallocate nearly one-third of its food production toward export crops, resulted in the shrinking of Haiti's rice industry, as it could no longer compete with the cheaper, subsidized U.S. rice imports. Haitian farmers were devastated, and rice production plummeted. Rural Haitian farm workers were reduced to near poverty (Mullin, 2018).

## A failed state, not a failed people

Prominent Haitian Americans include:

- singer Wyclef Jean
- artist Jean-Michel Basquiat
- writer Edwidge Danticat
- former Utah Congresswoman Mia Love
- current Florida Congresswoman Sheila Cherfilus-McCormack

The Chrysler 300 was designed by Ralph Gilles; Reggie Fils-Aimé is the former President of Nintendo America; Vanessa Cantave is the co-founder and executive chef of the catering company Yum Yum.

When we consider nations such as Haiti, we often concentrate on the failure(s) of the state and translate this as a failure of its people. While such state failure exists, as pointed out in this chapter, much of it is a consequence of external constraints. This failure, also associated with the caprice, malice, and troubles orchestrated by some of its leaders, must not cause us to equate the actions of these "state" actors with those of Haiti's people.

In this final section, we shall look at the continual struggle of these people to valiantly, against all odds, be successful, change the course of their destiny, and breathe free. The struggle to be free is associated with the decision to emigrate – by any means necessary. Investigating these decisions allows us to see the wonder of these great people.

## Immigration, quotas, and refugee status

Enslaved and free Haitians have been emigrating to the United States since the colonial period. The United States has the largest concentration of Haitian migrants in the world (687,000), followed by:

- the Dominican Republic (496,000)
- Chile (237,000)
- Canada (101,000)
- France (85,000)

But the largest group of Haitian immigrants arrived in 1972 and continues to this day. This number tripled between 1990 and 2018 (Olsen-Medina and Batalova, 2020). In 1972 thousands of Haitians, later termed "boat people," arrived in South Florida, seeking political asylum from the persecution of Haitian dictator Jean Claude "Baby Doc" Duvalier.

Cuban and Bahamian residents aided their journey, providing shelter, clothing, and water. They arrived with little more than the clothes on their backs. Rather than enjoying protected refugee status as articulated in the United Nations Convention and Protocol, the United States categorized the Haitians as economic refugees, not political refugees. The distinction is important because they could be deported without due process.

Despite the odds, Haitians continued to seek freedom in the United States. In 1980, between 300,000 and 400,000 entered the United States. Most of these were deported back to Haiti (Alexander, 2022). A second wave of Haitians fled after the 1991 military coup supplanted the democratically elected Jean-Bertrand Aristide.

Following this coup, tens of thousands of Haitians again took to boats heading for the United States. Thousands of Haitians were held at Guantanamo Bay to avoid U.S. legal entanglements. This was formalized by the executive order of George Bush in 2002. In this order, Guantanamo

Bay became the Migrant Operations Center for those people interdicted and detained at sea. This policy was continued under the Biden administration, affecting Haitian migrants disproportionally.

Another policy, initiated under the Obama administration and accelerated under the Trump administration, has led to an increased number of migrants being detained in Tijuana. This policy, known as "metering," only allows a specific number of people to enter the southern border daily. Despite formal U.S. policy, over 1,084,055 Haitians were residing in the United States in 2019. These policies, clearly rooted in anti-Black racism, disproportionately affect Haitians and subject them to mistreatment, cruelty and what many consider to be violations of basic human rights (Wolf, 2021). Haitians live in South Florida and New York City, and their story is one of success, not failure.

Political and economic instability not only leads to immigration, but these migrants often send money back to relatives through remittances. So even as the economy deteriorated due to export and foreign assistance declines and natural disasters, remittances increased. Remittances of slightly over US$3 billion accounted for 23 percent of Haiti's GDP in 2022 and were the largest source of Haiti's foreign exchange (Inter-American Dialogue, 2022).

5

# The Africans and the Making
# of the Americas

Africans have been central to the shaping and the making of the Americas from its founding. The first antislavery societies were established the same year the Declaration of Independence was penned. From then to the present day, our nation has been consumed with the idea and the reality of race. This chapter will explore this shaping and making. More formally, this chapter will examine the system of racial triangulation created to keep the Africans in their places. Racial triangulation, the intended outcomes of racial imperialism, has been associated with centuries of forced servitude, followed by the Civil War and Jim Crow laws, forced segregation, racial intimidation and terror, redlining, differential access to education and training, and finally, the cradle-to-prison pipeline. The Africans have repeatedly and consistently fought against each of these attempts to contain, restrain, and pervert their very being.

It would be inaccurate to reduce the various responses of the Africans as mere reactions to racial imperialism. In this chapter, I will demonstrate how the Africans creatively restructured racial imperialism. Therefore, the various aspects of racial triangulation developed to control the Africans by the imperial state have been responses to the continuous, organized, and deliberate acts of resistance, rebellion, and revolts orchestrated by the Africans. Consequently, shaping the Americas reflects the imperial state's reaction to the African's agency in asserting identity, liberty, and justice.

At the onset, we must clarify that there were hundreds of large-scale rebellions across the Americas. There were also innumerable individual acts of rebellion, from the destruction of equipment and crops, work stoppages and slowdowns, escapes, and even suicide. The day-to-day acts of rebellions were a constant part of the continual response of the Africans to racial imperialism. With this understanding, we begin by examining the impact of the Haitian Rebellion upon the United States.

# African rebellions in the United States

The Haitian Revolution, as the only successful slave rebellion in the Americas, also catalyzed several slave rebellions within the United States. The four most significant rebellions were Gabriel's Conspiracy, which took place in Richmond in 1800, the German Coast Uprising in 1811, Vesey's Rebellion in 1822, and the 1831 rebellion of Nat Turner. These rebellions ultimately led to our nation's most costly war – both in terms of lives and money – the Civil War. Of interest is that all the rebellions were orchestrated by highly educated, skilled Blacks in slave states. None of these rebellions were successful, but collectively, they represented the biggest threat to slavocracy. And what was that threat? A highly organized, educated, and determined group of Africans "yearning to breathe free." Examining these rebellions and their aftermath shows Africans' contributions to the making of the Americas.

## Gabriel's Conspiracy

The spring of 1800 found the United States in an existential moment as the Federalists and Republicans contested the nation's future. The period, marked by political unrest, chaos, and conflict, provided an enslaved man ironically named Gabriel the impetus for the most elaborate and extensive slave rebellion in Southern history (Egerton, 1993). Historians believe that if Gabriel's conspiracy had been successful, it would have significantly altered our political history and race relations. But what made this, of all preceding and later rebellions, so significant?

Richmond, in 1800, was a slave town with more enslaved people than free Whites. The city held a community whipping post where the enslaved were punished in the public square. Here, we find an enslaved person called Gabriel, just two decades after the American Revolution was celebrated. Black refugees and the success of the Haitian Revolution fueled their efforts (Nicholls, 2020).

Gabriel's conspiracy originated in an urban environment where many conspirators were free, highly skilled, and educated. Gabriel, a skilled blacksmith, enjoyed many freedoms, such as the ability to "decide where and for whom" he would work. So, while still legally an enslaved person, his role as a skilled bondman allowed him to have a portion of his earnings. Black artisans, carpenters, coopers, shoemakers, tanners, weavers, and blacksmiths enjoyed these special liberties. They also often worked in small shops within the city alongside White skilled laborers. However, skilled labor worked within an economic system controlled by merchants. These merchants often took advantage of Black skilled labor and failed to pay the agreed-upon labor cost. Black artisans, like Gabriel, were left in a capricious position.

The merchants, therefore, not the owners, were often seen as the principal enemy. For Gabriel, the cause of his problems was greed and deceit. Thus, his goals were freedom and the right to control the fruits of his labor – his earnings (Egerton, 1993).

Gabriel and fellow conspirators planned to seize the political crises gripping Virginia and the nation. Thus, the plot unfolded as the nation was embroiled in the war with Europe following the French Revolution and the conflict between the Federalists led by incumbent President John Adams and the Republican challenger Thomas Jefferson. The actual conspiracy involved hundreds of enslaved people throughout central Virginia who were counted on to rebel, enter Richmond, capture the Capital and State Armory, take Governor James Monroe hostage, and bargain for the freedom of Virginia's enslaved population. Two unplanned events, a terrible storm and the confessions of a few enslaved people to their masters of the plot, foiled the conspiracy. Gabriel and 25 conspirators were arrested, tried, convicted, and executed. The two informants were granted their freedom (Nicholls, 2020).

## German Coast Uprisings

The Haitian Rebellion convinced Napoleon of the Africans' determination, ingenuity, and grit. This rebellion ultimately led to his decision in 1803 to sell his territories in Louisiana. Thomas Jefferson consequently purchased the entire territory of Louisiana for approximately US$15 million (about 3 cents an acre). The United States acquired a total of 828,000 square miles, doubling its size. Then, seven years later, Louisiana erupted into violence as the largest slave revolt in U.S. history unfolded (Thompson, 1992).

The fear of a Black insurrection was a constant concern of Whites living in Louisiana. The rebellion on the evening of January 8, 1811 was their worst nightmare. Perhaps one of the most startling uprisings occurred in parts of the Territory of Orleans on January 8–10, 1811. Charles Deslondes, a Haitian-born mulatto enslaved person, served as an overseer on the plantation of Col. Manuel Andry. He organized and enlisted the support of several fellow enslaved people and maroons from adjacent colonies. After wounding the plantation owner and killing his son, the rebels seized weapons and gunpowder and began their insurrection. Deslondes organized the rebels into companies, appointing officers, flagmen, and drummers. Then, arming them with guns, swords, and farm implements, he led them toward New Orleans. Starting with an initial group of 64 to 125 enslaved men, they marched toward New Orleans. As they marched, another 200 to 500 enslaved persons joined the procession. En route, they burned five plantation houses and destroyed storage facilities and crops (Thompson, 1992).

The rebellion was short-lived as, on the second day, Deslondes and the rebels engaged two separate local militias organized to suppress the revolt. Deslondes's rebels, with limited arms, nevertheless marched to the beat of drums, waving flags and wearing stolen military apparel. The militias killed approximately 60 of the insurgents and wounded even more. In three separate sets of tribunals, 18 rebels were found guilty. They were all executed by firing squads. But killing them was not enough to intimidate other enslaved; in a gruesome display of barbarity and outright fear, their heads were decapitated and placed on spikes and displayed on poles that stretched 60 miles (Waters, 2023). Although it lasted only a few days, its effects across the country demonstrated its significance. The revolt caused several states to reorganize their militias, prompting new laws to control the enslaved (Thompson, 1992).

## Vesey's Rebellion

Denmark Vesey, a self-educated and formerly enslaved carpenter, contemplated the most sophisticated, encompassing, and detailed rebellion before and possibly after. Inspired by the Haitian Revolution, he planned a rebellion that may have involved as many as 9,000 enslaved and free Blacks in Charleston, South Carolina. Vesey's audacity alone merits a special place in American history. But who was this man, and what was his plan?

Denmark Vesey, born into slavery, was also apparently quite lucky. In 1799, after winning US$1,500 in a street lottery, Vessey purchased his freedom for US$600, and the rest he used to train to become a carpenter and rented a house on Bull Street, which he used for his carpentry shop. An avid reader, he was fascinated by the Haitian Revolution and read antislavery literature. His continual frustration with the plight of the Africans, either freed or enslaved, caused him to begin organizing. Vesey's Rebellion involved "skilled, literate, and privileged slaves" (Paquette and Egerton, 2004). The local African Methodist Episcopal Church provided the location for organizing and meetings with several of his co-conspirators. With the Bible as his reference point, Denmark challenged the institution of slavery. His plan was simple: to attack the guardhouses, seize arms from the arsenals, and kill as many Whites as they could while burning down the city and freeing all enslaved. An estimated 9,000 Blacks may have been involved in this plot. Denmark's plan also called for the assistance of free Black sailors, who, after the rebellion, would facilitate the formerly enslaved people to sail to the newly independent Haiti for refuge (National Park Service, nd). Egerton (1999) concluded it was "one of the most sophisticated acts of collective slave resistance in the history of the United States."

The plot was foiled when two conspirators reported the plan to their owners. Immediately, the mayor alerted the city militia and captured the insurgents. Vesey, along with 35 other enslaved people, were arrested, tried, and executed by a special court. According to the testimony of several at his trial, Vesey utilized several biblical texts that compared the Africans to enslaved Israelites in the Bible. And so, while plantation owners used the Bible to subvert and control the Africans, Vesey used it to encourage and challenge the Africans to fight for their freedom. As Vesey was being sentenced to death, the magistrate of the trial accused him of "attempting to pervert the sacred words of God into a sanction for crimes of the blackest hue" (Schipper, 2022). Ironically, after Vesey and fellow insurrectionists were tried and executed, White Charlestonians destroyed the church where they had met and, with local funds, built "a Citadel" to house a local militia consisting of 150 men. In 1843, that structure became home to the South Carolina Military Academy (National Park Service, nd).

The Charleston community, recognizing the impact of education among free Blacks, immediately passed laws prohibiting teaching African Americans to read, to assemble freely, and to migrate into the state. A permanent militia comprising 150 guardsmen was established at an annual cost of US$24,000. And finally, in December of 1822, the Negro Seamen Act placed restrictions on any vessel from another "state or a foreign port, having on board any free negroes or persons of color" (quoted in National Park Service, nd). This final act recognized the importance of these men as they circulated information about other slave insurrections across the Atlantic. Therefore, it was an attempt to control what information was available to the Blacks (free and enslaved).

## Nat Turner's Rebellion

Nat Turner's Rebellion of 1831 drove the wedge between Southern White enslavers and Northern White abolitionists. It convinced Southern Whites that their biggest threat was not the freed Africans but the rebellious ones. They feared that the enslaved would bring about anarchy as they sought vengeance, blood, and retribution. As Jefferson, a slaveholder, wrote regarding enslaved people, "we have the wolf by the ear, and we can neither hold him nor safely let him go" (Jefferson, 1820).

The timing of Turner's Rebellion, almost four decades to the day of the Haitian Rebellion, resulted in many Southern Whites fearing "similar scenes of bloodshed and murder might our brethren at the South expect to witness, were the disaffected Slaves of that section of the country [to] gain the ascendancy" (quoted in Horne, 2015: 1).

The conditions for a rebellion could not have been better, as the North and South were in a persistent state of agitation regarding the issue of slavery. The seminal event that sparked the flames was associated with the proposed admission of Missouri as a slave state. The 1820 Compromise, where Maine was admitted as a free state and Missouri as a slave state, preserved the balance between free and slave states. Further, with the prohibition of slavery west of the Mississippi, the southern boundary of Missouri, Congress aimed to preserve the balance. The uneasy truce was upset in 1831 with the Nat Turner slave rebellion in Virginia. The White Southerners were convinced that Northern abolitionists had facilitated the rebellion.

Much like Vessey, Nat Turner also utilized religion and the idea of salvation to convince the enslaved that their freedom was not only promised but necessary. Viewed as a prophet by the enslaved, his impact was tremendous. As a prophet of a vengeful God, he characterized slavery as evil and White enslavers as instruments of Satan. Turner repudiated the image of the smiling, grinning, happy enslaved person. Instead, he presented an African willing to do whatever was necessary, even shed blood, to ensure freedom. The Rebellion, in just one day, resulted in the bloodiest single day of violence perpetrated by enslaved people. In the end, at least 55 White people, including children, were killed, 30 enslaved men were tried and executed, and White mobs killed dozens more.

## Freedom oh freedom: Civil War and the African's determination to live free

In retrospect, none of the revolts of the enslaved had any chance of success. That was not the issue. Of the over 100 slave revolts that occurred across the decades and our country, none were successful. Many were ill-planned, the African freedom fighters ill-equipped, but one thing they had was faith in their struggle. The responses across the country ranged from grudging respect and admiration to abject fear and resentment. This bipolar response increasingly reflected the political alignment and realignment of the nation into two major factions – one desiring to free the Africans and the other to keep them enslaved. Neither had a clear plan for accomplishing either goal, but that did not stop the resulting political chaos. Ultimately, the confusion would erupt into a civil war, which did not resolve the issues.

## The Civil War

As early as 1808, with the Act Prohibiting the Importation of Slaves, the United States tried to control the increasing friction between the North and South concerning slavery. The act made it illegal to import enslaved people into the United States. However, it was still legal in nine states to own and sell enslaved people. But, even after the passage of this ban, hundreds of slave ship voyages brought captives to the United States, as well as Brazil and Cuba. These voyages continued the expansion of slave plantations and the trade it enabled. It is estimated that over 8,000 enslaved Africans reached U.S. territory, many coming up through the Gulf of Mexico (Barcia and

Harris, 2020). Cotton planters were the principal purchasers. Through African labor, cotton expanded westward.

The economic development, associated with human death and suffering, was part of the racial imperialism of the period that endures today.

The increasing importation of Africans added fuel to a blazing fire that resulted in the rapid expansion of the slave territories. Particularly, it entailed three interrelated events:

1. Manifest Destiny
2. the Indian Removal Act
3. the Mexican–American War

Individually, each of these would have had tragic consequences for the country and racialized groups, but collectively, they represented an inflection point that culminated in the Civil War.


*Manifest Destiny*

In the 19th century, Manifest Destiny, originally proposed by John L. O'Sullivan, predicted that God had destined the United States, White Americans, and their institutions to establish a heaven on earth. In many ways, Manifest Destiny articulated U.S. racial imperialism. In 1823, when President James Monroe advocated for westward expansion in what would become known as the Monroe Doctrine, he relied upon the presumed prophecies inherent in Manifest Destiny. These same prophecies buttressed Andrew Jackson's arguments as he signed the 1830 Indian Removal Act. And so, as U.S. territory expanded west of the Mississippi River, so did slavery – an estimated 200,000 enslaved persons crossed into the American frontier between 1830 and 1860 (Berry and Parker, 2023).

Texas became the focal point at which Manifest Destiny, slavery, and the competing interests of the North and South came to a head. Several historical figures, such as Davy Crockett, William B. Travis, and James Bowie, died during the Battle of the Alamo. Their deaths were not about freedom but rather to preserve slavery.

When Vincente Guerrero, then President of the Republic of Mexico, issued a decree that abolished slavery in 1829, Texas slaveholders immediately protested. One prominent landowner and politician, John Durst, exclaimed: "We are ruined forever should this measure be adopted." Immediately, Texans began scheming on how to avoid the ban on slavery. The scheme involved technically freeing the enslaved while forcing them into a contract to serve a specified number of years until they paid off the debt equal to their purchase price. Any cost of living, including clothing, food, or housing, would be deducted from their "wages," estimated to be about US$20 a year. Their children would assume the debt if the debts were not paid off by their death (McCullar, 2020).

Ultimately, when Mexico nullified these contracts, the slaveholders rebelled. Mexico responded by sending in troops to quell the rebellion and free all the enslaved people. When they converged on the Alamo, only one person was spared: an enslaved person by the name of Joe, the personal slave of William Travis. The dust had not settled over the Alamo as Sam Houston and a small yet determined group of volunteers defeated Santa Anna in the Battle of San Jacinto. Santa Anna signed the Treaties of Velasco, which acknowledged the Republic of Texas as an independent and sovereign state (McCullar, 2020).

Immediately, in 1836, slavery was enshrined in the Constitution of the Republic of Texas as it declared:

> All persons of color who were slaves for life previous to their emigration to Texas, and who are now held in bondage, shall remain in the like state of servitude … congress shall pass no laws to prohibit emigrants from bringing their slaves into the republic with them, and holding them by the same tenure by which such slaves were held in the United States; nor shall congress have power to emancipate slaves. (Texas Constitution, 1845)

All free Black people living in the Republic could only stay there with the approval of the Texas Congress (McCullar, 2020).

Mexico continued to regard Texas as their territory and invalidated any agreements signed by Santa Anna in prison. They sent several border raids to retake the territory. They also warned the United States that any attempts to annex the territory would be an act of war. The United States formally began annexation procedures after Polk was elected president in 1844. Believing in Manifest Destiny, Polk had campaigned on annexing Texas and expanding U.S. territory into the southwest to include Oregon, California, and New Mexico. After Mexico refused Polk's offer to purchase the land, and in 1845, the United States annexed Texas based on the Treaties of Velasco. Polk sent the U.S. military to enforce this annexation. These forces were soundly defeated by Mexican forces in 1846. Polk falsely claimed that Mexico had "invaded our territory and shed American blood on American soil." The U.S. Congress responded by declaring war, and the Mexican–American War had begun (Sexton, 2011). By 1848, the United States had won the war, and Mexico ceded the United States all the territory in New Mexico, Utah, Nevada, Arizona, California, Texas, and Western Colorado for US$15 million. Two years later, the Compromise of 1850 attempted to preserve the balance between free and slave states. Texas alone decided to sanction slavery. The balance was maintained as the District of Columbia agreed to abolish it. New Mexico and Utah chose to enact slave codes, while California became a free state. Congress ceded greater authority to the slave states with its Fugitive Slave Act, which made the return of runaway slaves a federal responsibility. The compromise only added fuel to the fire as it caused many moderate antislavery elements to become more determined to end slavery (Urofsky, 2023).

When the 1854 Kansas-Nebraska Act nullified the Missouri Compromise, Kansas became the focus of conflict between various pro- and antislavery factions. With the emergence of the Republican Party in the 1850s, prohibition in the slave territories took center stage.

Again, it was an enslaved African who pushed the needle. This time, it was a man by the name of Dred Scott. Dred Scott, having been relocated several times into and out of slave and free states, filed a legal claim asserting his freedom. The case went all the way up to the Supreme Court. In 1857, when the U.S. Supreme Court ruled in the Dred Scott case, the die was cast. In that decision, the Court ruled that an African had no standing or rights to citizenship. The Court also ruled that Congress could not regulate or prohibit slavery in federal territories. And it declared the Missouri Compromise of 1820 unconstitutional.

When Lincoln became president, the inevitability of conflict could not be ignored. Seven states – South Carolina, Mississippi, Florida, Georgia, Alabama, Louisiana, and Texas – immediately left the Union. When Confederate forces attacked Fort Sumpter, Lincoln requested 75,000 volunteers to fight back. Virginia, North Carolina, Tennessee, and Arkansas responded by joining the Confederacy. The Civil War had begun.

The Confederate States were intent on maintaining slavery. As Alexander Stephens, vice president of the Confederate States, in 1861, clearly states:

> The new [Confederate] Constitution has put at rest, forever, all the agitating questions relating to our peculiar institution – African slavery as it exists amongst us – the proper status of the negro in our form of civilization. This was the immediate cause of the late rupture and present revolution. ... The prevailing ideas entertained by ... most of the leading statesmen at the time of the formation of the old Constitution, were that the enslavement of the African was violation of the laws of nature; that it was wrong in principle, socially, morally, and politically. ... Those ideas, however, were fundamentally wrong. They rested upon the assumption of ... the equality of races. This was an error ...
>
> Our new government is founded upon exactly the opposite idea; its foundations are laid, its corner-stone rests upon the great truth, that the negro is not equal to the white man; that slavery – subordination to the superior race – is his natural and normal condition. (Alexander H. Stephens, March 21, 1861)

This view was in direct contradiction of the perspective of the African enslaved. As the Civil War ensued, and as many enslaved people began to desert their plantations and follow the military caravans, one could hear:

Oh freedom, oh freedom, oh freedom over me.
And before I'll be a slave, I'll be buried in my grave.
And go home to my Lord and be free.

While ostensibly, the Civil War was all about slavery, neither side was particularly concerned with the views of the enslaved people. The bloodiest and costliest war this nation has ever fought was all about preserving power; even leaders such as Abraham Lincoln only viewed the enslaved person as a pawn. Consider his statement:

My first impulse would be to free all the slaves, and send them to Liberia – to their own native land. But a moment's reflection would convince me, that whatever of high hope, (as I think there is) there may be in this, in the long run, its sudden execution is impossible.

If they were all landed there in a day, they would all perish in the next ten days; and there are not surplus shipping and surplus money enough in the world to carry them there in many times ten days.

What then? Free them all, and keep them among us as underlings? Is it quite certain that this betters their condition? I think I would not hold one in slavery, at any rate; yet the point is not clear enough for me to denounce people upon. What next? Free them, and make them politically and socially, our equals? My own feelings will not admit of this; and if mine would not, we well know that those of the great mass of White people will not. (October 16, 1854, speech at Peoria, Illinois)

Ultimately, Lincoln did what was expedient to force the rebellious slaveholding states back into the Union; he freed those enslaved people only in the states in the rebellion. That is, he released those enslaved people he had no control over.

No enslaved people were freed from those states loyal to the Union and not in the rebellion. And so, the Emancipation Proclamation held out the premise of the promise of freedom. A premise that never came to pass as the "great mass of White people" refused to allow it to come into being.

When asked about the emancipation of the enslaved person, William Lloyd Garrison remarked that emancipation was not enough; we must be free from the caprice of man's cruelty to man.

Frederick Douglass said the Negro must own their selves and their futures; they must have universal, equal rights and liberty. In an 1837 letter, Angelina

Grimke remarked that the freedom of Blacks was a human and moral right that could not be denied.

## The American paradox of race: the freedman's dedication to freedom

When the Emancipation Proclamation was issued on January 1, 1863, some four million Blacks (constituting 88 percent of all Blacks) were now free, but another 250,000 in Texas languished in slavery. Neither Lincoln nor Washington had any real impact on Texas, primarily because there were not enough Union troops to enforce the order.

Such force was not available until after the surrender of General Lee in 1865, and General Granger's regiment arrived two months later. Listen as Granger declares their freedom in his General Order Number 3:

> The people of Texas were informed that all enslaved people were free following a Proclamation from the Executive of the United States. This involves an absolute equality of rights and rights of property between former enslavers and enslaved people, and the connection heretofore existing between them becomes that between employer and hired laborer.
>
> The freedmen are advised to remain quietly at their present homes, and work for wages. They are informed that they will not be allowed to collect at military posts, and that they will not be supported in idleness either there or elsewhere.[1]

I cannot help but wonder if any Whites were advised to "remain quietly at their present homes, and work for wages ... that they would not be supported in idleness either there or elsewhere." Never in the history of this country was such a restriction or expectation placed on Whites. As we will see later, these were the seeds through which the infamous Jim Crow codes and laws would ensue. But for now, let us consider the response of the formerly enslaved person.

The responses of formerly enslaved people ranged from shock to exaltation, from acts of retribution to praise, and from prayers and celebration to cries of despair and loss. Some left not only the plantation but the South, seeking to re-establish connections with family and communities broken and shattered because of slavery.

Others stayed to attempt to take on freedom where they were enslaved. Regardless, these enslaved people challenged America to recognize their equality as they sought to establish themselves as free people within America. Ironically, one of the first things these free people aspired to do was to embrace education. It should be recalled that under slavery, it was illegal in many states to teach any Blacks – either free or enslaved – reading and writing.

But, even under slavery, Blacks facing severe punishment still found ways to support and encourage education. Therefore, it is not strange that after the war and emancipation, the now freedmen gathered in homes, cellars, sheds, meetinghouses, and even under the shade tree in the fields where they worked the crops to learn.

They learned from each other, teachers, clergy, or older family members. They not only learned to read and write, but they retained their history as a people. Imagine the scene recorded from South Carolina, as a six-year-old girl sits beside her mother, grandmother, and great-grandmother (over 75 years old), all embracing learning and reading for the first time (Coleman, 2023).

From the beginning, many of the freedmen distrusted the scalawags, carpetbaggers, and former masters, demanding to learn to read for themselves, to learn math, and to read the Bible firsthand. They established their schools – freedom schools – to accomplish this.

These freedom schools were sometimes funded by White aid and benevolent societies from the North, such as the American Missionary Association and the National Freedmen's Relief Association, Sabbath schools, and night schools. But most of the money to fund these schools came from the newly freed Americans, who privately sponsored their schools.

One example of these churches/schools is a small church known as Tolson's Chapel in Sharpsburg, Maryland. Tolson's Chapel was built by Blacks just two years after the end of slavery in 1863. Between 1868 and 1899, this one-room building was a church and school near the Civil War Battlefield of Antietam.

The schoolhouse's history in Tolson's Chapel illustrates how African Americans across the former slaveholding states created and sustained schools during Reconstruction. Here, the dreams of freedom were born as local Blacks sought to educate themselves and their children (National Parks Service, n.d.).

Consequently, as African Americans established their schools and advocated public education, they claimed education as a basic right as citizens. This dedication of the former enslaved to education laid the foundation for publicly funded schools for Blacks and Whites throughout the South and border states.

These newly freed Americans sought to become economically independent and exercise their full civil and political rights and the right to education. One of these efforts' most significant outcomes was the establishment of all-Black towns across America.

These Freedmen's Towns, or all-Black towns, were established by or for a predominantly African-American population. Many were founded by formerly enslaved people and existed in many of the former Southern states. For example, before the end of segregation, Oklahoma boasted dozens of these communities, while in Texas, some 357 freedom colonies have been verified and located (Sitton, 2007).

For a brief period, the promise of freedom flourished as Congress passed, and then slowly, the states ratified the so-called Reconstruction Amendments. These three amendments, the 13th, 14th, and 15th, abolished slavery and attempted to guarantee equal protection of the laws and the right to vote. So briefly, the illusion of freedom existed as the 13th Amendment prohibited involuntary servitude.

The principle of citizenship was ratified with the 14th Amendment for all born or naturalized and granted the right to vote and decide who could hold office. These rights were again reinforced with the 15th Amendment, which established that full citizenship rights could not be abridged due to race, color, or previous condition of servitude.

Of interest is that all debts of those associated with either the insurrection or rebellion against the United States and even the claim for the loss or emancipation of enslaved people were considered unenforceable, and all claims were held illegal and void. The problems were apparent as the Constitution denied women the right to vote for the first time.

Unfortunately, these amendments did not provide any enforcement provisions nor preclude the former states or their members from seeking to nullify, negate, or circumvent the laws.

No sooner than these amendments were ratified, and after the assassination of Lincoln, state laws and federal court decisions began to erode and nullify much of these throughout the late 18th century. Many states passed what would be known as Jim Crow laws that limited the rights of African Americans.

Decisions made by the Supreme Court, such as the Slaughterhouse Cases in 1873, undermined and prevented several guaranteed rights from being unenforceable by holding that these privileges or immunities could not be extended to rights under state law. In 1896, the *Plessy* v *Ferguson* case, which established "separate but equal," gave federal approval to all the Jim Crow laws.

These rights would not be guaranteed until the *Brown* v *Board* decision in 1954, the Civil Rights Act of 1964, and the Voting Rights Act of 1965.

The responses of Southern Whites to the newly freed persons were not limited to legislative or court actions.

## Responses by Whites: intimidation, lynching, and White racial riots

As the American Blacks celebrated their new freedom, many Whites in the South mourned the passage of what they believed was "their greatness." For many Southern Whites, this was personal and represented a communal defeat, marking the demise of the White man and a time of dismay.

They mourned the loss of traditions, customs, families, property, and a whole way of life built with Blacks' blood, sacrifices, and lives. Many considered leaving, while others began to retreat into nostalgia and fictitious memories of the Old South and mourning the lost cause of the Confederacy. The first Confederate memorial associations started appearing in 1865 and 1866 as they built cemeteries and monuments throughout the region (Cobb, 2017).

Others created groups, such as the Ku Klux Klan, which resorted to violence, murder, and terror to oppose this new freedom. The story of Tulsa and Black Wall Street, and hundreds of other Black colonies, illustrates the terror that ensued as the Africans sought to create their freedom.

No sooner than the 13th, 14th, and 15th Amendments were enacted – which provided legal and civil protections to formerly enslaved people – members of the Ku Klux Klan began systematic terrorist attacks against Black citizens for exercising their right to vote, running for office, and serving on juries.

Congress quickly responded by passing a series of Enforcement Acts of 1870 and 1871, which attempted to end such violence and empower the president to use military force to protect African Americans. The Act of 1870, for example, even prohibited groups of people from banding together "or to go in disguise upon the public highways, or the premises of another to violate another's constitutional rights." Legislative intent aside, these acts did nothing to diminish the harassment of Black voters across the South.

Seeing the lack of enforcement, the Senate passed two more Enforcement Acts, one known as the Ku Klux Klan Act, which was designated to enforce the 14th Amendment, and the Civil Rights Act of 1866. A second Enforcement Act passed in 1871 aimed to place national elections under the federal government's control and empower federal judges and U.S. marshals to supervise local elections (U.S. Senate, n.d.).

Then, the Third Enforcement Act of April 1871 gave the president the power to use the armed forces to combat those who conspired to deny equal protection of the laws and to suspend *habeas corpus*, when necessary, to enforce the act. These acts temporarily assisted in ending the violence and intimidation, but the formal end of Reconstruction in 1877 opened the floodgates for the disfranchisement and violence targeting African Americans.

Absent these protections, with the insurance of the Jim Crow laws throughout the South, it was essentially open season. Lynching became the most frequent weapon to terrorize Blacks and force them into submission. By 1877, lynchings were so normalized that they were flagrantly committed as public displays. They were advertised in local newspapers, and people dressed up and invited friends and neighbors to attend (Brown, 2020).

Large crowds and whole families would show up to watch Blacks get their "justice." Blacks were often punished for being prominent, free, and successful. Many Whites – rich and poor – used lynchings to keep Blacks "in their place." This perspective was expressed by none other than the founder of American sociology, Lester F. Ward:

These are fundamental and universal principles of ethnology, and when closely analyzed they will be seen to be all the result of the more general principle which makes for race improvement. When a woman of all inferior race yields to a man of a superior race there is a subconscious motive probably more powerful than physical passion, which is, indeed, the inspirer of the physical passion itself – the command of nature to elevate her race. When a woman of a superior race rejects and spurns the man of an inferior race it is from a profound though unreasoned feeling that to accept him would do something more than to disgrace her, that it would to that extent lower the race to which she belongs. And when the man of an inferior race strives to perpetuate his existence through a woman of a superior race, it is something more than mere bestial lust that drives him to such a dangerous act. It is the same unheard but imperious voice of nature commanding him at the risk of "lynch law" to raise his race to a little higher level.

In this last case, therefore, the philosophical student of races, however much he may deplore anything that tends to lower a higher race, sees reasons for partially excusing the "crime", since, although the perpetrator does not know it, it is committed in large measure under the influence of the biological imperative. It may be compared to the brave conduct of the male mantis or male spider in his zeal to perpetuate his race. On the other hand, the indignation and fury of the community in which such an act is performed is to be excused in a measure for the same reason. Although the enraged citizens who pursue, capture, and "lynch" the offender do not know any more than their victim that they are impelled to do so by the biological law of race preservation, still it is this unconscious imperative, far more than the supposed sense of outraged decency, that impels them to the performance of a much greater and more savage "crime" than the poor wretch has committed. (Ward, 1903: 371–372)

Often, the myth of the Black man as a sexual predator was used to fire up the masses. Other times, the real insult was that African Americans were perceived as being political and economic threats who wanted to foster integration, not sexual predators out to assault innocent White women.

Lynching and White riots were used to teach Blacks a lesson, put them in their place, and serve as a warning to any other Black person arrogant enough to challenge White supremacy. From the late 19th century to the middle of the 20th century, close to 5,000 Black people were lynched. In Mississippi alone, some 581 were lynched, while Georgia accounted for 531, and in Texas there were 493, with Blacks accounting for 72 percent of all lynch victims. Other victims included those Whites who helped Blacks or for being anti-lynching advocates. Also lynched were immigrants from Mexico,

China, and Australia. Blacks were accused of several dubious crimes including sexual aggression, murder, arson, robbery, and even vagrancy. But lynching was used to terrorize Blacks and to enforce segregation (NAACP, 2023).

But Blacks were not content to sit by and be lynched, as Blacks voted with their feet and initiated the largest domestic migration movement in modern history. Millions of Black people relocated from the most violent Southern regions to what was presumed to be a more tolerant North.

But the White mob was not content to lynch single individuals; soon, whole towns were annihilated.

## The Great Migration, segregation, redlining, and the birth of the ghetto

Blacks, as early as the 1900s, responded to lynchings with the greatest mass exodus our country has ever seen, called the Great Migration. But rather than a new day, they were greeted with new forms of racial violence. What guns and violence could not do, redlining and White flight did. In the process, newly created racialized zones came into being.

These zones, characterized as ghettos, were where overpolicing, underfunded schools, and limited social mobility served to create the cradle-to-prison pipeline, extreme levels of poverty and isolation. These truths account for the increasingly frustrated, violent, and hopeless.

My grandfather was part of the Great Migration. Born in rural Mississippi, he had been a sharecropper working on the same land where his grandfather had been enslaved. Even with seven sons, three daughters, and a wife laboring in the fields, he could barely scrape out an existence. In good years, there was just enough to make small repairs to the house, buy much-needed clothes for the fast-growing kids, and maybe a trinket for my grandmother.

Regardless of whether it was a good year or bad, lynchings and mob violence constantly terrorized Black communities. By 1915, my grandfather had had enough, so he packed up all his belongings and family and made the trek up North. They landed in East St. Louis, along with hundreds of others.

East St. Louis was the place to be. It was filled with opportunities, particularly in response to the labor shortages created during World War I and military production. Almost immediately, White business owners tried to block the new migrants from gaining either political or economic power. And while Blacks were only hired in the lowest-paying and lowest-skilled jobs, their White peers looked upon them as a threat. The Black population went from 6,000 to nearly 12,000 between 1910 to 1917 (Keys, 2017).

Things exploded as Blacks were hired to take the jobs of the largely White workforce that were on strike. The White workers lodged a formal complaint to the City Council on May 28. Ironically, a rumor surfaced at the same time about an attempted robbery of a White man by an armed Black man. White mobs began beating African Americans.

Tensions continued through the long, hot summer. Then, on July 1, after a White man shot into Black homes from a car, African Americans returned the fire at another oncoming Ford. Two White men were killed; they turned out to be police officers.

The next day, White mobs with pipes, baseball bats, and guns attacked and burned Black properties, and several Blacks were lynched across the city. After a week, nine Whites and hundreds of Blacks were dead, and it was estimated that the total property damage was US$400,000. Over 6,000 Blacks were forced to leave the city out of fear (PBS, 2023).

Similar race riots would take place in other cities, including Tulsa, Oklahoma, in 1921 and Rosewood, Florida, in 1923. In East St. Louis and elsewhere, an uneasy truce was established as Blacks and Whites coexisted in racially segregated zones. Segregation was not enough; banks, insurance companies, and businesses soon shunned the Black side of town. This shunning was officially known as redlining.

## Redlining and the creation of ghettos

In 1916, just across the river, in St. Louis, the residents voted on "a reform" ordinance that prevented people from buying homes in neighborhoods where more than 75 percent of the residents were of a different race. This became the first referendum in the country that sanctioned racial segregation in housing (Cooperman, 2014). Although this ordinance was declared unconstitutional by the U.S. Supreme Court (*Buchanan* v *Warley*) in the next year, many St. Louis communities responded by creating racial covenants, where residents and prospective new owners signed legal documents promising never to sell to an African American. From this point forward, the ownership of property was racialized and embedded into law and policies as new small and exclusive suburban municipalities emerged (Lipsitz, 2011). These covenants remained in effect until the U.S. Supreme Court ruled them unconstitutional in 1948 (*Shelley* v *Kraemer*).

What racial covenants could not accomplish, redlining did (Cooperman, 2014). Redlining was first coined in the 1960s by John McKnight to describe the discriminatory practice of banks excluding certain areas for investment based on community demographics (see Jackson, 2022). These practices expanded to cover a range of financial investments, including development, insurance, and even healthcare and were sanctioned at all levels of government. These discriminatory practices designated Black and Brown communities as "hazardous" and unworthy of investment and development due to the racial composition of the residents.

In 1934, the Federal Housing Administration, under Roosevelt's New Deal, declared that neighborhoods with poor housing markets, declining public health, unemployment, and economic immobility were reasons to deny mortgages to residents. The reality was that these neighborhoods were comprised of large numbers of "undesirable populations," including immigrants, people of color, those of the Jewish faith, and people with low incomes (Lockwood, 2020).

Then, in 1965, the Federal Highway Act began constructing highways to create more efficient routes connecting the suburbs and cities. They made "controlled access" expressways that deliberately divided redlined neighborhoods but did not provide access to the very residents affected. Thus, residents in these communities could not use the new routes to the resources, markets, jobs, and services in other parts of the city.

All of this led to decreasing availability of healthcare, employment, affordable food, and quality housing in poorer neighborhoods. In a word, all of this led to the creation of "the ghetto." What followed was predictable; as crime rates rose and property values and taxes sank, racially biased policing intensified, as did the cradle-to-prison pipeline, and despair replaced hope.

## Cradle-to-prison pipeline: school underfunding and overpolicing of Black bodies and neighborhoods

Through each period, Africans not only survived but developed strategies for thriving. Racial structures continued to evolve to thwart these efforts. The next phase of racial triangulation involved the creation of what the Children's Defense Fund calls the cradle-to-prison pipeline. African Americans and Latinos are, respectively, 5 and 1.3 times more likely than their White counterparts to be incarcerated. In some states, such as New Jersey, Blacks are more than 12.5 times more likely to be incarcerated than White Americans (Ghandnoosh and Barry, 2023). The cumulative effects of decades of redlining segregation have produced hyper-segregated, intensively poor areas where race and class fuel the cradle-to-prison pipeline. Added to this is the underfunding of schools and the overpolicing of Black bodies.

Over 60 years ago, the Supreme Court in *Brown* v *Board of Education* ruled that segregated schools were unconstitutional. Today, even though the student population is significantly more diverse, schools remain segregated by race, ethnicity, and economic status. Over a third of students (approximately 18.5 million) attended schools where 75 percent or more of the student body was of a single race or ethnicity. A full 14 percent of students attended highly segregated schools where the student body consisted of 90 percent or more of a single race or ethnicity (GAO, 2022). Schools with a high concentration of Black and Hispanic students are also more likely to be underfunded when compared to other schools. The underfunding of schools increases the likelihood of failure. This underfunding of schools, which starts as children begin school, amounts to an annual cost of US$150 billion. The data reveals that school expenditures are significantly and positively related to student outcomes such as reading, math, and higher completion rates (Century Foundation, 2020). Across 37 states, poor students receive substantially less, about US$800 per student, than their more affluent peers. Just US$500 per student more in a school with 500 students, you could hire three more teachers, buy every student a laptop, or provide intensive targeted support for students in need (Morgan, 2022).

## The continual cost of racial violence

Today, the cost of racial violence costs the U.S. economy some US$16 trillion (Akala, 2020). And what are the costs of all this violence? During the period of slavery in the United States, if enslaved people had been reimbursed for their time in forced servitude, the total has been estimated to range from US$18.6 trillion to US$6.2 quadrillion (compounded annually from 3 percent to 6 percent). Add another US$35 trillion to US$16 quadrillion for loss of land and property. Finally, no one has calculated the cost of pain and suffering over these 400+ years, but again, it would be in the quadrillions (all figures derived from Darity et al, 2022). This has been the cost of White violence perpetrated against Blacks.

Black history is American history; Black liberation is the essence of American liberation. Only when we realize the promises of the Declaration of Independence – of life, liberty, and the pursuit of happiness – will we experience these promises.

Although victimized repeatedly, we have not succumbed to becoming victims. We have been and continue to be overcomers. We have rebuilt what has been destroyed and relocated to avoid violence and continual abuse. We have never abandoned our quest to be free, achieve in every field of human endeavor, or live authentically.

And what of these accomplishments, under duress?

- Mathew Henson and Admiral Robert Peary explored the North Pole in 1909.
- Jesse Owens demonstrated to Hitler what a Black man could do by winning four gold medals in the Berlin Olympics in 1936.
- Jackie Robinson became the first Black to enter the major baseball leagues in 1947, even though Blacks played the sport for over 60 years.
- We have Althea Gibson, Venus Williams, Coco Gauff, and Naomi Osaka, who might be the world's best tennis player.
- With pen and prose, Gwendolyn Brooks won the Pulitzer Prize for poetry in 1950.

We have this amazing young poet, Amanda Gorman, the youngest inaugural poet in U.S. history: an award-winning writer, cum laude graduate of Harvard, who shows what the future looks like. We have Barack Obama, who became the first Black president of the United States, and Kamala Harris, the first Black female vice president of the United States.

We do not wait for or expect freedom from legislation or judicial decrees. We are free by virtue of being humans. We will continue to survive, thrive, and set new achievement standards by any means necessary. It is more than our right; it is our mandate from the Creator of all.

We will settle for full accountability and responsibility for past wrongs. While we recognize that reparations are due, we have no confidence that any will come soon. No, we will not take any more promissory notes. We will, however, demand that schools and courts, political institutions and economic systems, police and legislatures act responsibly, equitably, and justly for us and our prosperity.

To guarantee these premises, we promise to do the following: litigate, validate, agitate, propagate, and instigate a continual revolutionary struggle. We shall do more than overcome; we will more deliberately, meticulously, and strategically utilize and maximize our votes, economies, and communities to foster change and new realities.

# 6

# Unsung Warriors: Black Women

The most disrespected person in America is the Black woman.
The most unprotected person in America is the Black woman.
The most neglected person in America is the Black woman.[1]

Black women's identities have been prescribed and conscribed almost from the beginning of our nation. These representations of the African woman in America have rarely reflected the contributions to the American project. Even when there is an attempt to acknowledge their true histories grudgingly, it barely scratches the surface. Black women have blazed the trail, set the bar, and creatively constructed their identities and realities from the Revolutionary War to the Civil War, from the Industrial Revolution to the era of civil rights, and from "Hidden Figures" to "the Black Lives Matter Movement." This chapter acknowledges the various ways Black women have been both sterilized and characterized, yet they remain resilient, resistant, and rebellious, unsung warriors. Explored, therefore, will be the classic stereotypes that have attempted to racialize and minimize her. But this chapter will also explore their responses and their active engagement in creating, sustaining, and maintaining feminine identities that are uniquely African, Black, and proud. We begin with Nina Simone's 1966 classic as she captures the four principal character types:

1. She heralds "Aunt Sarah" as a strong, resilient woman who declares, "My skin is black/My arms are long/My hair is wooly/My back is strong/ Strong enough to take the pain/Inflicted again and again/What do they call me? /My name is Aunt Sara."
2. Then there is "Saffronia," a mixed-race woman whose skin was described as "yellow" and who was forced to live "between two worlds." In this in-between place, she is buffeted by the Black and Whites. "My father was rich and white; he forced my mother late one night."

3. Then there is "Sweet Thing," accepted by both Blacks and Whites, whose primary attributes were neither good looks nor fine hair but because she could satisfy the sexual needs of men: "Whose little girl am I? /Anyone who has money to buy."

4. Nina's lament ends with the bitter tale of a woman who has endured generations of oppression and suffering. She cries out, "My skin is brown/ My manner is tough/I'll kill the first mother I see/My life has been rough/ I'm awfully bitter these days/Because my parents were slaves." And in a scream that rages through the ages, she declares, "My name is Peaches!" (Davis, 2003).

These four characterizations were also reflected in the work of Patricia Hill Collins as one of several controlling images established by the racial order not only to define but limit Black feminine realities. Four such images were the Mammy, Jezebel, Sapphire, and the Welfare Mother, all created to control how Black women were perceived within Western institutions (Hill Collins, 1991). Black women, a part of virtually every aspect of American history, were forbidden from reading and writing and often restricted to the kitchen, the field, and nearly invisible.

Even today, Black women are often not considered normal, typical, or worth our attention. Because of the misperceptions, misrepresentations, stereotypes, and outright racialized sexism, they are least likely to be viewed as worth our attention. They are, therefore, "often overlooked when we discuss racism and sexism; even then, they are most likely to be discriminated against" (Coles and Pasek, 2020).

In many ways, Black women are the epitome of what can only be termed "unsung warriors." Among these legendary warriors is, of course, the matriarch or the Mammy.

## Matriarch a.k.a. the Mammy

Select enslaved Black men were often forced to have sex with multiple Black women, much like the breeding of animals, to produce prized slaves. Sex was, therefore, a reward to those Black men and women deemed worthy of such rewards.

But like other animal stock, fathers were not needed and were often sold as quickly as the pregnancies were confirmed. Black men, therefore, became disposable in this system (Clarke, 1971).

Although discarded, that did not mean that Black fathers and mothers did not do their utmost to preserve contact. Records demonstrate that one of the most pressing needs of Black mothers and fathers during Reconstruction was to reconstruct their families (see, for example, Williams, 2012). Records also indicate that absent this, the extended family of grandparents, mothers, and fathers, and an entire system of what has been called "fictive kinship" came into being to preserve and maintain fully functioning families in the Black community.

The system survived Reconstruction but was almost immediately under attack in the next wave of anti-Black racism. Even today, the myth of a matriarchal Black family and the domineering Black woman survives.

Warrick Dunn constantly praises his late mother, Betty Smothers, a single parent who worked as a police officer in Baton Rouge, Louisiana, to raise six children. Unfortunately, her life was cut short on January 7, 1993, when two robbers ambushed her while she was working off-duty to escort a businesswoman to make a night deposit.

At 18, Dunn was left to raise his five younger siblings. In 1997, Dunn signed a multimillion-dollar contract to play professional football with the Tampa Bay Buccaneers, but he never forgot the mother who got him there (Lee, 2021).

Mothers like Betty Smothers are not some rarities but part of the success stories of millions of kids. Kids without these unsung warriors would not have had a chance. It is no accident that Black mothers have been forced to bear the brunt of parenting from the beginning of the African presence in America.

The system of slavery required slaves and did not require strong Black families. The system, therefore, was created to break the Africans' spirit, foundation, and community. And while the Africans were enslaved, the family distorted, and the community displaced, they never became slaves; the family survived, and the community endured. Through all these assaults, one figure – the Black matriarch – stands tall. She provided the spiritual glue, the grit, and the love that uplifted the child and the man, encouraged the community, and sustained the family.

Strong Black women have long fought to transform this country:

- Women like Harriet Tubman helped over 100,000 people escape from slavery.
- Strong Black women like Ida B. Wells-Barnett and Mary Church Terrell not only fought to end lynching but also were among the first to fight for women's right to vote.

But unfortunately, their struggle often gets buried under the attention given to White suffragettes.

Jacqueline Jones (1982) recounts the story told to Zora Neale Hurston (1938) by her grandmother:

"Ah was born back due in slavery," Nanny tells her granddaughter, "So it wasn't for me to fulfill my dreams of whut a woman oughta be and to do." Nanna consistently articulated her desires to be a good mother, love her family and endure. She never embraced nor denied the harsh realities of slavery and being denigrated. "Ah didn't want to be used for a work-ox and a brood-sow, and Ah didn't want mah daughter used dat way neigher. It sho wasn't mah will for things to happen like they did."

She persisted and held on to her faith silently while wearing the bondage of slavery. "Ah wanted to preach a great sermon about colored women sittin' on high, but they weren't no pulpit for me." (Hurston, 1938: 31–32, quoted in Jones, 1982: 1)

So, while outwardly the enslaved Black woman was a fieldworker with her head held down, inwardly, she was a rebellious servant, physically powerful and a devoted mother and wife (Jones, 1982). The myth of Black women being docile, controlled, and always smiling is one of the most prevailing myths within the racial state. Such ideas are comforting and do not challenge the presumed liberalness of some Whites.

The Mammy is often depicted as a heavyset Black female maid who is overly loyal to her White masters. The myth led to Black people being punished when they were not "kind and nice." Therefore, to preserve White comfort, Black people must conform. Hence was born, and still maintained, the Mammy (Thompson, 2020). One of the first Mammy figures to appear was Aunt Chloe in Harriet Beecher Stowe's *Uncle Tom's Cabin* (1852). Black women during slavery were often charged with various domestic duties, including nursing, rearing the owners' children, cleaning the house, and preparing meals.

The commercialization of the Mammy figure was accomplished as Aunt Jemima, the "slave in a box," became a national success (Manring, 1998). Aunt Jemima, first appearing in 1889, was finally retired by Quaker Oats in 2020. Aunt Jemima is based on a 19th-century minstrel show celebrating the racialized characterization of "the Mammy." The first Aunt Jemima was a formerly enslaved person, Nancy Green, who died in 1890 (Olson and Ott, 2020). But Aunt Jemima, as with most of the mammies, was more the "figment of White imagination than a factual part of the average master's home" (Hipskind, 2009).

Southern Whites so loved the Mammy that, in 1923, the U.S. Senate voted to build a monument "in memory of the faithful slave mammies of the South." The Southern Congressman who argued for this monument stated: "The traveler, as he passes by, will recall that epoch of southern civilization" when "fidelity and loyalty" prevailed. "No class of any race of people held bondage could be found anywhere who lived freer from care or distress" (Horwitz, 2013).

White supremacy and Southern nostalgia, with its "benevolent planters and happy enslaved people," were certainly in vogue. The enslaved people, most likely taking care of young White children, were very young (Clinton, 1995). And Blacks in mass rejected the character while lynchings were still in vogue.

As our nation entered the 20th century, Mammy again was embraced in songs like "Mammy's Little Coal Black Rose" (1916). Built in 1916, the Dead Heroes of the Confederacy monument in Arlington Cemetery features a frieze which includes "a turbaned and heavyset mammy, holding up a white child for a departing rebel to embrace" (Horwitz, 2013).

Al Jolson relives his earlier minstrel performances in the 1930 Technicolor release of the film *Mammy*. This led to the first Black woman, Hattie McDaniel, receiving an Oscar as Mammy in *Gone with the Wind* (1939). Mammy is most recently portrayed in *The Help* (2011) (Thompson, 2020).

The next wave of anti-Black racism, under the guise of uplift and welfare, again targeted the Black family and the relationship between Black parents and their children. Under the welfare system, the presence of a Black man in the family meant either reduced or no subsidy payment. Therefore, in a strange game of hide and seek, Black men were noticeably absent when the social worker came to check on the family (Carten, 2016).

These Black men, who were also being denied jobs and careers in a White-male-dominated labor force, became easy targets for the increasingly hostile and militarized industrialized penal system that came into being. The cradle-to-prison pipeline, fueled by a fierce "war on drugs and crime" targeting Black men, meant that the prisons across America were soon filled with Black men, while in the community, Black women were forced to take on both the roles of mother and father (Carten, 2016).

Today, "Black women are three times more likely to die from a pregnancy-related cause than White women. The leading factors associated with this disparity include access to quality healthcare, structural racism, and sexism" (C.D.C., 2023). Yet, these realities do not hinder the continuation of the Mammy stereotype. But Mammy was not alone; Jezebel was also a frequent target.

## Jezebel

Celia, at the age of 19, killed a man who was trying to rape her. Because she was enslaved and because it was 1855, she could not use the current laws of Missouri in her defense. Those laws stated that a woman could use deadly force if in "imminent danger of forced sexual intercourse." But the judge ruled that Celia had no rights as an enslaved woman; she could not refuse her "master." And so, Celia was convicted of murder, sentenced, and hanged on December 21, 1855 (Equal Justice Initiative, 2016).

Amid the Memphis riots of 1866, multiple Black women were gang-raped by a White mob. None of their perpetrators were ever tried, but that did not stop the women from being the first group of women to speak out on sexual assault before Congress. From that time to now, Black women have been at the forefront of challenging sexual assault (Chabane, 2020).

The sexual abuse of Black women has been chronicled repeatedly throughout history. Thousands of prominent White men, such as South Carolina Congressman Strom Thurman, a Dixiecrat, avid segregationist, and one of the longest-serving members of Congress in U.S. history, went to his grave without admitting that he had sexually abused, raped, and impregnated the 16-year-old Black maid working in his father's house (King, 2022).

Over their lifetimes, more than 18 percent of African American women will be sexually assaulted (West and Johnson, 2013). But this only measures those that report the abuse. For every 15 Black women raped, only one tends to report her assault (West and Johnson, 2013). Sexual assaults of Black women are linked to the presumed hypersexualized myth accompanying the Jezebel stereotype.

For this reason, regardless of status or success, Black women are more likely to be criticized for their dress. Consider the story of Texas A&M coach Sydney Carter, who faced criticism for wearing a tight pink pantsuit and heels on the court (Bernabe, 2022). She and other Black women must deal with the racial/sexual stigma associated with their presumed hypersexuality. They suffer from the controlling stereotype known as Jezebel.

Jezebel, the hypersexualized Black temptress, has a long history in America's racial myths. She first appears in slavery, as she is projected as being a lust-driven, enthusiastic sexual predator. As early as the mid-1400s, European enslavers used this as the justification for rape and a means of forcing women to reproduce with enslaved Black men.

Next, the Black woman becomes more feral, with few moral qualms, as her sexuality and sexual cravings drive her. These images continue today as the promiscuous, sex-crazed Black woman is vilified in movies, music, and even sex dolls.

Perhaps the first popularized Jezebel of the 18th century was a native of South Africa, kidnapped as a child, who became the epitome of "savage femininity." Her name was Saartjie Baartman, or, more pejoratively, "Venus Hottentot." Baartman was born in 1789, the year of the French Revolution. Kidnapped and forced to perform, she debuted to massive crowds in London in 1810 at age 20 (Frith, 2009).

Her career continued to blossom in France. Although Baartman never performed naked, she did wear skin-colored tights that gave the illusion of such. And this did not stop French royalty from erotically fantasizing about this "Black woman" (Frith, 2009).

Tragically, in just six years, Baartman died of pneumonia and alcoholism. The obsession with her sexuality did not end in her death, as Napoleon's surgeon general and others pillaged her body. They mutilated Baartman's body, making castes of her body parts (with special attention to her supposedly elongated labia), boiled her bones, and placed her brain and genitals in preservation fluid, pickling them for posterity. They remained displayed at the National Museum of Natural History until the 1970s. In 1994, with Nelson Mandela, the first elected Black president of South Africa, Saartjie Baartman finally returned home (Frith, 2009).

Actress Aida Overton Walker was one of the first Black women to make it big as Jezebel. She often played the role of either a maid or a tragic octoroon. As one of the most celebrated Black vaudeville actresses, Walker performed before royalty and starred in the first all-Black Broadway musical. But Walker's most prized role was as Salome, "a powerful seductress who could demand a saint's head in return for a glimpse of her body" (Linchong, 2024).

What is strange is that Walker and her husband fought hard against the racist stereotypes of the day. They worked to produce a "clean, refined, artistic" representation of Blacks and their realities (Curtis, 2023).

Perhaps one of the most notorious Jezebels was none other than Josephine Baker. Freda Josephine McDonald, born on June 3, 1906, was the daughter of entertainers. Her family worked throughout the Midwest but barely made enough to eat.

Josephine often took odd jobs, forced to dance in the street to survive. At 15, she ran away and began performing in an African-American troupe. Soon after, Josephine met her husband, took his last name, and became Josephine Baker. She arrived in New York as an accomplished dancer in several Vaudeville shows, just in time to experience the Harlem Renaissance.

She performed to mostly White audiences, dancing, and singing, often in a banana skirt. It was no surprise that Baker was wildly received in Berlin in 1926. She was projected as primitive and natural, pre-dating modernity, and was the epitome of the noble savage (Lewis, 2022).

Josephine Baker's arrival in Germany coincided with the *nacktkultur* (nudist) movement. The timing was not the best, or perhaps it was, as the emerging Nazi movement attempted to cleanse the country of "immorality." They targeted Josephine Baker and her shows as they sought to build a nation based upon Aryan strength, morality, and virtues.

She became the symbol of decadence and "racial impurity." Baker was again met with notoriety when she traveled to Austria, as the headlines declared her to be the "Black Devil" and "Jezebel." Leaflets heralded her performance in Vienna as the "brazen-faced heathen dance(r)." Using this as a backdrop, Josephine Baker became a spy funneling secret messages of information heard during performances behind enemy lines (Lewis, 2022).

Hip-hop has reinforced these narratives, particularly the Jezebel and, as we will see, Sapphire. Hip-hop, evolving in the early 1970s among Black and Latino youth, began as a statement of protest against a culture that had become saturated with sex, violence, and drugs. Or as hip-hop artist Lauren

Hill (1998) observes, "Hip-hop started out in the heart. ... Now everybody tryin' to chart". Hip-hop groups such as Public Enemy ("Fight the Power," 1989), N.W.A. ("F★★★ Tha Police," 1988), Queen Latifa ("U.N.I.T.Y.," 1993), and Tupac Shakur ("Changes," 1992) all provided strong messages challenging institutional racism, police misconduct, and oppressive poverty.

But soon after rocking our world, hip-hop swerved deeply into the erotic, the sexual and the violent as:

- LL Cool J talked about feeling "kind of horny" and wanting to "Blow your socks off, make sure your G spots off" in his 1996 track "Doin It."
- More recently, in Kanye West's 2005 single "Gold Digger," he stereotyped women as only wanting him for his money.
- This was followed by G-Eazy's 2017 single "No Limit," which described Black women as only engaging in sex for money, gifts, and other objects of value.
- These activities were further legitimized by female artists such as Cardi B in her top-selling version of "No Limit" (2017) where she rapped about only engaging in sex for money.

The overly sexualized Black female was most recently projected in the Super Bowl performance of Rihanna as she sang her hit song "Bitch Better Have My Money" (2015). As in the past, Black feminists questioned the song and her performance. While some recognized that the performance legitimated people engaged in "sex work and trade," they argue that it did not reflect the authenticity of Black women (Mock, 2014).

Others have argued that Rihanna glorified violence against Black women and gave vent to the "kidnapped female" trope. A third analysis suggests that Rihanna's work is situated within Audre Lorde's theory of the practice of eroticism.

Lorde (2006) asserted that:

> The erotic is a resource within each of us that lies in a deeply female and spiritual plane, firmly rooted in the power of our unexpressed or unrecognized feeling. To be perpetuated, oppression must corrupt or distort those various sources of power within the culture of the oppressed that can provide energy for change. For women, this has meant a suppression of the erotic as a considered source of power and information within our lives. (Lorde, 2006: 87)

The debate lingers, but what is clear is that the image of the Black Jezebel is alive and well in America.

What is also clear is these images, while representing the lives of single women, do not represent the lives of others. And even though Rihanna might embrace the sexual and the erotic in her life and music, others have not adopted or, according to some, legitimized their victimization, exploitation, and abuse.

And so, while Rihanna might be celebrated for her endurance and authenticity, others see her as a justification for Chris Brown's victimization and assault, helping to preserve the patriarchal exploitation of Black women (Crumpton, 2020). Currently, Jezebel is popularized by current Black hip-hop stars such as City Girls, Cardi B, and Megan Thee Stallion.

## Sapphire a.k.a. Peaches

During the 2022 Grand Slam semifinal of the U.S. Open, Nick Kyrgios, annoyed by how the matches were going, took out his frustration on a pair of his rackets. He cracked his racket by banging it repeatedly on the ground. Then, not satisfied, he took another racket, "reared back, and hit that one on the sideline, too" (Associated Press, 2022).

There was no response from tennis officials or the public. And in this total silence, one only concludes that "boys will be boys." Now compare this to what happened just four years earlier, again at the U.S. Open. This time, frustrated Serena Williams broke her racket after losing a call. She was immediately sanctioned with "a code violation for coaching, a penalty points for breaking her racket, and a game penalty for calling the umpire a thief." Later, she was fined an additional US$17,000. As pointed out by several commentators, Williams was penalized for being an "angry Black woman" (Prasad, 2018).

Even being the most visible Black woman in America did not shield Michelle Obama. Hence, few were surprised as the absurdity of negative stereotypes struck again on a July 14, 2008 *New Yorker* magazine cover. In this artist's rendition, Michelle Obama was an angry and gun-toting militant. The front cover shows her, with afro, bandolier, and assault weapon, along with her Muslim husband "performing what rightwing commentators have called a 'terrorist fist bump' while burning the U.S. flag in the fireplace of an Oval Office, decorated with a portrait of Osama bin Laden" (Goldenberg, 2008). Such imagery has a long, almost 300-year history in our country.

As slavery ended and the country reeled in the social, economic, and political upheaval that followed our bloodiest, self-inflicted wound, known as the Civil War, the Black woman became one of the principal victims. Negative stereotypes depicting her as overly aggressive, ill-tempered, hostile, ignorant, and overbearing became one of the dominant tropes. Or, more simply, perhaps she was being criticized for being a strong Black woman.

Maybe some would argue that her race and gender preclude her from being rational or even justified in her anger. The irrationality of the attacks targeting Black women has given rise to a new term – *misogynoir* – coined by Moya Bailey (2021). The term refers to a unique form of anti-Blackness and misogynistic representation that targets Black women and shapes their identities within visual culture and digital spaces.

Consequently, rather than dealing with the need for change, detractors would hide Black women behind a mythical "angry Black women syndrome." Perhaps she is stigmatized, ostracized, and penalized for being a Sapphire.

The first Sapphire stereotype can be seen in the early 1830s as White minstrels portrayed Negro Wenches. The term "Negro Wenches" often referred to presumed loose women in servitude (Kelley, 2014). These White men, covering their skin with burned cork and grease paint, performed as Black men and women. They portrayed Black women as "grotesque, loudmouthed, masculine and undeserving of the protections afforded to White ladies in American society" (Kelley, 2014).

These portrayals were intended to be cruel, ridiculous, and menacing. The obvious disdain in which they projected Black women was reinforced by the more "gentile" portrayal of White women on the same stages. These stereotypes helped preserve and strengthen the negative stereotypes while justifying the rape, exploitation, and control of Black people (Kelley, 2014).

During the period shortly after the Civil War until the mid-1900s, and long before the name Sapphire was used, angry Black women were popularized as "Sassy Mammies." Pilgrim (2008) explains that even during the era when Jim Crow was being rigidly enforced, these women were often symbolically allowed to cross racial boundaries, were characterized as able to chastise men, White and Black, beat their children, and rule their house with an iron hand (or rolling pin).

Yet, their freedom and assertiveness suggested that life for Black people was not bad. Here was a woman accepted by Whites and allowed to be uniquely sassy, bold, and clearly in charge.

In 1939, Ernestine Wade began playing the role of Sapphire in the radio show *Amos and Andy*. Here, the image of the Sapphire materialized as the "emasculating, finger-waving, neck-snapping … (woman who) complained incessantly about her husband's shortcomings" (Kelley, 2014).

The Sapphire character had become full-blown when Aunt Ester appeared in the *Sandford and Son* situation comedy in 1972. Ester, now projected as a Bible-toting, angry, frustrated woman, continually chastises her "fish-eyed fool" of a brother-in-law – Fred Sanford. Soon after the show closed, C.B.S. resurrected the Coon minstrel show as Florida Evans and her family living in the Cabrini-Green projects in what was hailed as *Good Times*. Living in extreme poverty, a new Sapphire – Willona Woods – goes through a series of "worthless boyfriends, an ex-husband, politicians, and other men with questionable morals and work ethics" (Pilgrim, 2008).

A new level of White hate emerged to greet Shirley Chisholm in 1972, who declared that she was "unbought and unbossed" in her campaign to become the first Black person to run for the presidency of the United States. Dismissed by White male journalists and politicians, she garnered the strongest support from other Black women.

But Chisholm had a greater vision. She was out to create a coalition to favor women's rights and those of Black Americans and Indigenous people. Her main goal was to target the infamous segregationist former governor of Alabama, George Wallace, famous for saying, "Segregation now, segregation tomorrow, and segregation forever" (Little, 2024). Black men even rejected Chisholm, as the left endorsed Senator George McGovern, who subsequently lost to Nixon in a landslide.

At age six, Kaia Rolle was forcibly bound with zip ties and escorted from her Florida school in Orlando because she was having a "temper tantrum," according to her teachers (Toohey, 2020). Research has long identified Black girls as being over-penalized, criminalized, and institutionalized by educators, counselors, caseworkers, police, and judges. They face harsher discipline policies for doing nothing more than their White peers. They are nearly six times more likely to receive school suspension than their White counterparts (Crenshaw et al, 2015).

The angry Black woman associated with the Sapphire myth has been equally vilified and reflected in many contemporary institutional settings. Similarly, she is represented as aggressive, ill-tempered, bitter, overbearing, hostile, and just plain angry. Some even go so far as to imply that this accounts for the lack of Black women in the labor force (at 7 percent) and even fewer in leadership positions. Among the top corporations in America, Black women only account for one in 25 top posts in the C-Suite (McKinsey & Company, 2022).

Nowhere is this more apparent than among Black women in the academy. Their experiences document the enormous amount of departmental and university service they perform even as they experience increasingly higher demands to function as a professional. They are more likely to be scrutinized, censored, and rebuked for their authenticity, voice, and refusal to serve on another committee.

The extraction of free labor "from the most overworked faculty" in the university only adds to their precarity as they challenge the spaces within the colonizing university's neoliberal system. Such spaces as "ethnic studies, emerging and interdisciplinary fields" place them under incredible stress as they must compromise health and lives to make an impossible system work (Williams, 2023).

Black women in academia know about the fear, the isolation, and the absolute horror that their profession is destroying them. They, therefore, work to create peer mentoring, sister circles, and supportive relationships that help them deal with the gendered and racialized trauma in academia (Allen and Turner, 2022).

The reality is that these "angry Black women" are assertive, successful, and in control of their own identities, bodies, and sexuality. They therefore challenge both the Black and White patriarchy, White supremacy, and hegemonic structural sexual racism.

While some would attempt to silence these strong Black women, some have used their anger to lead the way for change. Such leadership is found in the Black Lives Matter movement, which three courageous women started. These women, Alicia Garza, Patrisse Cullers, and Opal Tometi, started the movement in 2013 after an all-White jury found George Zimmerman innocent after killing Trayvon Martin, an unarmed Black teenager.

A year later, they spearheaded a nationwide protest as another Black man, George Floyd, was killed as police knelt on his neck during his arrest in Minneapolis (B.B.C., 2020). Black Lives Matter has become the consciousness, the strength, and the continuous call for change as the chants "never forget" and "never again" are heard throughout our land.

# The New John Henry, Stereotypes, and Authentic Black Masculinity

Malcolm X, in 1962, asked:

> Who taught you to hate the texture of your hair? Who taught you to hate the color of your skin? To such an extent, you bleach to get like the white man. Who taught you to hate the shape of your nose and the shape of your lips? Who taught you to hate yourself from the top of your head to the soles of your feet? Who taught you to hate your own kind? Who taught you to hate the race that you belong to so much so that you don't want to be around each other? No ... you should ask yourself who taught you to hate being what God made you.[1]

## John Henry and the objectification of Black masculinity

Many know the story of John Henry, famous in Black folk ballads. The story describes a strong Black man, pitted against a machine, who died "with his hammer in his hand." John Henry, for decades, has been a symbol of Black masculinity and defiance, resistance, and perseverance.

It is a story of a man who refused to submit, but constantly needed to prove himself worthy. But rather than being rewarded, he was forced to prove himself continually. Finally, in his struggle against the racist system that repeatedly tried to suppress, oppress, and reduce him to an object, he faced the ultimate test: man against machine. And in his final contest against a steam-powered drill, this hero won the battle but lost the war. He collapsed two steps ahead of the machine, driving the last steel drill into the rock.

Sherman James and Associates adapted the story into a psychological construct – John Henryism – to characterize a "strong behavioral predisposition to cope actively with psychosocial environmental stressors"

(James, 1994: 163). According to James's formulation, three characteristic features were associated with this construct:

1. efficacious mental and physical vigor;
2. a strong commitment to hard work; and
3. a single-minded determination to succeed.

In this chapter, I want to discuss how the battle wages on. These unsung warriors, heroes, and heroines continue to navigate toxic racial environments. And even as they chart new paths and scale new mountains, they continue to bear the tremendous weight of operating within racialized spaces.

Such individuals are constantly suspected and overly scrutinized, rather than being applauded and encouraged by society, and they are often ridiculed, punished, and negatively characterized. If they dare to speak out, they are more likely to receive sanctions, condemnations, and marginalization. Because of their burdens, both on and off the job, they are more likely to obtain lower performance evaluations, promotions, and job security.

The modern John Henry more likely to be in prison then college, have increased health risks, a higher likelihood of being isolated, impoverished, and afflicted with physical and mental incapacitating illnesses, all leading to early death. Let us begin.

## The racial construction of Black masculinities

> I am what time, circumstance, history, have made of me, certainly, but I am also, much more than that. So are we all.
>
> Baldwin, 1955/2012: ii

In a previous chapter, we argued that to destroy the alliance forged between the Irish and African servants, the White planter class created the myth of Whiteness and convinced the Irish that they were White. Along with this myth came the presumption of privileges presumed to be associated with being White.

These myths of Whiteness and privilege continue to be utilized, as seen in the most recent M.A.G.A. (Make America Great Again) movement, where poor Whites are being urged to serve as the frontline troops once again for the White war against Black, Brown, Indigenous, and Asians who would dare to presume equality.

What was not discussed, and the focus of this section, is how this same process created a whole slew of stereotypes purposefully aimed at the "Black man." Fear of the Black man runs deep, and is a method devised by the White structure to convince the Black man that he, not the system, was the problem. The weapon used for this purpose was the multiple ways his identity was manipulated to produce his worst nightmare.

A search of the internet reveals a whole litany of words used to describe the Black man. Some nicer words include dim-witted, bumbling, lazy, angry, sexually aggressive, forsaken, sad, betrayed, suffering, unloved, and ridiculed.

The most vile would be ape, Coon, Jungle Bunny, Kaffir, monkey/porch monkey, zibabo, spade, spook, and of course n★★★★★/n★★★★(h). Attached to these words are such stereotypical characters as Zip Coon, Sambo/Uncle Tom (Remus), Jim Crow, and Buck/Mandingo. And for most of this same period, there has been a constant rejection of these images as Black men and women have fought for the very soul of our community. Tracing these stereotypes to their origins helps us understand how and why they came into being and how and in what ways Blacks continually recreated their identities.

Our journey begins with the Black Dandy, aka Zip Coon, Slick and the Jacked-Legged Preacher.

## The Black Dandy

The Black Dandy's first incarnation pre-dates the United States, as Europeans first explored Africa and kidnapped young children, primarily boys, in the 15th and 16th centuries. These children became much like pets, as the European elite dressed them in elaborate clothes, providing education and training to make them the "luxury" enslaved.

As the British extended their control over the Americas, Black people in fancy dress were presented as a form of slave luxury, often seen on exhibit at carnivals and cross-dressing festivals, with favored-slave status. By the turn of the century and the Harlem Renaissance, the Black Dandy re-emerged suited up, wearing top hats and strolling with canes (White and White, 1998). We can identify multiple examples of the Black Dandy throughout history.

## Zip Coon

Zip Coon, in the early Minstrel shows, was often represented in his "bright, loud, exaggerated clothes: swallow-tail coat with wide lapels, gaudy shirts, striped pants, spats and top hat." Zip's days were spent sleeping, hunting, and shuffling along. When he was not doing these things, he was stealing chickens or dancing (Lemons, 1977).

Zip Coon first appearance was in 1834, popularized in Minstrel shows. Later, his melody was used in the more popular song "Turkey in the Straw," published in 1861. And then, in 1916, "Turkey in the Straw" re-emerged as "N★★★★★ Love a Watermelon, Ha! Ha! Ha!" performed by Harry C. Browne and produced by Columbia Records (Traditional Tune Archive, 2023).

This last version served to become one of the most obvious racist themes within America. Strange, on many hot days, as the ice cream truck lumbered through neighborhoods in our country, few would connect to the song being played on the speakers. You remember "Eeny, Meeny, Miny, Moe." And no, it had nothing to do with "catching a tiger by its toes." Next time that ice cream truck appears in your neighborhood, and you hear the song, remember where it originated (Johnson, 2014).

As the 19th century approached, the Black Dandy was viewed as threatening for many in a racialized America, where Black people, particularly Black men, were assigned specific positions and identities. By refusing to conform to these "White expectations," they challenged the racial framing of Black masculinity (Berger, 2016).

## Slick

In the 1970s, a new ethnic subgenre emerged known as Blaxploitation. One of the most infamous in this category was the 1973 movie *The Mack*. In this film, the lead character, during the civil rights movement, opts to become a "pimp" instead (King, 2013).

Of note is that the pimp was just the most recent incarnation of the "Black Dandy" known as Zip Coon. The movie appealed to the prejudice and fascination of Whites through the creation of a hypervisible, hypersexed, violent, and lawless Black man (Eshun, 2016). Hip-hop would take these creations to new highs and lows as the pimp became normalized, stylized, and romanticized.

Calvin Broadus, Jr., a.k.a. Snoop Dogg, is one of Billboard's top 10 hip-hop artists. He is one of the founding fathers of gangsta rap and the West Coast sound (Lamarre et al, 2023). Snoop Dogg has gone from church boy to gangsta to pimp. He has gone from Snoop Dogg to Snoop Lion to plain Slim. He brags about being the pimp for the stars and athletes, dealing in sex, drugs, and women across multiple states (Renshaw, 2013).

By whichever name you choose – Slick, Pimp, or the Mack – the Black Dandy has been a mainstay throughout American and European history. This is a sometimes famous, sometimes infamous, sometimes strange, sometimes loved, sometimes reviled Black character. It has evolved from fiction, reality, and myth. And, of course, Snoop Dogg's best friend and mentor is none other than Archbishop Don "Magic" Juan, a former pimp.

The Black Dandy continues to evolve. The image ranges from the noble to the commoner, from the height of respectability to the lowest of thugs. The duplicity of these characterizations is rarely represented in one person. One of the most versatile of the latest Black Dandies is seen in the persona of Don "Magic" Juan.

Don "Magic" Juan (born Donald Campbell) has worked through many personalities associated with the Black Dandy. Born in Chicago on November 30, 1950, he is not only a former pimp but also a hip-hop artist, actor, fashion designer, and preacher (Hoekstra, 2000).

As a pimp, Don Juan recruited prostitutes and promoted them out of the record store he operated during the 1970s in Chicago. He modeled himself after Iceberg Slim, Superfly, and other media pimps. He fell in love with flashy cars and clothes (Hoekstra, 2000).

Then one day in 1985, while smoking P.C.P., he had a vision – God told him to turn his life over to God, and four years later, he was ordained as a minister by Dr. F.L. Johnson of the Christian Ministers Congress Non-Denominational Council, Inc (Hoekstra, 2000).

This was followed by his opening of the Magic World Christian Kingdom Church of the Royal Family. Since 1974, taken from a scene from *The Mack*, Don Juan has celebrated his birthday by throwing what has since been known as the Players Ball. The Players Ball has become an annual gathering of pimps in Chicago, drawing some of the most famous and infamous pimps across America to the city.

Although the Black Dandy has often been cast as romanticized and vilified, we should also note that many Black men have worn this mantle. Some have also been preachers and again condemned. Let us look at some of these Black Dandies, Jack-Legged Preachers.

## Jack-Legged Preachers

Few historical and contemporary figures stand out as much as the Black preacher. Think for a moment. Some of the most significant movements toward liberation, equality and democracy within this country have been led by these men.

We would have to include Richard Allen, a formerly enslaved person, who, with Absalom Jones, started the African Methodist Episcopal Church. And who could forget such giants as Adam Clayton Powell, Marcus Garvey, Ralph Abernathy, Andrew Young, Fred Shuttlesworth, Malcolm X and Dr. Martin Luther King, Jr.?

The list is only getting started. Black preachers can be found throughout the history of America. And they are at once one of the most villainized and idealized personas. For many, they are nothing more than a "Jack-Legged Preacher."

The Jack-Legged Preacher is often characterized as illiterate, vile, crooked, and even a servant of Satan. As a result, he is often looked down upon, ridiculed, and suspected. Infamous preachers such as Rev. Ike or Daddy Devine come to mind. And while the history of Black preachers defies the logic of his stereotype, the negative denotations remain. So let us look at this character and see why he has been so vilified.

Several of these preachers can be identified. One was John Jea, who with his entire family was kidnapped and sold into slavery in New York. He was only two, and the year was 1773. He was forced to go to church by his master as a form of punishment, but strangely he became not only a devout Christian, but a noted preacher (Bell, 2013).

But, one of the most infamous and certainly most vilified Black preachers would have to be Nat Turner. Few have been so feared by White plantation owners, representing their most dreaded outcome. And why Nat Turner, you ask? He was first and foremost an educated preacher who dared to use religious lessons found in the Bible to encourage, organize and execute a four-day rebellion of enslaved and free Blacks in Southampton County, Virginia, in August of 1831.

In the aftermath, after the White planter elite witnessed the deadliest slave revolt in U.S. history unfold (killing between 55 and 65 White people), a deliberate program was instituted that would prevent such a thing from ever happening again:

- Almost immediately, Southern White legislators made it illegal to educate enslaved and free Blacks.
- Blacks could not assemble freely.
- Even their worship services were under the watchful eye of a White minister (White et al, 2020).

These laws did not stop Black preachers from preaching or Black people from reading, even though the Bible they were given was severely limited.

The official *Holy Bible for Negro Slaves* was an interesting document. Rather than the traditional 66 books in the King James version, this one only contains parts of 14. It was used to indoctrinate enslaved people into their plight.

It starts with the creation story, skips to Joseph getting sold into slavery, then skips over the Israelites' liberation from slavery. No mention of their freedom is ever made. Then only those parts of the New Testament which highlight submissiveness, servanthood, and allegiance to the master are found. The whole Book of Revelation is missing. This "Holy Bible" went hand-in-hand with the laws prohibiting reading by the enslaved people and proscribed which religious tenets would be preached (Strong, 2018). And into this void steps the Black Preacher.

Of the 4,467 people lynched between 1884 and 1941, 3,300 were Black. One of the principal focuses of lynching was a determined attempt "to destabilize the Black community and focus on the successful and the influential – people like preachers or prominent business owners" (Foley, 2020).

Such was the case of I.T. Burgess, a preacher from Putnam County, Florida, who was hanged in 1894. He was accused of instigating a revolt. A year later, Lucious Turner, a West Point, Georgia, preacher, was shot for apparently writing an insulting note to the sister of two White brothers.

And lastly, Ida B. Wells talks about a Reverend King, a minister out of Paris, Texas, who in 1895 was beaten with a Winchester rifle and forced to leave town. His offense? He preached against the horrific lynching of handyman Henry Smith (Foley, 2020). These dates hide the hundreds of black churches that were also targeted, such as the 1882 destruction of the Emanuel African Methodist Episcopal church in Charleston, South Carolina.

What is strange is that rather than decreasing in numbers, they have increased in the 1990s and our current era. Neither threats, bombings, or even murders have kept the Black preachers silent or their congregations impotent. This was seen when over 100 Black pastors created a "Wall of Prayer" in support of the family of Ahmaud Arbery as they sought justice during the courtroom trial of his killers.

## Sambo and Uncle Tom

On August 30, 1861, without President Lincoln's approval, General John C. Freemont took it upon himself to issue a proclamation emancipating the slaves owned by Missouri Confederate sympathizers. As the cartoon in Figure 7.1 indicates, Lincoln was ambivalent at best in terms of his support of emancipation.

Not wanting to anger bordering states, Lincoln was more concerned with saving the "Union" than freeing the slaves. Hence the cartoon depicts papers floating in the water labeled "Freemont proclamation" and the ship flying a pennant with the simple words "Proclamation" in the background. The Sambo pejorative referring to all the enslaved is more than a coincidence. Sambo was, in many ways, the embodiment of the "perfect" slave, at least in the minds of the Confederacy. So, who was this "Sambo"?

One of the earliest Sambo caricatures appears in the 1808 short story "Sambo and Toney: A Dialogue in Three Parts" by Edmund Botsford. Sambo seems highly intelligent, thoughtful, and Christian in this earliest of portrayals.

Therefore, we see two representations of the slave: Christian Sambo and non-Christian Toney. According to this portrayal, neither Sambo nor Toney is stupid or dense. Botsford, a Baptist minister, was not perfect. However, he believed that Christianity would help ease some of the harsher aspects of slavery for both the enslaved person and the enslaver. He observed that "slavery in its best state is a great evil" and that only through Christianity could the enslaved person become cooperative and accepting and the enslavers become less violent and more tolerant (Ford, 2011: 161).

Sambo appears in print in Harriet Beecher Stowe's book, *Uncle Tom's Cabin*. In this book, Sambo, a slave overseer working for the cruel enslaver, Simon Legere, is juxtaposed against Uncle Tom, a pious, God-fearing, compassionate man. In a strange twist, Uncle Tom refuses to reveal the whereabouts of two slave women hiding.

These women had been sexually abused by their masters. Knowing that he would be beaten to death for refusing, Uncle Tom held fast. For this,

**Figure 7.1:** Lincoln: "I'm sorry to have to drop you, Sambo, but this concern won't carry us both!"

LINCOLN—"*I'm sorry to have to drop you, Sambo, but this concern won't carry us both !*"

Source: Frank Leslie's illustrated newspaper, vol 12, no 308 (1861, October 12), p 352 via Library of Congress Prints and Photographs Division Washington, D.C., https://lccn.loc.gov/2003668332

he was tormented and beaten to death by Sambo. And in his dying breath, Uncle Tom forgives Sambo.

While Stowe aimed to produce an anti-slavery book, it still presents these two diametrically opposed Black male characters – one a noble, Christian hero, the other docile, violent, and dedicated to his master. In a strange twist, Uncle Tom has become villainized as an ultimate Black "sellout." But in Stowe's book, Tom is a heroic and courageous Black man who used his charm and insider position as a house servant to gain access to writing materials, food, and information by which and through which he aided other enslaved Black people not only to survive, but to escape slavery.

Conversely, Sambo has been rendered the impotent, docile, ignorant, servile, and linguistically challenged buffoon. The next section will see how these two characters have continued through history.

## Uncle Tom

Harriet Beecher Stowe wrote *Uncle Tom's Cabin* to combat the 1850 passage of the Fugitive Slave Act, requiring northerners to return runaway slaves to slavery and the South. Poring over slave narratives of slaves escaping along the Underground Railroad, she came across the account of Josiah Henson (1848).

Henson became the ideal by which Uncle Tom took literary life, and along with other texts, Stowe assembled the other characters to compile *Uncle Tom's Cabin*. The book, over time, outsold the Bible; it has become one of the most successful books of the period, and by the late 1950s, it was being dramatically portrayed in Minstrel shows and theaters throughout the United States and England.

The story so inflamed radical conservatives that alternative and revised perspectives were offered. Southern White planters were redeemed, and Black people again were submerged into inferiority in the novels that appeared. One such book, *The Clansman*, the source of the first feature-length film, *The Birth of a Nation*, was written as a counter to the literary accomplishments of *Uncle Tom's Cabin* (Turner, quoted in Martin, 2008).

Over the decades, Uncle Tom has been stripped of his humanity and transformed into the docile, castrated, happy-to-please-Whites-at-any-cost stereotype. Uncle Tom is repackaged and appears as Bill "Bojangles" Robinson in the Shirley Temple films of 1930. In these movies, the singing and dancing companion becomes the tender companion of his child patron, Little Eva.

Another repackaging was taken from the *Uncle Remus* tales of Joel Chandler Harris in the 1880s. In 1946, Uncle Remus was adapted by Disney for its film *Song of the South*.

Uncle Tom became a reality as Black men and women were forced to live under Jim Crow. To violate the laws, norms, and rules of Jim Crow would mean risking their homes, jobs, and even lives. One of the main jobs that Black men could have during this time was that of the Pullman sleeping car porters. For many Whites, this perfectly represented the humble Uncle Tom. But, as we will see in the last section, the Black Pullman became the frontline troops for the modern civil rights movement.

Uncle Tom became a fixture in many homes as Mars Food launched its new Uncle Ben's Rice in 1947. Over the past seven decades, it has been the best-selling rice in the United States. The company even invented the myth that the rice originated from a Black Texas farmer "known for his high-quality rice."

The actual character was the head waiter at a Chicago restaurant, Frank Brown, whose face has been on the packages since its inception. To redeem what for years had been seen as a humble, racist character, the company tried to elevate Ben to the chairman of the Board in 2007 (Elliott, 2007). Then in the aftermath of the George Floyd murder, Mars joined other companies to remove the racist images of Uncle Ben (Booker, 2020).

*Django Unchained* (2012) again repackages Uncle Tom in the staunchly loyal and suspicious head house slave Stephen Warren. Stephen, devoted to death and contrary to the original Uncle Tom, betrays the trust of the enslaved person's rebellion led by Django. He dies as Django watches from a distance as an explosion destroys the slave mansion. And so, we come full circle from the original *Uncle Tom's Cabin*.

Black males portrayed in films have traditionally provided overtly racist and negative characterizations. Starting with D.W. Griffith's *Birth of a Nation* (1915), Black men are blatantly characterized as rapists, dumb, and violent. As a sexual threat to White women, they had to be kept in check. Other films, such as *Hallelujah* (1929), would blame the absent Black male for the loss of the Black family, as they migrated to large cities such as New York, Chicago, or Los Angeles. These images help promote a racist political agenda where the lives and realities of Black men are characterized by deviants, drug dealers, and overly sexualized characters (Miller, 1998). These characterizations continued into the present, including roles played by Paul Robeson (Emperor Jones), Sidney Poitier, and James Earl Jones in shows during the 1970s and 1980s. The list includes Morgan Freeman playing Hoke in *Driving Miss Daisy* (Zanuck et al, 1989). And, in real life, several Black men have been negatively labeled, including O.J. Simpson, Detroit Mayor Dennis Archer, Karl Malone (Utah Jazz basketball player), Kanye West (rapper), and, of course, Clarence Thomas (Justice on the U.S. Supreme Court). Each has been stigmatized and faulted for not representing "a true Black man." Not only are their values questioned, but their actions and "authenticity." Often, such men are called "Uncle Toms," a character that goes all the way back to "Sambo."

## Sambo

It was through the popularity of the Minstrel shows of the 1830s that Sambo became a common theme among White, working-class audiences. Sambo, sometimes Tambo, or Zambo, or Jim Crow, represented that happy slave who was loud, cheerful, and without a care. Even as slavery ended and separate but equal became the law of the land, Sambo, always knowing his place, "provided comfort as he enjoyed his ignorance, danced through his travail and never had to worry about a thing." Then, as America discovered radio and television, Sambo and Toney became *Amos and Andy*. And much like the earlier Minstrel shows, two White men performed in blackface and preserved America's lovable Sambo.

In the early days of motion pictures, Lincoln Theodore Monroe Andrew Perry (1902–1985) took Sambo to a new level with the character "Stepin Fetchit." Fetchit, billed as the "Laziest Man in the World," who was touted as being slow-witted, shuffling, and head-scratching, became one of the highest-paid actors in Hollywood. He was the first Black actor to earn US$1 million and the first to be featured in a film (Lamparski, 1982; Clark, 2005).

Sambo succumbed to the civil rights movement as major Black comedians and activists such as Godfrey Cambridge and Dick Gregory refused to play the role (Boskin, 1986).

## Mandingo: from Nat Turner to George Floyd

Slave merchants and owners created the sexualized, strong, brutish, animalistic Black man known as Mandingo. Mandingo, though paraded as being a physically powerful Black man, had to be continually and often brutally subdued and forced into labor. He was the chief protagonist in *Birth of a Nation* (1915) after emancipation, who raped the innocent daughters of Whites throughout the South. This trope led to the thousands of lynchings of black men as White men sought revenge for these presumed wrongs.

The Mandingo trope, highly influenced by the story of Nat Turner, projects the Black male as angry, hostile, and rebellious. Many Black men, intentionally or unintentionally, have embraced the Mandingo trope as the hypersexualized or angry Black male. Public figures such as Bill Cosby or R. Kelly have a long history of rape and sexual imposition, and there were decades in which they appeared to be above the law. Their behavior and the lack of immediate prosecution demonstrate the power of such behavior and how it has been normalized. The internalization of these stereotypes has obvious outcomes, as we have seen. Still, the less obvious reactions to these stereotypes by police and educators, judges, politicians, and everyday citizens have led to repeated tragedies. George Floyd and Michael Brown joined over 200 mostly Black men killed by police since 2020 (Raham, 2021).

This normalization applauds and rewards Black hypersexuality. Consider the long list of Black male hip hop stars recently making the news, including:

- Mystikal
- Lil Mosey
- Cash Out

A long list of Black professional athletes includes:

- N.F.L. players Darren Sharper and Thomas Henderson;
- N.B.A. players such as Tom Payne;
- former heavyweight boxing champion Mike Tyson.

Nat Turner was an enslaved person who learned to read and write and became a preacher. After a vision from God, he planned and executed one of the most effective, sustained slave rebellions in U.S. history on August 21, 1831. In this rebellion, 60 Whites were killed, but over 200 Blacks were massacred as Whites sought revenge. The Turner Rebellion was the worst nightmare for the White slavocracy as "visions of angry Black men hell-bent on exacting revenge" disturbed the gentile vision of the "happy slave" (James, 2010).

In response, Black people across the South were forced to endure even more "cruel, barbaric and traumatizing forms of control." Nine states – Virginia, Alabama, Delaware, Georgia, Louisiana, Maryland, North Carolina, South Carolina, and Tennessee – passed a whole range of laws to limit Black people's mobility. These laws banned the free assembly of Blacks, independent religious services, and preaching to a crowd of more than five.

Teaching Blacks to read or write became illegal (Coleman, 2023). The Turner Rebellion also fostered similar slave insurrections in places like Maryland. But instead of enslaved people, free Black residents planned and orchestrated slave insurrections. Panicked slaveholders in the state pushed legislation that enacted repressive laws targeting free and enslaved Black residents.

One very aggressive plan, produced by the publicly funded Maryland Colonization Society, sought to force even free Black Marylanders back to West Africa, create separate Black public schools, and exclude and discriminate against hiring Black skilled workers.

All of these were upheld as Maryland native and Chief Justice Roger B. Taney and six other Supreme Court justices ruled in the 1854 Dred Scott decision that the "enslaved African race" and free people of color had no claim to either freedom or citizenship under the U.S. Constitution. The backlash to this decision extended to so-called free states such as Ohio and Indiana, even barring free Blacks from settling in the state.

The angry Black man has historically been a top media personage, as witnessed by such people as Jack Johnson, a.k.a. The Great Black Hope. But while there is a parkway honoring Jackie Robinson and Paul Robeson has a postage stamp named after him. Many have forgotten Johnson, who was condemned for his "Unforgivable Blackness" (Ward, 2004). Johnson earned the label as the first Black World Heavyweight champion in 1908, defeating James Jeffries, who had been tagged the "Great White Hope."

Many Whites looked on in horror as their "Hope" was lost and began attacking Black people throughout America. Dozens of riots erupted across the United States as Whites vented their frustration and fear of this "angry Black Man." Lynchings also spiked as 67 Black men were killed for no reason then, and Whites were angered that Black Americans dared to celebrate Johnson's victory. Even the films of Johnson's victory caused so much rioting that Congress in 1912 banned the interstate transportation of boxing films. This law was in effect until 1940 (Gustkey, 1990).

These events legitimized the angry Black man stereotype and the fear, anxiety, and retribution within White racial frames. Rebecca Latimer Felton, a writer and politician, summed up for many the White attitude toward Black males and lynching: "If it needs lynching to protect woman's dearest possession from the ravening human beasts, then I say lynch a thousand times a week if necessary" (Felton, quoted in Brockell, 2022). Between 1880 and 1950, annually an average of 60 lynchings occurred (Equal Justice Initiative, 2020).

The largest mass execution for rape ever reported in the United States occurred in 1951, as seven Black men were accused, convicted, and executed for the rape of a White woman. Seventy years later, the governor of Virginia pardoned all seven. Justice delayed is still justice denied. White mobs frequently lynched Black men under the presumption of sexual transgressions against White women. Though routinely, these accusations were fabricated, they reflected the fears of Whites.

These fears had little to do with the presumed violence and hypersexuality of the Black men but with the need to enforce the segregation of the races. The murder of 14-year-old Emmett Till in 1955 was one of the last lynchings. Till's offense was allegedly flirting with a White woman. It was not until 2017, sixty years later, that the accuser, Carolyn Bryant Donham, recanted her accusation that Till had "grabbed her by the hand and waist and acted lewdly." The two White men, Bryant and Milam, were acquitted of Till's kidnapping and murder by an all-male, all-White jury in September of 1955 (Kimble, 2017).

Black men, uncontrolled, were a threat to public safety and the decency of White women. "Black brutes" became reviled, paraded, and promoted, as seen from Hollywood to sports. Mandingo first appears in the classic 1933 film *King Kong*, then again in 1976. In each of these, a 25-foot-tall gorilla goes to his death in pursuit of a White woman. This same trope reappears in the *Lord of the Rings*. Consider the wraiths and orcs, both with dark skin, broad faces, and dreadlocks. These racial overtones continue the negative portrayal of Black males (Yatt, 2002). Such portrayals either promoted and played on the notions of "Black male hypersexuality" targeting innocent White females (Bates, 2005) or were overly violent (Yatt, 2002).

In the real world, when leaders such as Malcolm X argued that Blacks must use "any means necessary" to obtain their rights, Whites cringed with fear and looked at him as a dangerous Black man. They suddenly loved the peaceful and comforting presence of Rev. Dr. Martin Luther King, Jr., who was viewed as less threatening (James, 2010).

In 2008, the *Vogue* magazine cover depicted N.B.A. legend LeBron James and a blonde in a pose eerily reminiscent of one representing King Kong and a blonde woman. These portrayals continued the trope of Black men as brutes and monkeys who must have a White woman. This cover would appear during the same year that a Black man, Barack Obama, was running for president (Morris, 2008).

The angry Black male has been normalized, but in different ways. On the one hand, this recognizes that we all get mad sometimes. And on the other hand, it reflects the righteous indignation advocated by Malcolm X. Still, one condition can be termed "toxic masculinity" that reflects a more troubling internalization of these negative stereotype. Several examples are readily available: For example, consider the story of Ja Morant, who plays for the Memphis Grizzlies. Ja Morant, one of the brightest stars in the N.B.A., has a Nike shoe brand, a top-selling jersey, and is on the winning team. But he also has a list of violent episodes where he is accused of shoving, beating, and threatening behavior. But, while these incidents have been reported to the police, there have yet to be any charges (Hensley-Clancy, 2023).

## The reality of being Black

Typologies, stereotypes, tropes, internalized racism, victimization, racial trauma – pick the word that best suits you. Regardless of the words you choose, they neither fit nor do they adequately describe what it entails to be Black in America. While normalization of these terms has resulted in static representations and niches such as the Black Entertainer, Athlete, Welfare Queen, and Criminal/Thug, none of these attests to the resilience, determination, drive, and realities that Blacks have created.

But what they do accomplish is the preservation of White racial troupes, stereotypes, and myths of what it means to be Black. Further, to maintain these illusions, stiff penalties are rendered to Blacks who dare to step out of line. The repeated lynching of thousands of Blacks was essentially retribution for those who dared to step across the racial line and dared to be different.

The internalization of these stereotypes has obvious outcomes, as we have seen. Still, the less obvious reactions to these stereotypes by police and educators, judges, politicians, and everyday citizens have led to repeated tragedies. George Floyd and Michael Brown joined over 200 mostly Black men killed by police since 2020 (Raham, 2021).

Unarmed Black people, in general, and Black men in particular are more than three times more likely to be fatally shot by police (Lett et al, 2021). Half of the 250 kids expelled daily from preschool are Black boys (Novak, 2023). Black boys lost an average of 132, and Black girls lost 77 days per 100 students enrolled, compared to just 21 days for their White peers due to out-of-school suspensions (Camera, 2020). Not only are Black men more likely to be criminalized, but they serve 19.1 percent longer than their white counterparts for similar crimes (U.S. Sentencing Commission, 2017).

Unfortunately, even during these challenges, Black males have been subject to over-policing. When Jack Johnson dared to not only defeat the Great White Hope but then to marry a White woman, he was quickly arrested, condemned, and even arrested for "White slavery" (carrying a woman, White, across state lines for sex).

The fact that it was his wife did not seem to matter at the time. Or consider the case of Trayvon Martin, who was killed because he was wearing a hoodie and was presumed to be a gang member. And the irony is that George Zimmerman was acquitted as the all-White jury agreed with this assessment.

One of the strangest cases of misidentification was witnessed when Harvard Professor Henry Louis Gates was arrested by local police officers as he attempted to enter his Cambridge, Massachusetts, home (Pilkington, 2009). Even having the wrong hairstyle can cause police to overreact, as Clarence Evans learned. While playing with his kids outside his own home, Evans was accosted and forced against his car by a White deputy who mistook him for a suspect. Even after proving that Houston Police had wrongly targeted him, the police officials and union "saw nothing wrong with the encounter" (Miller, 2019).

Strangely, as education and income go up, the intersection of race and gender demonstrates that if you are White or a Black woman, there is a reduced risk of discrimination and depression. However, the opposite is true for Black men, who are targeted as "dangerous, threatening and inferior." Consequently, research demonstrates that these conditions lead to an increased risk of depression among higher-status Black men (Assari et al, 2018) and boys (Assari and Caldwell, 2018).

But being wealthy, or even one of only five Black Republicans in Congress, did not keep a man from being stopped seven times in one year for driving a new car in the wrong neighborhood (Vega, 2016). A scary conclusion reached by researchers reporting in the *New York Times* revealed that Black boys, even from some of the most affluent families and neighborhoods in America, still earn less in adulthood than their White peers. More troubling is that Black boys from the highest economic group are likelier to end up poor, while White boys from the same tier are likelier to remain rich (Badger et al, 2018).

Student demonstrators, quietly sitting at lunchroom counters, were dragged away by angry patrons, hosed, and beaten – all because they stepped out of their place and tried to cross the sacred line separating White and Black diners (Bates, 2019). The Rev. Dr. Martin Luther King, Jr., jailed for contempt of court for marching on Good Friday, would write his manifesto "Letter from Birmingham Jail" while incarcerated (Brown-Nagin, 2022).

After sprinters Tommie Smith and John Carlos raised their fists in protest during the 1968 Summer Games, they were immediately banned from the U.S. team and the Olympic Village. Death threats and jeers heralded their return to the U.S. Four years later, this time in Munich, track athletes Wayne Collert and Vince Matthews were punished because they "did not face the flag" during the Olympic ceremony. They were barred from Olympic competition because they were "unquestionably ... defiant." And in 1996, the N.B.A. suspended Mahmoud Abdul-Rauf because he refused to stand during the national anthem (Litsky, 2010).

More recently, quarterback Colin Kaepernick was barred from playing professionally when he refused to stand for the anthem at N.F.L. games (Johnk, 2017). And who can forget when Fox News host Laura Ingraham rebuked Cleveland Cavelier's LeBron James, telling him to "shut up and dribble" (Sullivan, 2018)?

Among entertainers, Paul Robeson, outspoken activist against lynching, was among the first to face the House Un-American Activities Committee in 1949 for "propagating communism in the United States" (King, 2011). The State Department denied Robeson a passport, and he was effectively confined to the United States and forced to do concerts across fences.

More recently, reminiscent of the 1960s COINTELPRO (a series of covert and illegal projects involving the surveilling, infiltrating, discrediting and disrupting of domestic American political organizations), the F.B.I. aggressively targeted and handed down stiff criminal charges as prosecutors tried to disrupt and destroy the global response to the police killing of George Floyd (M4BL, 2021).

Historically, predominantly White legislative bodies have removed Black elective officials from office, effectively disentrancing their constituents. These statewide bodies have punished the respective officials and denied their constituents their political rights.

These state-mandated expulsions have typically been for minor, if not manufactured, infractions, while the penalties have been severe. In all cases, the sentences were more related to the political stance of the Black elected officials than their minor offenses. The first occurrence happened in September of 1868, as 33 Black state legislators were expelled from the Georgia State Assembly – simply because they were Black (Holliday, 2018).

Similar expulsions would occur throughout the South, as in Reconstruction, the rising tide of Black voters and elected officials were systematically disenfranchised and expelled from office. The next major wave of expulsions would come 100 years later as the modern civil rights movement got underway. Centrist Black elected officials such as Adam Clayton Powell and Julian Bond were either legislatively expelled or denied admission to the positions to which they were elected. Again, the real losers were the voters from their districts, Harlem and Atlanta, who were legislatively disenfranchised (Edelman, 2023; History.com, 2024).

This brings us to the situation in Tennessee, where Republican lawmakers expelled two Black men, Justin Jones and Justin Pearson, in 2023. Though they were reappointed within days, the trauma was real, and they still must go through a special election. All the while, they must remain obedient or else face another expulsion, with their voters disenfranchised.

Through it all, Black men have been and continue to be active agents in creating their masculinities. And while none of them, or us for that matter, are perfect, we should neither vilify nor romanticize these identities. Black masculinities continually challenge the stereotypes as they reimagine, reproduce, and realign their identities.

## Authentic Black masculinity

There is no single Black masculine type. Black masculinity is complex, multilayered, multisituated, and multigenerated. There is no inherent, intrinsic, or natural Black gendered role. The system and the community structure gender role orientation, adaptation, and realities. Between these two extremes, the individual navigates exercising choice. To ignore Black male agency is to ignore Black male realities. Under those situations where Black male agency is constricted either by systemic racism or circumscribed by the community, then their ability to effectively navigate is also affected. Several possibilities exist to alter the effects of systemic and community limitations. Examining some of these possibilities demonstrates how Black males can successfully create authentic selves devoid of the stigmas and traumas often projected upon them. In this closing section, let's explore just a few examples of what is already happening.

After dealing with years of depression and suicidal thoughts, Kid Cudi decided to seek mental health treatment and started a movement. Cudi realized that many Black men caught up in hypermasculinity, racial-induced traumas, and denial find themselves in an environment of isolation and frustration. Mental health issues become multiplied as the cultural stigma associated with Black masculinity only compounds the problem. Kid Cudi realized that the cool, tough, super macho was detrimental to Black men's mental health. And when you add racism, stereotypes, and systemic oppression, limited space is provided for being vulnerable, sensitive, or open. This accounts for the increased violence perpetrated by and among Black males (Miller, 2016).

Authentically embracing oneself and choosing to acknowledge sadness, depression, anxiety, and fear are necessary for healing. Encouragement is also needed to challenge and embrace each other and seek help. Kid Cudi began a movement in many ways when he kicked out the hashtag #YouGoodMan on social media (Kornhaber, 2016).

A new breed of Black heroes has started popping up in movies and T.V. series. From Black Panther to Black Lightning, new Black male images are being produced. These heroes, exhibiting hope and optimism, accomplishment, and consistency, have surfaced to concentrate on what is good, right, and brilliant about being a Black man. In a real world with real problems, these portrayals present Black male leadership, role models, and possibilities. Rather than seeing the constant vilification, we are given a validation of positivity.

Research is also being produced that counters the misinformation that continually reifies the myth that Black men are more likely to be incarcerated, unemployed, and poor. The reality is that millions of Black men are doing quite well. The poverty rate, for example, has fallen by 18 percent in the last three decades. Alternatively, the number of Black males in the middle and upper classes has also increased by nearly 18 percent (Wilcox et al, 2018).

Black students with just one Black teacher are likelier to graduate and attend college (Gershenson et al, 2022). Black male teachers increase students' likelihood of developing better learning and problem-solving skills. Black male teachers can utilize their lived experiences to provide inspiration, compassion, advice, and tough love. Specifically, Black male students will be more likely to succeed if a Black male teacher guides the way (Callahan, 2020).

Black mentoring programs, such as the Black Male Initiative, have effectively established community and meaningful engagement for Black males at higher education institutions. These programs have provided a means of countering systemic racism, fostered students' persistence, and reinforced Black male identities. Success comes about as Black males are more fully integrated into a supportive community and benefit from peer mentoring and support (Brooms, 2018).

8

# Conclusion: Songs of Freedom

Throughout our history of trials and triumphs, our songs have been of freedom; as we plowed the fields of justice and planted the seeds of equality, we sang of a brighter day to come. That day is today, as we "lift up our eyes unto the hills." Our faith, resilience, and determination have brought us a new song of freedom.

We have now come full circle. And what have we learned? What is the truth? For far too many, the story and reality of Africa springs from the imagination of Europeans. It is a story of initial contact situations in which the Europeans discovered Africa and the Africans (see Chapters 1 and 2). This story is part mythology, part apology, and part ideology, as Europeans emerge as White, superior conquerors, and the Africans are defined as Black, inferior, and victimized. We explored how even what is considered science is replete with racial overtones. Much like the father of American psychology, Samuel A. Cartwright (1851), who argued that enslaved Africans seeking to escape were mentally ill (drapetomania), the father of American sociology, Lester Frank Ward, is notable in that he advocated Social Darwinism, arguing that Western civilization's oppression of Africans was a result of the survival of the fittest. Ward went so far as to assert that lynching was a necessary consequence of the inferiority of Blacks (see Chapter 5).

Thus, from its beginning, sociology was imbued with scientific racism and White supremacy. For upper-class Whites, racism, and oppression were not only justified but encouraged. Following suit from the University of Chicago, Robert Park would argue that the failure of Blacks and other "lesser" groups to assimilate demonstrated that they had not quite developed. At best, they imitated, albeit imperfectly, the traditions of more advanced Europeans (Park, 1919). According to these scholars, the Africans suffered from a culture of poverty, ghetto mentalities, and generational poverty. Consequently, either because of biological or cultural defects, the Africans were in a constant state of failure (see Chapter 2).

In previous chapters, we explored the counterarguments of W.E.B. Du Bois and Mary Church Terrell. We explored the core African ideas

(Chapters 2 and 3). We also examined how the Africans embraced agency, authenticity, and viewing that reality from the perspective of the Africans (Chapters 4 and 5). We investigated how Black women and men reacted to and rejected stereotypes (Chapters 6 and 7). These are just some of the truths we have visited.

The truth, I suggest, is a song by James Brown in 1968 when he declared, "Say it loud: I'm Black and I'm proud." Go ahead, get your funk on, make that move, and repeat after me, "I'm Black and I'm proud." In this final chapter, we shall explore the rich music produced by Africans in America. In the process, we shall understand that this music was more than soul, hospel, hip-hop or funk. African music was an assertion of being, a testament of faith, and a clarion call to the Universe – I am. These were songs of protest and process, anger and love, action and determination. They were songs that called out the racism faced by Blacks. But they were more than a complaint, as Brown asserted: As Blacks, "we demand a chance to do things for ourselves" (Brown et al, 1968). Self-empowerment and self-identification originating with and by Black people are not externally rendered but internally endorsed.

Time does not allow for a total review of the rich musical genres and messages Africans have produced. But here, let us consider just one of these sites: the United States and its principal proponents, African Americans.

As we begin, you might ask how, given the atrocities visited upon the African, caged in seas of violence, rippling with contempt, bigotry, and despair, can the caged bird sing? The African bird continues to sing because of hope, promise, and the possibilities of a new day. The African bird can sing because they know how to survive, thrive, and overcome. And the African bird can sing because it has the keys to the Universe, their cage, and their future. Those keys are love, joy, and wonder for self and community. They are keys of life, justice, and humanity that they brought into this land from the beginning. Those keys are evident in Black soul, gospel, blues, jazz, R&B, hip-hop, and rap.

Black soul, gospel, blues, jazz, R&B, hip-hop, and rap all share one thing: stories of survival, resistance, determination, and empowerment. Perhaps the oldest of these is the Gospel. So, say it loud, say it clearly, say it right now "I am Black and proud." Today, I sing a new song.

## Gospel: the soul of America

For far too many scholars and conventional history, the history of African heritage begins with the discovery of Africa by Europeans. But, such a perspective only renders the African as an object, not the subject of his own story. Being an object means that Africans respond to the European definition of reality. Such an object has no real identity save that connected with the European.

Alternatively, being an agent means that the African creatively engages, makes choices, and is the architect of their past and future. Which of these perspectives is central to understanding the realities of Blacks; are they the creation of another or the result of their designs?

Academic objectivity, the idea that academia is fair, honest, and based on science and scholarship, has long been demonstrated to be both myth and ethnocentric. This is particularly true when understanding other cultures and peoples based on something other than Western origin. Our history, psychologies, sociologies, anthropologies, and so on, all spring from a particular ethnocentric, a.k.a. Eurocentric, frame of reference.

This means we evaluate, interrogate, and interpret African American history and culture through a racial lens constructed on White Western standards (Metcalfe, 1970). One of the first lenses through which to view the Blacks in America is through gospel music.

As pointed out by Metcalfe, gospel and spirituals, one of the first cultural forms identifiable for Black Americans, has its roots in Western African music. Even earlier, Work (1915) situates the origins of African-American gospel music in Ethiopian legends. Ethiopian legends place Ethiopians as living in two dimensions, "one in the east, the land of the rising sun, and the other in the west, the land of the setting sun. Consequently, the Ethiopians dwelt in perpetual light" (Work, 1915, quoted in Metcalfe, 1970: 16).

The music that came out of this experience, whether gospel, blues, soul, hip-hop or rap, reflects these elements of music: music from the Sons of Light that has survived the valleys of shadow and death, which has been so long a part of the Black American sojourn.

Using what was known as the talking drum, these songs were only accompanied by drums. Again, the talking drum comes from Nigerian and other West African communities. Other instruments are a simple washboard, harmonica, and guitar. But the musical voices could often be heard when Africans arrived in America, singing of freedom and a brighter day tomorrow.

One of the most important figures of Black resistance to slavery was Harriet Tubman, or Moses as she was affectionately known. After her escape, she discussed how she was "a stranger in a strange land." And while she was free, she believed all her brothers, sisters, friends, mothers, and fathers should also be free (Bradford, 2012). Tubman and other slave insurrectionists used songs to communicate, coordinate, and orchestrate the struggle for freedom.

These songs became a code whose words gave directions for escape routes and plans. With biblical references and connections to peoples, places, and stories, the words meant different things to the audience, depending on whether they were White or Black. So, being bound for Canaan land, for a White person, might mean dying and going to heaven, but for the enslaved, it meant escaping to Canada.

A couple of songs were quite useful, such as the following, which Tubman would use:

- "Wade in the Water," tells enslaved people to escape in the water to avoid being seen.
- "Steal Away," which meant that they were planning to escape.
- "Sweet Chariot" indicates that escape is imminent, and a "band of angels" is coming to take them to freedom. The "sweet chariot" – the Underground Railroad – would be coming low (to the South) to take them to the North or freedom (carry me home).

Contrary to popular wisdom, the Africans were neither willing nor happy slaves. Enslaved people revolted over 100 times. Many of these revolts were failures, lacked planning, and doomed the perpetrators to torture and death. Yet, the Africans continued to resist and fight for freedom. One of the earliest songs recorded, sung by Black Union soldiers as they escaped the plantations, was the "Freedom Song." It goes like this:

Oh freedom, oh freedom, oh freedom over me.
And before I'll be a slave, I'll be buried in my grave.
And go home to my Lord and be free.
No more master, no more master, no more master calling me.
And before I'll be a slave, I'll be buried in my grave.
And go home to my Lord and be free.
No more misery, no more misery, no more misery over me.
And before I'll be a slave, I'll be buried in my grave.
And go home to my Lord and be free.
Oh freedom, oh freedom, oh freedom over me.
And before I'll be a slave, I'll be buried in my grave.
And go home to my Lord and be free.

It is not without irony that a central theme of many African-American spirituals is freedom. These songs can be heard as far away as South Africa during the struggle against apartheid (1948–1994) and the song "Freedom is Coming" (Hawn, 2018).

As Blacks began to escape from the South, in what has come to be known as the "Great Migration," a new musical form came into being: colorful melodies with arrangements that, while using White songs, were made Black through syncopation – the rhythmic recasting of words, accentuating normally weak beats. This new music, also associated with the rise of Pentecostal churches, featured "shouting," "speaking in tongues," and the "circle dances" that came out of Africa.

One of the most significant composers of this period was Rev. C.A. Tindley, who wrote "I'll Overcome Someday," which became the basis of the American civil rights movement's "We Shall Overcome" by Reverend Gary Davis. Perhaps the most prolific and well-known songwriter was Thomas A. Dorsey. Who could forget his "Precious Lord Take My Hand" or Aretha Franklin's father, Reverend C.L. Franklin?

The list would be incomplete if we did not include Robert Martin, Sister Rosetta Tharpe, and Mahalia Jackson, who famously sang "Precious Lord" on the U.S. Capitol steps under the shadow of Lincoln's statue.

Gospel music captured religious experiences, preserved the West African cultural roots, and provided both hopes and dreams of freedom.

## Blues: a tonic for whatever ails you

B.B. King (2005, quoted in Shriver and Jones, 2015) says, "Blues is a tonic for whatever ails you." I am reminded of a skit on the Flip Wilson show. In this skit, Flip played a club owner looking for an entertainer to sing and play the Blues. One of the applicants was White, and he said, "Everybody knows the Negro gave the Blues to America." His wife (in the "Geraldine" voice) said, "Jus' a minute, honey! The Negro didn't give the Blues to America. America gave the Blues to the Negro."

And so it is; it has not been a bed of roses for Blacks here in America. As my mother and her sons prepared to go to church early on many Sunday mornings, I would dress while listening to B.B. King and other blues songs. I remember my mom asking, in frustration once, "Son, it's Sunday morning; must you play the blues?" My response was, "It makes me feel good." Why?

Racial trauma historically has been ignored and submerged under denial, fear of rejection, and caprice on the part of various racist structures, practices, and policies. Racial trauma can result from multiple communities in which we exist, have existed, or have avoided:

- It can result from dealing with various institutional actors such as police hiring, supervisory personnel, and colleagues.
- It can result from policies and laws built into the system/structures.
- It results from covert and overt actions.

Let me begin by stating I grew up in an apartheid city, where Whites lived on one side, Blacks on the other. I attended exclusively Black schools until college, when I formally entered the White university and White spaces. I am a Vietnam veteran, and post-traumatic stress disorder for being Black and a combat veteran are separate but related entities. Yet, through it all, blues has been my friend. And now let us walk down that road paved with song, sorrow, and uplift.

One of the classic blues songs, written by Abel Meeropol and sung by Billie Holiday in 1939, is "Strange Fruit." With this, the protest song was launched onto the American scene, as it protested the continual lynching of Black Americans with lyrics such as "Southern trees bear a strange fruit/ Blood on the leaves and blood at the root." This declaration of protest was the beginning of the civil rights movement (Margolick, 2000) and brilliantly articulated the racial trauma of the period.

No one can forget, or should be ignorant of, the 1964 song by Nina Simone, "Mississippi Goddam." This song articulated the racial trauma associated with the murders of Emmett Till and Medgar Evers and the bombing of the 16th Street Baptist Church in Birmingham, Alabama. Between 1882 and 1968, an estimated 4,700 Americans were lynched; of these, 3,500 were Blacks. And Mississippi was at the top of the list (Burke, 2024).

Lynchings in America were public events; hell, they were parties, as Whites would come from all over the country to participate and celebrate this strangely local custom. Killing Blacks, burning Black towns, and rape of Black women were all part of the racialized trauma. And the strange fruit that this produced was rarely punished by any court: strange fruit indeed.

## Soul, hip-hop, and rap: the conscience of America

Strange, whenever there is a conversation about diversity, equity, and inclusion, it implies this is accomplished when White spaces accommodate the token Black, Brown, Red, or Yellow person. Ironically, integration has always been defined as when people of color enter White spaces.

But when Whites were required to come into Black spaces, they fled. White flight, often paid for with public funds (Federal Housing Administration), has historically produced and continues to produce "Vanilla suburbs and Chocolate cities." In our modern era, gentrification preserves White spaces by displacing poor Blacks.

But Whites have always had a strange fascination for all things Black, Brown, Red, and Yellow. Voyeuristic excursions into the ghettos were and continue to be in vogue. They called it slumming, checking out the "Dark" villages, their music, culture, and essence – but only for a moment, only for the night. White America would face the reality of segregated, displaced, humiliated, and down-casted people in these moments. Or at least, what they thought were such.

Little did they know, or even now would admit, that they were, in effect, confronting their inner selves, insecurities, and self-righteous indignations as they projected their "own stuff" into these other spheres. Thus, these spheres, particularly in the music genres known as soul, hip-hop, and rap, were and continue to be the conscience of America.

As Black people in academia, corporations, industries, or almost any other institutional setting in America, we must navigate in White spaces.

And given the paltry number of us in these spaces, whenever we are not present, our absence is more than noticed; it is often a source of concern for White supervisors. This is particularly so when we are senior personnel in these spaces.

How dare we have other lives, other things that are more important than being on display in White spaces? Do we not know we must be there to preserve the illusion of inclusion? Ever notice how many Blacks in White spaces always have their music with them, in the ear, turned up loud, and bumping? Thank God for soul, hip-hop, and rap – the soothing sounds that calm a troubled spirit.

What is so special about these sounds? Soul, hip-hop, and rap combine all the other Black diaspora genres. Here, you will find gospel and jazz, blues and improv. Here, you will find the heart, mind, and soul of Black existence. The soul is the essence, the embodiment of spirituality, rationality, actuality, and totality of people of African heritage in America.

Soul reflects the cultural consciousness, pride, intensity, sensitivities, and emotional fervor of a people who continue to rise, strive, and remain agents of their destiny. Here, the vision and the promise, the history and dilemmas, the future and the dreams of Black people are wrapped up in rhyme and timed to a funky beat – harmonically gifted voices blended in rhapsodies that transcend time, space, and circumstances.

Think about it – the Temptations, the Supremes, Miracles, Commodores, Earth Wind, and Fire, Sly and the Family Stone, Aretha Franklin, Diana Ross, Patti Labelle, Smokey Robinson, Stevie Wonder, and Teddy Pendergrass – these are just the tip of the great mountain of Black talent. This mountain not only survives but helps a people survive; it not only reveals but attests to the greatness of those people that moved a people, causing America to pop its fingers – that rocked its world.

In 1967, when 24-year-old Aretha Franklin taught America how to spell "RESPECT," she challenged Blacks to be confident, independent, empowered, and sassy. This message, rejecting sexism, racism, homophobia, and misogynistic objectification of Blacks in general, but the Black woman in particular, became the anthem for the civil rights movement.

Posthumously, Otis Redding's "Sitting on the Dock of the Bay" was released a year later. The soul of Black America was revealed here as he brought Black R&B together with funk, folk, and our realities. But Otis and his Bar-Kays were killed in a tragic plane crash. He never saw his song top the pop and R&B charts. In 2011, Kanye West and Jay-Z sampled "Otis" with "try a little tenderness" and won the Grammy for Best Rap Performance for a song in 2012.

When the Staple Singers in 1971 stepped out on the stage and sang "Respect Yourself," they spoke for a community of "Black folk" that was frustrated with the world. This was a direct rejection of a world that was dismissive of, afraid of, and simultaneously obsessed with all things Black. Reminiscent of an earlier period known as the Harlem Renaissance, Blacks again asserted their value, resolve, and need to teach their young and reclaim their heritages by, first and foremost, "respecting themselves." Funk exploded all across America.

A year later, chronicling the confused, mixed-up world of the 1970s, the Stylistics released their hit song "People Make the World Go Round." And what was their message for America and a troubled world? That "ups and downs" are what make the world go round and that people are responsible for those "ups and downs."

Harold Melvin and the Blue Notes were among the most popular Philadelphia soul groups of the 1970s; their music spanned soul, R&B, doo-wop, and disco. Among this group of stars was none other than Teddy Pendergrass. Just before he left the group to launch his phenomenal career as a soloist, he led the group in what has become a timeless classic: "Wake Up Everybody."

This song, released in 1975, is resonating today on the right. Have you ever wondered why so many on the right are obsessed with "woke?" It is spelled out in the lines calling out lying politicians and sinful preachers and highlighting society's change, "The world has changed so very much/ From what it used to be."

When Spike Lee was looking for a song to connect to his 1989 film *Do the Right Thing*, he came to Public Enemy, and they produced "Fight the Power." Public Enemy had been blazing a trail with such albums as *It Takes a Nation of Millions to Hold Us Back* and *Fear of a Black Planet*.

"Fight the Power" is ranked number two in *Rolling Stone*'s 500 Greatest Songs of All Time list. Why? Let us consider. "Fight the Power" incorporates and makes so much of Black culture real, reclaims civil rights, and brings together Black gospel and, of course, the funk of James Brown. "Fight the Power" is a revolutionary song, calling for Blacks to stop swinging and realize that they must transcend the liberal notion of racial equality and understand that we are not the same.

You see, equality means never comparing yourself to another. Parents would say their children are the same. And while, as a parent, I may love all my children, I love them uniquely, separately, and individually. They are not the same. They are all special. And so are we as Black Americans. We must challenge the power structure to "give us what we want: what we need," not whatever is left on the table of greed.

The song is a call for intelligent activism, reminiscent of the first song of Blacks in America ("We would rather die on our feet than live as slaves on our knees"), we must have freedom or death, and we are never the less still Black and proud.

Neither America nor the world was ready for Tupac when he dropped into our world. Tupac's mother and family were heavily involved in the Black Panthers Black Liberation Army. Tupac is among the best-selling musical artists in the world. His records sold over 75 million worldwide. To understand his overwhelming influence, consider the top eight of his greatest hits:

1. "Keep Ya Head Up"
2. "How Long Will They Mourn Me?"
3. "Letter 2 My Unborn"
4. "Hit 'Em Up"
5. "California Love"
6. "Changes"
7. "Trapped"
8. "Dear Mama"

Today, nearly three decades after his death on September 13, 1996, Tupac Shakur still is one of the most iconic figures in hip-hop. His music reflects the contradictory realities of being Black, proud, and despised in America. Tupac's music captures the anger and ecstasy, the frivolity and the sublimity, the essence and the insanity of being a Black man.

A man whose very life continues to be a character, a caricature, a fantasy. Strangely, many consider Tupac to be the essence of a "thug angel." One who never transcends the streets, the gangster, the drug starved, pimp hustler – all the mimes racist America must create to protect themselves from all that is Black!

It was Tupac who redeemed the Black criminal who romanticized T.H.U.G.L.I.F.E., but many do not know that it is an acronym for "The Hate U Give Little Infants F★★★ Everybody." Tupac realized the Black body had long been criminalized, racially profiled, and subjected to racially biased policing and sentencing (the cradle-to-prison pipeline). And all these realities were byproducts of a racist America. So when he signed to the record label Death Row, he was at once the hottest and most dangerous performer in America. And, of course, he realized that "All Eyez (were) on Me."

I could go on, but who can forget his tribute to his mother, "Dear Mama," which acknowledged this Black woman's tremendous impact on his life? This single mother from a low-income setting filled him with love, tenderness, determination, and hope: Dear Mama.

## The truth is wrapped up in our dreams.

In closing, I remember a story I encountered a few years ago.

A little boy starts his 2.8-mile trek to school on a frigid rural road in southern China. By the time little Wang Fuman gets to school, frost covers his eyebrows and hair. His lips and cheeks are red and chapped. A photo posted by his teacher dubbed "Frostboy" has gone viral as this little hero touched people worldwide. One viewer responded, "Don't forget your dreams" (Hernandez, 2018). I am reminded that every journey begins with a dream and ends with a journey.

When Martin Luther King, Jr. articulated his dream, it reflected the contemporary reality of Jim Crow and the audacious hope for a brighter day. Specifically, King's reflections were presented between the harsh truth Langston Hughes laments in "A Dream Deferred" and the hope expressed in Stevie Wonder's "Hold On to Your Dream." While Hughes asked whether a dream deferred would "fester like a sore,"[1] Stevie Wonder challenges us to remember that "there's always tomorrow" (1996).

King's dream (King, 1963) continued a theme that runs throughout the experiences of Blacks in America. While his dream continued this historic theme, it nevertheless ushered in a distinctly new set of possibilities. Today, as we contemplate keeping the dream alive, I think it is time for a new set of dreams and possibilities by a new set of dreamers, dream keepers, and dream makers.

King's dream was so important because it was not a simple reaction to the bitter reality of dreams deferred for far too long. It was more than a resignation to the righteous indignation of generations of Blacks whose patience wore thin as they waited for America to make good its promises of freedom, dignity, and justice. King, the dreamer, refused to submit to the calls for retribution and violence, calling instead for resolve and determination. The genius of King's dream was to articulate a sustainable community for Blacks. It has endured and pointed to hope even as we watch the re-emergence of state-sanctioned violence targeting Blacks and the continued racial gaps in educational outcomes, social mobility, wealth accumulation, health care, and sustained high levels of Black incarceration. This achievement takes on more relevance when we consider that the leading cause of death for Black men between the ages of 18 and 38 is most likely to be another Black man. King's dream challenges the system of slavery, then racism, that pitted Blacks against each other. A system that teaches, encourages, and rewards Black antagonism, conflict, and competition. Rather, the dream articulated a community of families where respect replaced envy, deference replaced destruction, and achievement replaced defeat. This dream, now almost 55 years in the making, continues to foster hope and triumph and calls for justice. However, I wonder if it is time for new dreams and dreamers.

My grandmother used to say, "Don't let nobody steal your dreams, for they are your strength, they help you climb life's peaks and valleys, they help you avoid despair. For only they can keep you from drowning in sorrow, only they can help you face tomorrow."

## Dream keepers

This past week, while going through some last-minute Christmas cards, I came across a real gem that once again reaffirmed the importance of not only dreams, but equally important dream keepers. Let me share with you here a letter from a kid named Chris:

> To Whom it May Concern:
> First off, I'd like to admit that I was selling marijuana on high school campuses and I'm sorry. I made a very big mistake that will change my life forever. My decisions were immature and very stupid, and I regret doing it. I should have thought about my actions before … now my future is bleak. I am truly sorry and begging for a second chance to start my life over and walk from this situation into my dreams. If I can get a second chance, I promise I will use it to pursue those dreams.

Chris is not unlike the other two million kids arrested each year across this country. What made Chris's story different is that he was allowed to become a dreamer rather than just another statistic. His life was altered by what Gloria Ladson-Billings refers to as "dream keepers." Expanding on her designation, a dream keeper challenges us to envision alternative realities that empower and improve the lives of young people. The dream keepers helped Chris not to obsess over his failure, but to grasp a new reality. He was allowed to dream again. These dreams helped him to refocus, redirect, and rechannel his anxieties, fears, and frustrations into alternative possibilities. Oh. The end of the letter reads: "Florida State University Announces the graduation of Christopher Jermaine Butler, with the degree of Bachelor of Science with a major in Information Technology, Friday evening, December 15, 2017" (PBS, 2016).

From slavery to the present, dreams have pointed to the possibility of freedom. Though objectively, one may be constrained, dreams allow one to escape subjectively. But dreams without purpose-driven tasks are fantasies, and fantasies are illusions that temporarily distort but do not substantially change our realities. Dreams help you turn horror into hope, problems into possibilities, failures into futures, and rejection into what Bob Marley termed redemption songs. For Marley, redemption came from the revolutionary understanding that tasks without dreams were toil, and dreams without tasks or purpose were fantasies. Those who only know toil or fantasies live in slavery. Songs of redemption that envisioned a new day gave meaning and purpose to the struggle. They allowed those mired in the belly of the beast to keep hope alive and to sing a change that is going to come. Alongside dream keepers are what I choose to call dream makers – those individuals who motivate young people to articulate, refine, and pursue their dreams.

## Dream makers

Dream makers are parents and family, teachers and mentors, friends and other community members, for it takes a village to raise a child. Dream makers are what make democracy and the American dream work. They are everyday people who stand up and fight for change, dispel animosity, and seek alternative futures where everyone can maximize their potential. Therefore, where some have fallen astray and find their paths blocked with hatred, misery, and despair, dream makers point to love, kindness, and hope.

So, while some point to the ever-increasing objectification of identity, the increasingly fragmented families and communities, and the increasing fragility of life itself, dream makers point out that we need not more machines but more humanity. Therefore, while some live behind barricades of hate, dream makers espouse a future where we all can live lives free and open. In addition, as King observed, while our technology allows us to travel to the moon, many of us need to learn how to travel next door. As we attempt to achieve his beloved community, the first step is to get to know each other.

Unfortunately, while our knowledge has increased, we have become more cynical, distrustful, and complacent. Dream makers are needed to help us reassert the goodness of universal brotherhood, the power of unity, and the endurance of love and justice. We must become what King dreamed we could be – drum majors for justice, drum majors for peace, and drum majors for righteousness. In doing this, we will make the dream a reality, renew our spirits, and then be able to "cash the check" issued by our nation in the words of the Constitution and the Declaration of Independence. This promissory note held that all people, regardless of status – be they Brown, Tan, Red, Black, White, Muslim, Hindu, Jew, gentile, straight, gay, trans, immigrant, homeless, or elderly – are guaranteed the unalienable rights of life, liberty, and the pursuit of happiness. As we pursue our dreams, we will continue to take the high road that leads to the place of justice. We, therefore, will not drink from the cup of bitterness or hatred. We will recognize that we are all part of this great family called humanity, regardless of accidents of birth.

We recognize that as we pursue our dreams, we can never be satisfied if Blacks, Hispanics, Native Americans, Jews, and Muslims are victims of unspeakable horrors of police brutality, indiscriminate searches, and seizures or denied access because of their religion. We cannot ignore the plight of immigrants and refugees whose only crime is having been born on the wrong side of a border. Neither can we ignore the continual harassment, discrimination, and intimidation faced by women.

Homophobia has no place in our churches, schools, or our community. Poverty knows neither race, religion, gender, nor nationality. Poor Whites in Appalachia and the rural South, displaced workers in the rust belt and urban slums, unemployed and underemployed in the deep South and South of the borders need real jobs, real opportunities, and real deals so they can feed their families, educate their children, heal their sick, and truly make America great again.

Let freedom ring for all these members of our extended family and community. We cannot continue to uphold a system that strips children of their identity or denies them the dignity of nobility simply because they do not have the proper papers. Sickness and homelessness can no longer be tolerated in the richest country in the world. Neither can we continue to allow the high dropout rates, achievement gaps, income, and health disparities which allow poverty to continue unabated generation after generation. No, we are not satisfied and will not be satisfied until justice rolls down like waters and righteousness like a mighty river.

You see, I, too, have a dream. That all the Wang Fumans of the world will breath free and sing that old Negro Spiritual – free at last, free at last, thank God almighty we are free at last. And so, even with these difficulties, even though at times it appears that the world and its leaders have gone crazy, I remain hopeful, I remain determined, and I remain convinced that the dreams, dreamers, dream keepers, and dream makers will continually shine beacons of light toward a brighter tomorrow. Yes, I have a dream that dreams will return.

*Dreams return*

>What happens when dreams return?
>Do they sparkle with hope and glisten with song?
>Do they prance along voyeuristic roads?
>Where wonder and surprise forever unfold.
>What happens when dreams return?
>Do they fill cups with promise and souls with laughter?
>Do they shatter despair and vanquish frustration?
>Where each day overflows with possibilities.
>Or do they point the way to unbridled futures?
>Don't give up or in ... hold on to your dreams ...
>Pursue them with passionate determination.
>Nurture them diligently with excellence and resolve.
>Keep getting up till your dreams become reality.
>Then, dream a new dream as dreams return.

There is no shortage of examples we can draw upon. The experiences of Blacks are a testament to the realities of love, sacrifice, hope, despair, visions, empowerment, and dreams found in soul, hip-hop, and rap, which have given America its essence, realities, and conscience. Thank you, and keep the dreams alive; pursue the truth, and they will continually set you free.

# Notes

## Chapter 2

[1] https://www.etymonline.com/word/genus
[2] This section draws extensively from *Encyclopedia Britannica* (2023).
[3] Unless otherwise noted, much of this section is derived from Dickson et al (2023).
[4] Unless otherwise noted, much of this section is derived from Khan (2009).

## Chapter 3

[1] Russia and Asia would take distinctively different paths toward imperialism.
[2] Gun sales have increased by 26 percent, while hate groups have dramatically risen since President Obama was elected. According to the Southern Poverty Law Center, these changes have been "fed by antagonism toward President Obama, resentment toward changing demographics, and the economic rift between rich and poor" (see Southern Poverty Law Center, http://www.splcenter.org/what-we-do/hate-and-extremism

## Chapter 5

[1] https://www.battlefields.org/learn/primary-sources/general-order-no-3

## Chapter 6

[1] https://genius.com/Malcolm-x-who-taught-you-to-hate-yourself-annotated

## Chapter 7

[1] https://genius.com/Malcolm-x-who-taught-you-to-hate-yourself-annotated

## Chapter 8

[1] https://www.poetryfoundation.org/poems/46548/harlem

# References

**Chapter 1**

ADL (2021) "Extremists See Critical Race Theory as Evidence of 'White Genocide'." *Anti-Defamation League*. https://www.adl.org/resources/blog/extremists-see-critical-race-theory-evidence-white-genocide

Bell, D. (1987) *And We Are Not Saved*. Basic Books.

Bleiweis, R., Boesch, D., and Gaines, A.C. (2020) "The Basic Facts About Women in Poverty." *American Progress*. https://www.americanprogress.org/article/basic-facts-women-poverty/

Brubaker, R., Loveman, M., and Stamatov, P. (2004) "Ethnicity as Cognition." *Theory and Society*, 33(1): 31–64.

Cineas, F. (2020) "Critical Race Theory, and Trump's War on It, Explained." *Vox.com*. https://www.vox.com/2020/9/24/21451220/critical-race-theory-diversity-training-trump

Clark, J. (2021) "Fact Check: 3 Common Claims About Critical Race Theory." *Louisville Public Media*. https://www.lpm.org/news/2021-07-09/fact-check-3-common-claims-about-critical-race-theory

Coates, R., Ferber, A., and Brunsma, D.L. (2021) *The Matrix of Race: Social Construction, Intersectionality, and Inequality*. SAGE.

Cooper, P. (1993) *When Stories Come to School*. Teachers and Writers Collaborative.

Delgado Bernal, D. (1998) "Grassroots Leadership Reconceptualized: Chicana Oral Histories and the 1968 East Los Angeles School Blowouts." *Frontiers: A Journal of Women Studies*, 19(2): 113–143.

Du Bois, W.E.B. (1899) *The Philadelphia Negro*. University of Pennsylvania Press.

Du Bois, W.E.B. (1903) *The Souls of Black Folks: Essays and Drawings*. A.C. McCurg & Co.

Durden, T. (2021) "Dear CRT: Focusing on Family Engagement." *Kaplan Learning Center*. https://blog.kaplanco.com/ii/dear-crt-focusing-on-family-engagement

Gross, T. (2021) "Uncovering Who Is Driving the Fight Against Critical Race Theory in Schools." *NPR*. https://www.npr.org/2021/06/24/1009839021/uncovering-who-is-driving-the-fight-against-critical-race-theory-in-schools

Hardin, N. (2021/2023) "What is Critical Race Theory?" Alliance Defending Freedom.

Hill Collins, P. (2009) *Black Feminist Thought: Knowledge, Consciousness, and the Construction, Intersectionality, and Inequality.* SAGE.

King, M.L., Jr. (1963) "Letter from a Birmingham Jail." https://www.africa. upenn.edu/Articles_Gen/Letter_Birmingham.html

Lather, P. (1998) "Critical Pedagogy and its Complicities: A Praxis of Stuck Places." *Educational Theory*, 48(4): 487–497. https://doi.org/10.1111/j.1741-5446.1998.00487.x

Marx, K. (1867) *Capital: A Critique of Political Economy Vol 1.* Progress Publishers.

Meehan, K. and Friedman, J. (2023) "Banned in the USA: State Laws Supercharge Book Suppression in Schools." *Pen America.* https://pen.org/report/banned-in-the-usa-state-laws-supercharge-book-suppression-in-schools/

Miller, L. (1966) *The Petitioners: The Story of the Supreme Court of the United States and the Negro.* Pantheon Books.

Miller, R., Liu, K., and Ball, A.F. (2020) "Critical Counter-Narrative as Transformative Methodology for Educational Equity." *Review of Research in Education*, 44(1): 269–300. https://doi.org/10.3102/0091732X20908501.

Mould, M. (2011) *The Routledge Dictionary of Cultural References in Modern French.* Routledge.

National Center for Education Statistics (2021) "Digest of Education Statistics." Available at: https://nces.ed.gov/programs/digest/d21/tables/dt21_306.10.asp

Phelan, M. (2019) "The History of 'History is Written by the Victors'." *Slate.com.* https://slate.com/culture/2019/11/history-is-written-by-the-victors-quote-origin.html

Robinson, C.J. (2019) *Cedric J. Robinson: On Racial Capitalism, Black Internationalism, and Cultures of Resistance*, edited by H.L.T. Quan. Pluto Press. https://doi.org/10.2307/j.ctvr0qs8p

Sapolsky, R., Ehrlich, P. and Wojcik, J. (2003) "Appeal of the Rare." *Discover.* https://www.discovermagazine.com/mind/appeal-of-the-rare

Szasz, T.S. (1970) *The Manufacture of Madness: A Comparative Study of the Inquisition and the Mental Health Movement.* Syracuse University Press.

Villenas, S., Dehyle, D., and Parker, L. (1999) "Critical Race Theory and Praxis: Chicano(a)/Latino(a) and Navajo Struggles for Dignity, Educational Equity, and Social Justice." In Parker, L., Dehyle, D., and Villenas, S. (eds) *Race Is … Race Isn't: Critical Race Theory and Qualitative Studies in Education* (pp 31–52). Westview. https://doi.org/10.4324/9780429503504-3

Wilson, W.J. (1980) *The Declining Significance of Race.* University of Chicago Press.

World Population Review (2023) "State Rankings: Critical Race Theory Ban Status." https://worldpopulationreview.com/state-rankings/critical-race-theory-ban-states

## Chapter 2

Abbink, J. (1998) "A Historical-Anthropological Approach to Islam in Ethiopia: Issues of Identity and Politics." *Journal of African Cultural Studies*, 11(2): 109–124. DOI: 10.1080/13696819808717830

Abdelfatah, R. (2021) "'Black Moses' Lives On: How Marcus Garvey's Vision Still Resonates." *NPR*. https://www.npr.org/2021/02/08/965503687/marcus-garvey-pan-africanist

Adewale, A. and Schepers, S. (2023) "Colonialism and the Struggle for Independence." In Adewale, A. and Schepers, S. (eds) *Reimaging Africa* (pp 91–113). Palgrave Macmillan. https://doi.org/10.1007/978-3-031-40360-6_5

Asbridge, T.S. (2005) *The First Crusade: A New History: The Roots of Conflict between Christianity and Islam*. Oxford University Press.

Bar-on, A. (1999) "Social Work and the 'Missionary Zeal to Whip the Heathen Along the Path of Righteousness'." *The British Journal of Social Work*, 29(1): 5–26.

Belcher, W.L. (2012) *Abyssinia's Samuel Johnson: Ethiopian Thought in the Making of an English Author*. Oxford University Press.

Bernal, M. (2002) *Black Athena: The Afroasiatic Roots of Classical Civilization, Volume 1: The Fabrication of Ancient Greece*. Rutgers University Press.

Bond, S.E. (2017) "Why We Need to Start Seeing the Classical World in Color." *Hyperallergic*. https://hyperallergic.com/383776/why-we-need-to-start-seeing-the-classical-world-in-color/

Bonfante, L. (2011) "Classical and Barbarian." In Bonfante, L. (ed) *The Barbarians of Ancient Europe: Realities and Interactions* (pp 1–36). Cambridge University Press.

Bowersock, G.W., Brown, P., and Graber, O. (1999) *Late Antiquity: A Guide to the Postclassical World*. Belknap Press of Harvard University Press.

Boxill, B. (2005) "Rousseau, Natural Man, and Race." In Valls, A. (ed) *Race and Racism in Modern Philosophy*. Cornell University Press, 150–168.

Brindley, E. (2003) "Barbarians or Not? Ethnicity and Changing Conceptions of the Ancient Yue (Viet) Peoples, ca. 400-50 BC." *Asia Major*, 16(1): 1–32. http://www.jstor.org/stable/41649870

Brubaker, R. and Cooper, F. (2000) "Beyond 'Identity'." *Theory and Society*, 29: 1–47.

Buccus, I. (2020) "The History of Liberalism is Entwined with Racism." *Daily Maverick, Opinionista*. https://www.dailymaverick.co.za/opinionista/2020-03-08-the-history-of-liberalism-is-entwined-with-racism/

Butzer, K. (1981) "Rise and Fall of Axum, Ethiopia: A Geo-Archaeological Interpretation." *American Antiquity*, 46(3): 471–495. doi:10.2307/280596

Carmichael, S. (1966) "Black Power." *Enclopedia.com*. https://www.encyclopedia.com/history/dictionaries-thesauruses-pictures-and-press-releases/black-power-speech-28-july-1966-stokely-carmichael

Carmichael, S. (Kwame Ture) and Hamilton, C. (1967/1992) *Black Power: The Politics of Liberation*. Vintage.

Carroll, W.H. (1993) *A History of Christendom, V3*. Christendom Press.

Christian, M. (2019) "A Global Critical Race and Racism Framework: Racial Entanglements and Deep and Malleable Whiteness." *Sociology of Race and Ethnicity*, 5(2): 169–185. https://doi.org/10.1177/2332649218783220

Clairmonte, F.F. (1970) "The Race War by Ronald Segal." *The Journal of Modern African Studies*, 8(3): 507–509.

Cole, J.B. and Guy-Sheftall, B. (2003) *Gender Talk: The Struggle for Women's Equality in African American Communities*. One World.

Cooper, A.J. (1892) *A Voice of the South*. Aldine Printing House.

Cooper, L. (1994) "Critical Storytelling in Social Work Education." *Australian Journal of Adult and Community Education*, 34(2): 131–141.

Cronon, E.D. (1955) *Black Moses: The Story of Marcus Garvey and the Universal Negro Improvement Association*. University of Wisconsin Press.

Delgado, R. (1989) "Storytelling for Oppositionists and Others: A Plea for Narrative," *Michigan Law Review*, 87(8): 2411–2441.

Diamond, J. (1994/2023) "How Africa Became Black." *Discover*. https://www.discovermagazine.com/planet-earth/how-africa-became-black

Dickson, G., Madden, T.F. and Baldwin, M.W. (2023, October 24) "Crusades." *Encyclopedia Britannica*. https://www.britannica.com/event/Crusades

Diop, A. (1954) *The African Origin of Civilization: Myth or Reality*. L. Hill.

Du Bois, W.E.B. (1897) "The Conservation of the Races." The American Negro Academy, Occasional l Papers No. 2.

Du Bois, W.E.B. (1903/2009) *The Souls of Black Folk*. The Journal of Pan African Studies E Book. https://www.jpanafrican.org/ebooks/3.4eBookSoulsofBlackFolk.pdf

*Encyclopedia Britannica* (2023, February 3) "Al-Andalus." *Encyclopedia Britannica*. https://www.britannica.com/place/Al-Andalus

Erskine, A. (1995) "Culture and Power in Ptolemaic Egypt: The Museum and Library of Alexandria," *Greece & Rome*, 42(1): 38–48. doi:10.1017/S0017383500025213

Fanon, F. (1952/2008) *Black Skin, White Masks*. Grove Press.

Fawad, A. and Yu, W.J. (2016) "Confucian Philosophy and Chinese Ethnic Minority Policy: A Case Study of Xinjiang." *Journal of Historical Studies*, 2: 36–53.

Fawcett, E. (1952/2020) *Conservatism: The Fight for a Tradition*. Princeton University Press.

Flikschuh, K. and Ypi, L. (2014) *Kant and Colonialism: Historical and Critical Perspectives*. Oxford University Press.

Friedman, S. (2018) "Operation Solomon: From Ethiopian Jews to Ethiopian Israelis." *Jewish Museum London*. https://jewishmuseum.org.uk/2018/ 10/24/operation-solomon-from-ethiopian-jews-to-ethiopian-israelis/ #:~:text=And%20who%20are%20the%20Ethiopian,King%20Solomon%20 and%20Queen%20Sheba

Garvey, M. (1923/2009) *Philosophy and Opinions of Marcus Garvey*, edited by A. Jacques-Varvey. The Journal of Pan African Studies. https://archive. org/details/ThePhilosophyOpinionsOfMarcusGarveyOrAfricaForThe Africans/mode/2up

Gavins, R. (2016) "Murray, Pauli." In *The Cambridge Guide to African American History* (p 200). Cambridge University Press. doi:10.1017/ CBO9781316216453.217

Gobineau, A. de (1853) *An Essay on the Inequality of the Human Races: The Hidden Causes of Revolutions, Bloody Wars, and Lawlessness.*

Goldenberg, D.M. (1999) "The Development of the Idea of Race: Classical Paradigms and Medieval Elaborations." *International Journal of the Classical Tradition*, 5(4): 561–570.

Guevara, C. (1961) "Economics Cannot be Separated from Politics." https:// www.marxists.org/archive/guevara/1961/08/08.htm

Guevara, C. (1964) "On Development." https://www.marxists.org/archive/ guevara/1964/03/25.htm

Hall, E. (1989) *Inventing the Barbarian: Greek Self-Definition through Tragedy*. Clarendon Series/Oxford University Press.

Hall, J.M. (1997) *Ethnic Identity in Greek Antiquity*. Cambridge University Press.

Hartley, L.P. (1970) *The Go-Between*, 3rd edn. Penguin.

Harvey, M. (2001) "Deliberation and Natural Slavery." *Social Theory and Practice*, 27(1): 41–64. http://www.jstor.org/stable/23559041

He, B. (2004) "Confucianism Versus Liberalism Over Minority Rights: A Critical Responses to Will Kymlicka." *Journal of Chinese Philosophy*, 31(1): 103–123. https://ssrn.com/abstract=2030098

Hellenthal, G., Bird, N., and Morris, S. (2021) "Structure and Ancestry Patterns of Ethiopians in Genome-wide Autosomal DNA." *Human Molecular Genetics*, 30(R1): R42–R48. https://doi.org/10.1093/hmg/ddab019

Henton, L. (2022) "What Martin Luther King, Jr. Said About Systemic Racism." *Texas A&M Today*. https://today.tamu.edu/2022/01/15/ what-martin-luther-king-jr-said-about-systemic-racism/#:~:text= %E2%80%9CJustice%20for%20black%20people%20will%20not%20 flow%20into,published%20in%201969%20titled%20%E2%80%9CA%20 Testament%20of%20Hope.%E2%80%9D

Hillenbrand, C. (1999) *The Crusades: Islamic Perspectives*. Fitzroy Dearborn Publishers. https://archive.org/details/crusadesislamicp0000hill/page/n3/mode/2up

History.com (2009/2022) "Marcus Garvey." https://www.history.com/topics/black-history/marcus-garvey

Hubbard, J.W. (1931) "The Cause and the Cure of African Immorality." *International Review of Mission*, 20(2): 241–253. https://doi.org/10.1111/j.1758-6631.1931.tb04062.x

Isaac, B. (2006) "Proto-Racism in Graeco-Roman Antiquity." *World Archaeology*, 38(1): 32–47. http://www.jstor.org/stable/40023593

Johnson, N.D. and Koyama, M. (2018) "The State, Toleration, and Religious Freedom." GMU Working Paper in Economics No. 18-18. https://ssrn.com/abstract=3187817

Johnson, S. (1775) https://archive.org/details/bim_eighteenth-century_taxation-no-tyranny-an-_johnson-samuel_1775_0/page/n89/mode/2up?q=yelps

Jordan, W.D. (1968/2012) *White Over Black: American Attitudes toward the Negro: 1550–1812*. University of North Carolina Press.

Judy, R. (1991) "Kant and the Negro." *Surfaces*, 1. https://doi.org/10.7202/1065256a

Kant, I. (1796/2006) *Anthropology from a Pragmatic Point of View*, edited by R.B. Louden. Cambridge University Press.

Kendi, I.X. (2016) *Stamped from the Beginning*. Bold Type Books.

Kennedy, R.F. (2017) "Why I Teach About Race and Ethnicity in the Classical World." *The Medium*. https://eidolon.pub/why-i-teach-about-race-and-ethnicity-in-the-classical-world-ade379722170

Khan, M.A. (2009) *Islamic Jihad: A Legacy of Forced Conversion, Imperialism, and Slavery*. IUniverse.

Khatun, A. (2020) "The Whitewashing of Empire and History Within British Schools." *Amaliah*. https://www.amaliah.com/post/53452/whitewashing-empire-history-within-british-schools

King, M.L., Jr. (1963) "Letter from a Birmingham Jail." https://www.africa.upenn.edu/Articles_Gen/Letter_Birmingham.html

Kleingeld, P. (2014) "Kant's Second Thoughts on Colonialism." In Flikschuh, K. and Ypi, L. (eds) *Kant and Colonialism* (pp 43–67). Oxford University Press.

Kleingeld, P. (2019) "On Dealing with Kant's Sexism and Racism." *SGIR Review*, 2(2): 3–22.

Kwong, L. (2015) "What's in a Name: Zhongguo (or 'Middle Kingdom') Reconsidered." *The Historical Journal*, 58(3): 781–804. doi:10.1017/S0018246X14000570

Lather, P. (1998) "Critical Pedagogy and its Complicities: A Praxis of Stuck Places," *Educational Theory*, 48(4): 487–497.

Levine, D. (2014) *Interpreting Ethiopia: Observations of Five Decades.* Tschai Publishers.

Lewis, R. (2009) "Marcus Garvey's Global Vision." *76 King Street, Journal of Liberty Hall: Legacy of Marcus Garvey*, 1. https://www.google.com/books/edition/76_King_Street_Journal_of_Liberty_Hall_T/p4JoPdCQZ24C?hl=en&gbpv=1&dq=marcus+garvey+biography&pg=PA65&printsec=frontcover

Li, C. (2006) "The Confucian Ideal of Harmony." *Philosophy East and West*, 56(4): 583–603. http://www.jstor.org/stable/4488054

Liestman, D. (1993) " 'To Win Redeemed Souls from Heathen Darkness': Protestant Response to the Chinese of the Pacific Northwest in the Late Nineteenth Century." *The Western Historical Quarterly*, 24(2): 179–201. https://doi.org/10.2307/970935

Locke, J. (1823) *The Works of John Locke.* Printed for Thomas Tegg [etc.].

Luu, C. (2020) "Black English Matters." *Daily JSTOR.* https://daily.jstor.org/black-english-matters/

Mahmud, T. (1999) "Colonialism and Modern Constructions of Race: A Preliminary Inquiry." *University of Miami Law Review*, 53(4): 1219–1246.

Martin, B.L. (1991) "From Negro to Black to African American: The Power of Names and Naming." *Political Science Quarterly*, 106(1): 83–107. https://doi.org/10.2307/2152175

McCoskey, D.E. (2002) "Race Before 'Whiteness': Studying Identity in Ptolemaic Egypt." *Critical Sociology*, 28(1–2): 13–39. https://doi.org/10.1177/08969205020280010401

McCoskey, D.E. (2006) "Naming the Fault in Question: Theorizing Racism among the Greeks and Romans [Review of *The Invention of Racism in Classical Antiquity*, by B. Isaac]." *International Journal of the Classical Tradition*, 13(2): 243–267.

McCoskey, D.E. (2012) *Race: Antiquity and Its Legacy (Ancients & Moderns).* Oxford University Press.

Mellinkoff, R. (1993) *Outcasts: Signs of Otherness in Northern European Art of the Late Middle Ages.* University of California Press.

Mill, J.S. (1869) *On Liberty.* Longmans, Green, Reader, and Dyer.

Miller, R., Liu, K. and Ball, A.F. (2020) "Critical Counter-Narrative as Transformative Methodology for Educational Equity," *Review of Research in Education*, 44(1): 269–300.

Millett, P. (2007) "Aristotle and Slavery in Athens." *Greece & Rome*, 54(2): 178–209. http://www.jstor.org/stable/20204189

Mills, C.W. (1997) *The Racial Contract.* Cornell University Press.

Moore, C. (1974) "Were Marx and Engels White Racists? The Prolet-Aryan Outlook of Marxism." *Berkeley Journal of Sociology*, 19: 125–156. http://www.jstor.org/stable/41035216

Muthu, S. (2003) *Enlightenment against Empire.* Princeton University Press.

Nikuze, D. (2014) "The Genocide against the Tutsi in Rwanda: Origins, Causes, Implementation, Consequences, and the Post-genocide Era." *International Journal of Development and Sustainability*, 3(5): 1086–1098.

Nkrumah, K. (1963) *Africa Must Unite*. Heinemann.

Painter, N.I. (2011) *The History of White People*. W.W. Norton and Company.

Parry, J. (1996) *The Rise and Fall of Liberal Government in Victorian Britain*. Yale University Press.

Petts, D. (2011) *Pagan and Christian: Religious Change in Early Medieval Europe*. Bristol Classical Press.

Poser, R. (2021) "He Wants to Save Classics From Whiteness. Can the Field Survive?" *The New York Times*.

Pradella, L. (2014) "New Developmentalism and the Origins of Methodological Nationalism." *Competition & Change*, 18(2): 180–193. https://doi.org/10.1179/1024529414Z.00000000055

Raz, G. (2014) "Conversion of the Barbarians' [Huahu] Discourse as Proto-Han Nationalism." *The Medieval History Journal*, 17(2): 255–294. https://doi.org/10.1177/0971945814545862

Richard, F.G. and MacDonald, K.C. (2015) "From Invention to Ambiguity: The Persistence of Ethnicity in Africa." In Richard, F.G. and MacDonald, K.C. (eds) *Ethnic Ambiguity and the African Past* (pp 15–54). Left Coast Press, Inc.

Said, E.W. (1979) *Orientalism*. Vintage Books.

Said, E.W. (1985) "Orientalism Reconsidered." *Cultural Critique*, 1: 89–107.

Schuenemann, V.J., Peltzer, A., Welte, B., Van Pelt, W.P., Molak, M., Wang, C., Furtwängler, A., Urban, C., Reiter, E., Nieselt, K., Teßmann, B., Francken, M., Harvati, K., Haak, W., Schiffels, S. and Krause, J. (2017) "Ancient Egyptian Mummy Genomes Suggest an Increase of Sub-Saharan African Ancestry in Post-Roman Periods." *Nature Communications*, 8(1): 1–11. https://doi.org/10.1038/ncomms15694

Segal, R. (2001) *Islam's Black Slaves: The Other Black Diaspora*. Farrar Straus Giroux.

Smith, A. (1776/2000) *The Wealth of Nations*. W. Strahan and T. Cadell.

Stanley, B. (2010) "From 'the Poor Heathen' to 'the Glory and Honour of All Nations': Vocabularies of Race and Custom in Protestant Missions, 1844–1928." *International Bulletin of Missionary Research*, 34(1): 3–10. https://doi.org/10.1177/239693931003400102

Steinman, E. (2012) "Settler Colonial Power and the American Indian Sovereignty Movement: Forms of Domination, Strategies of Transformation." *American Journal of Sociology*, 117(4): 1073–1130.

Stuurman, S. (2008) "Herodotus and Sima Qian: History and the Anthropological turn in Ancient Greece and Han China." *Journal of World History*, 19(1): 1–40. https://www.jstor.org/stable/2007945

Talbot, M. (2018) "The Myth of Whiteness in Classical Sculpture." *The New Yorker*. https://www.newyorker.com/magazine/2018/10/29/the-myth-of-whiteness-in-classical-sculpture

Taylor, M. (2014) "Conservative Political Economy and the Problem of Colonial Slavery, 1823–1833." *The Historical Journal*, 57(4): 973–995. http://www.jstor.org/stable/24531972

Tunick, M. (2006) "Tolerant Imperialism: John Stuart Mill's Defense of British Rule in India." *The Review of Politics*, 68(4): 586–611. http://www.jstor.org/stable/20452826

Valls, A. (ed) (2005) *Race and Racism in Modern Philosophy*. Cornell University Press.

Ward, J.K. and Lott, T.L. (eds) (2002) *Philosophers on Race: Critical Essays*. Wiley-Blackwell.

Ware, T. (2015) *The Orthodox Church: An Introduction to Eastern Christianity*. Penguin Books.

Weiming, T. (2024, February 15) "Confucianism." *Encyclopedia Britannica*. https://www.britannica.com/topic/Confucianism

Wells-Barnett, I.B. (1892/2005) *Southern Horrors: Lynch Law In All Its Phases*. Project Gutenberg Ebook of Southern Horrors.

West, B.A. (2008) *Encyclopedia of the Peoples of Asia and Oceania*. Facts on File.

Whitmarsh, T. (2018) "When Homer Envisioned Achilles Did He See a Black Man." *Aeon*. https://aeon.co/essays/when-homer-envisioned-achilles-did-he-see-a-black-man

Wills, M. (2019) "Whitewashing American History." *Daily JSTOR*. https://daily.jstor.org/whitewashing-american-history/

Winkelmann, J.J. (1764) *Geschichte der Kunst des Alterthums*. Akademischen Verlage.

Yates, B. (2017) "Ethnicity as a Hindrance for Understanding Ethiopian History: An Argument Against an Ethnic Late Nineteenth Century." *History in Africa*, 44 : 101–131. doi:10.1017/hia.2016.13

## Chapter 3

Acemoglu, D., Johnson, S. and Robinson, J.A. (2002) "Reversal of Fortune: Geography and Institutions in the Making of the Modern World Income Distribution." *The Quarterly Journal of Economics*, 117(4): 1231–1294. https://doi.org/10.1162/003355302320935025.

Adi, H. (2012) "Africa and the Transatlantic Slave Trade." *B.B.C.* https://www.bbc.co.uk/history/british/abolition/africa_article_01.shtml

Adi, H. (2022) *African and Caribbean People in Britain*. Penguin.

Agutierrez, R.A. (1991) *When Jesus Came, the Corn Mothers Went Away: Marriage, Sexuality, and Power in New Mexico, 1500–1846*. Stanford University Press.

Akinbode, A. (2021) "Nzinga Mbande: The African Queen Who Fought Portuguese Colonialism for 37 Years." https://www.thehistoryville.com/nzinga-mbande/#:~:text=Queen%20Nzinga%20Mbande%20of%20the%20Ambundu%20Kingdoms%20of,40%20years%2C%20from%20the%2016 20s%20to%20the%201660s

Asiwaju, A.I. (1985) *Partitioned Africans: Ethnic Relations Across Africa's International Boundaries 1884–1984*. St. Martin's Press.

Atlantic Charter (1941, August 14) https://www.nato.int/cps/en/natohq/official_texts_16912.htm https://web.archive.org/web/20211208233557/https://www.nato.int/cps/en/natohq/official_texts_16912.htm

Barry, B. (1998) *Senegambia and the Atlantic Slave Trade*. Cambridge University Press.

Barton, K.C. (1997) " 'Good Cooks and Washers': Slave Hiring, Domestic Labor, and the Market in Bourbon County, Kentucky." *The Journal of American History*, 84(2): 436–460. https://doi.org/10.2307/2952566

Bell, D. (1989) *And We Are Not Saved*. Basic Books.

Bellah, R.N. (1975) *The Broken Covenant: American Civil Religion in Time of Trial*. Seabury Press.

Blaut, J.M. (1989) "Colonialism and the Rise of Capitalism." *Science & Society*, 53(3): 260–296. http://www.jstor.org/stable/40404472

Boxell, L., Dalton, J. and Leung, T.C. (2019) "The Slave Trade and Conflict in Africa, 1400–2000." Munich Personal RePEc Archive, MPRA Paper 94468. Stanford University. https://mpra.ub.uni-muenchen.de/94468/

Braga, R. (2020) "Portugal, Colonialism and Racial Justice: From Denial to Reparation." *OpenDemocracy*. https://www.opendemocracy.net/en/democraciaabierta/justicia-racial-colonialismo-portugal-negacionismo-reparaci%C3%B3n-en/

Braveheart-Jordan, M. and DeBruyn, L. (1995) "So She May Walk in Balance: Integrating the Impact of Historical Trauma in the Treatment of Native American Indian Women." In Adleman, J. and Enguídanos, G.M. (eds) *Racism in the Lives of Women: Testimony, Theory, and Guides to Antiracist Practice* (pp 345–368). Harrington Park Press/Haworth Press.

Briney, A. (2020) "A Brief History of the Age of Exploration." *Thought.com*. https://www.thoughtco.com/age-of-exploration-1435006

Carney, J. and Rosomoff, R.N. (2011) *In the Shadow of Slavery: Africa's Botanical Legacy in the Atlantic World*. University of California Press.

Casely, H.J.E. (1903/2007) *Gold Coast Native Institutions. With Thoughts upon a Healthy Imperial Policy for the Gold Coast and Ashanti*. Sweet & Maxwell. https://archive.org/details/goldcoastnativei00hayfiala/page/n3/mode/2up

Coates, R.D. (2003) "Law and the Cultural Production of Race and Racialized Systems of Oppression: Early American Court Cases." *American Behavioral Scientist*, 47(3): 329–351. https://doi.org/10.1177/0002764203256190

da Silva, F.R. (2021) "The Profits of the Portuguese–Brazilian Transatlantic Slave Trade: Challenges and Possibilities." *Slavery & Abolition*, 42(11): 77–104.

Deetz, K.F. (2018) "How Enslaved Chefs Helped Shape American Cuisine." *Smithsonian Magazine*. https://www.smithsonianmag.com/history/how-enslaved-chefs-helped-shape-american-cuisine-180969697/

de Sousa, A.N. (2021) "How Portugal Silenced 'Centuries of Violence and Trauma'." *Aljazeera*.

Diamond, J. (1997/2017) *Guns, Germs, and Steel: The Fates of Human Societies*, 20th anniversary edn. W.W. Norton & Company.

Doesticks, P. and Butler, P. (1859) *Great Auction Sale of Slaves, at Savannah, Georgia*. American Anti-Slavery Society. https://archive.org/details/greatauctionsale00does

Emmanuel, K. (2015) "What Africa's Slaves Brought to American Cuisine." *Pulse.com*. https://www.pulse.com.gh/ece-frontpage/what-africas-slaves-brought-to-american-cuisine/2rkxxvd

*Encyclopedia Britannica* (2023) "British Empire." *Encyclopedia Britannica*. https://www.britannica.com/place/British-Empire

Esseks, J.D. (1971) "Political Independence and Economic Decolonization: The Case of Ghana Under Nkrumah." *Western Political Quarterly*, 24(1): 59–64. https://doi.org/10.1177/106591297102400110

Fage, J.D. and McCaskie, T.C. (2023, November 7) "Western Africa." *Encyclopedia Britannica*. https://www.britannica.com/place/western-Africa

Fitzgerald, C. (2016) "African American Slave Medicine of the 19th Century." *Undergraduate Review*, 12: 44–50. http://vc.bridgew.edu/undergrad_rev/vol12/iss1/1

Flemming, A. (2020) "The Origins of Vaccination." *Nature.Org*. https://www.nature.com/articles/d42859-020-00006-7

Fonchingong, T.F. (2006) "The State and Development in Africa." *African Journal of International Affairs*, 8(1&2): 1–21.

Ganeshram, R. (2022) "In the Late 18th Century, Philadelphia was a City of High-End Cuisine: However, Few Know that Many of its Culinary Masters were of African Descent like Hercules Posey." *B.B.C.* https://www.bbc.com/travel/article/20220201-hercules-posey-george-washingtons-unsung-enslaved-chef

Gbadamosi, N. (2022) "Africa's Stolen Art Debate Is Frozen in Time." *Foreign Policy*. https://foreignpolicy.com/2022/05/15/africa-art-museum-europe-restitution-debate-book-colonialism-artifacts/

Gilroy, P. (2004) *"There Ain't no Black in the Union Jack": The Cultural Politics of Race and Nation*. University of Chicago Press.

Green, E. (2013) "Explaining African Ethnic Diversity." *International Political Science Review*, 34(3): 235–253. https://doi.org/10.1177/0192512112455075

Griffiths, I. (1986) "The Scramble for Africa: Inherited Political Boundaries." *The Geographical Journal*, 152(2): 204–216. https://doi.org/10.2307/634762

Hall, M. (2000) *Archaeology and the Modern World: Colonial Transcripts in South Africa and the Chesapeake*. Routledge.

Harris, C.I. (1993) "Whiteness as Property." *Harvard Law Review*, 133(9).

Harris, J.B. (2011) *High on the Hog: A Culinary Journey from Africa to America*. Bloomsbury USA.

Harris, J. (2023) "9 Facts About the Transatlantic Slave Trade." *History.com*. https://www.history.com/news/transatlantic-slave-trade-facts

Hassan, M.-R.S. and Robleh, S.M. (2004) "Islamic Revival and Education in Somalia." In *Educational Strategies Among Muslims in the Context of Globalization: Some National Case Studies* (vol 3, pp 141–163). Brill.

Hawthorne, W. (2001) "Nourishing a Stateless Society during the Slave Trade: The Rise of Balanta Paddy-Rice Production in Guinea-Bissau," *The Journal of African History*, 42(1): 1–24. http://www.jstor.org/stable/3647213

Helo, A. and Onuf, P. (2003) "Jefferson, Morality, and the Problem of Slavery." *The William and Mary Quarterly*, Third Series, 60(3): 583–614.

Higginbotham, A.L. (1978) *In the Matter of Color: Race and the American Legal Process*. Oxford University Press.

Hoffman, P.T. (2017) *Why Did Europe Conquer the World?*. Princeton University Press.

Hublin, J., Bailey, S.E., Freidline, S.E., Neubauer, S., Skinner, M.M., Bergmann, I., Le Cabec, A., Benazzi, S., Harvati, K. and Gunz, P. (2017) "New Fossils from Jebel Irhoud, Morocco, and the Origin of Homo Sapiens." *Nature*, 546(7657): 289–292. https://doi.org/10.1038/nature22336

Huttenback, R.A. (1973) "The British Empire as a 'White Man's Country': Racial Attitudes and Immigration Legislation in the Colonies of White Settlement." *Journal of British Studies*, 13(1): 108–137. http://www.jstor.org/stable/175372

Iliffe, J. (1967) "The Organization of the Maji Maji Rebellion." *The Journal of African History*, 8(3): 495–512. http://www.jstor.org/stable/179833

James, P. (2004) "300 Years of African American Invention and Innovation." *The MIT Press Reader*. https://thereader.mitpress.mit.edu/300-years-of-african-american-invention-and-innovation/

Jasanoff, M. (2020) "Misremembering the British Empire." *The New Yorker*.

Khilnani, S. (2022) "The British Empire was Much Worse than You Realize." *The New Yorker*. https://www.newyorker.com/magazine/2022/04/04/the-british-empire-was-much-worse-than-you-realize-caroline-elkinss-legacy-of-violence

Krause, J. (2021) "Islam and Anti-Colonial Rebellions in North and West Africa, 1914–1918." *The Historical Journal*, 64(3): 674–695. doi:10.1017/S0018246X20000357

Lester, A. (2022) "The British Empire and Race: A Debate with Robert Tombs." *Snapshots of Empire.* University of Sussex. https://blogs.sussex.ac.uk/snapshotsofempire/2022/02/01/the-british-empire-and-race/

Lewis, M. and Clark, W. (1989) *The Journals of Lewis and Clark.* Penguin/Random House.

Lim, W. (2020) "The Racial Contract: Interview with Philosopher Charles W. Mills." *Harvard Political Review.* https://harvardpolitics.com/interview-with-charles-w-mills/

Linsley, B. (2013) "Feeble to Effeminacy: Race and Gender in the British Imperial Consciousness 1837–1901." *Grand Valley Journal of History*, 2(2): Article 1. https://scholarworks.gvsu.edu/gvjh/vol2/iss2/1

Longmore, J. (2007) "'Cemented by the Blood of a Negro'? The Impact of the Slave Trade on Eighteenth-Century Liverpool." In D. Richardson, S. Schwarz and A. Tibbles (eds) *Liverpool and Transatlantic Slavery* (pp 227–251). Liverpool University Press.

Martin, D. (2007) *Rebuilding Brand America: What We Must Do to Restore Our Reputation and Safeguard the Future of American Business Abroad.* AMACOM.

McKinley, C.E. (2023) "Contemporary Forms of Historical Oppression: Experiences and Consequences of Gendered IPV and Sexual Violence Experiences." In *Understanding Indigenous Gender Relations and Violence* (pp 67–84). Springer. https://doi.org/10.1007/978-3-031-18583-0_6

Michalopoulos, S. and Papaioannou, E. (2011) "The Long-Run Effects of the Scramble for Africa." NBER Working Paper No. 17620. https://www.nber.org/system/files/working_papers/w17620/w17620.pdf

Mills, C.W. (1997/2020) *The Racial Contract.* Cornell University Press.

Mondragon, B. (2022) "Uprooted: Doorway Gardens and African Plant Cultivation in the Colonial Atlantic World." *History in the Making*, 15: Article 10. https://scholarworks.lib.csusb.edu/history-in-the-making/vol15/iss1/10

Monticello (nd) "Thomas Jefferson and Sally Hemings: A Brief Account." https://www.monticello.org/thomas-jefferson/jefferson-slavery/thomas-jefferson-and-sally-hemings-a-brief-account/

Morrissette, P.J. (1994) "The Holocaust of First Nation People: Residual Effects on Parenting and Treatment Implications." *Contemporary Family Therapy*, 16: 381–392. https://doi.org/10.1007/BF02197900

Mohamoud, A.A. (2006) *State Collapse and Post-conflict Development in Africa: The Case of Somalia (1960–2001).* Purdue University Press.

Moyd, M. (2017) "Resistance and Rebellions (Africa)." *International Encyclopedia of the First World War.* https://encyclopedia.1914-1918-online.net/pdf/1914-1918-Online-resistance_and_rebellions_africa-2017-06-20.pdf

Mulcare, D. (2008) "Restricted Authority: Slavery Politics, Internal Improvements, and the Limitation of National Administrative Capacity." *Political Research Quarterly*, 61: 671–685.

Murrin, J.M. (2000) "The Jeffersonian Triumph and American Exceptionalism." *Journal of the Early Republic*, 20(1): 1–25. https://doi.org/10.2307/3124828

Mutter Edu Staff (2022) "Medicinal Practices of Enslaved Peoples." *The College of Physicians of Philadelphia*. https://collegeofphysicians.org/programs/education-blog/medicinal-practices-enslaved-peoples

Nagel, J. (2000) "Ethnicity and Sexuality." *Annual Review of Sociology*, 26(1): 107–133.

Newman, B. (2020) "Throne of Blood: It's Time for the British Royal Family to Make Amends for Centuries of Profiting from Slavery." *Slate*.

Nkrumah, K. (1945) "Fifth Pan-African Congress, Declaration to Colonial People of the World (Manchester, England)." https://www.modernghana.com/news/236966/nkrumah-and-pan-africanism.html

NMAAHC (nd) "The Historical Significance of Doulas and Midwives." *National Museum of African American History and Culture, Smithsonian Institute*. https://nmaahc.si.edu/explore/stories/historical-significance-doulas-and-midwives

Norton, K. (2022) "How African Indigenous Knowledge Helped Shape Modern Medicine." *NOVA*. https://www.pbs.org/wgbh/nova/article/smallpox-epidemic-boston-onesimus-african-indigenous/

Nunn, N. (2017) "Understanding the Long-run Effects of Africa's Slave Trades." *Vox EU. CEPR*. https://cepr.org/voxeu/columns/understanding-long-run-effects-africas-slave-trades

O'Brien, C.C. (1996) "Thomas Jefferson: Radical and Racist." *The Atlantic*.

Ojo, O. (2008) "The Organization of the Atlantic Slave Trade in Yorubaland, ca.1777 to ca.1856." *The International Journal of African Historical Studies*, 41(1): 77–100. http://www.jstor.org/stable/40282457

O'Rourke, K.H., Prados de la Escosura, L. and Daudin, G. (2010) "Trade and Empire." In Broadbery, S. and O'Rourke, K.H. (eds) *The Cambridge Economic History of Modern Europe, Vol.1 1700–1870* (pp 96–121). Cambridge University Press.

Paice, E. (2019) "The First World War in East Africa." *British Library. World War One*. https://www.bl.uk/world-war-one/articles/the-first-world-war-in-east-africa#:~:text=Outbreak%20of%20the%20First%20World, fostered%20a%20degree%20of%20entente

Pasley, J. (2019) "15 American Landmarks that were Built by Slaves." *IBW21*. https://ibw21.org/editors-choice/15-american-landmarks-that-were-built-by-slaves/

Perry, M. (2016) "Uncovering the Brutal Truth about the British Empire." *The Guardian*. https://www.theguardian.com/news/2016/aug/18/uncovering-truth-british-empire-caroline-elkins-mau-mau

Pettigrew, W.A. (2016) *Freedom's Debt: The Royal African Company and the Politics of the Atlantic Slave Trade, 1672–1752*. Omohundro Institute and UNC Press.

Pinckney, T.C. and Kimuyu, P.K. (1994) "Land Tenure Reform in East Africa: Good, Bad or Unimportant?" *Journal of African Economies*, 3(1): 1–28. https://doi.org/10.1093/oxfordjournals.jae.a036794

Pruitt, S. (2021 [updated 2023]) "How Portugal's Seafaring Expertise Launched the Age of Exploration." *History*. https://www.history.com/news/portugal-age-exploration

Rahal, M. (2022) "The Algerian War: Cause Célèbre of Anticolonialism." *JSTOR Daily*. https://daily.jstor.org/algerian-war-cause-celebre-anticolonialsm/

Rawls, J. (1971/1999) *A Theory of Justice*. Belknap Press. https://daily.jstor.org/algerian-war-cause-celebre-anticolonialism/

Ray, V. (2019) "A Theory of Racialized Organizations." *American Sociological Review*, 84(1): 26–53. https://doi.org/10.1177/0003122418822335

Robinson, D. (1975) "The Islamic Revolution of Futa Toro." *The International Journal of African Historical Studies*, 8(2): 185–221. https://doi.org/10.2307/216648

Rodney, W. (1982) *How Europe Underdeveloped Africa*. Howard University Press.

Roque, A.C. (2018) "The Sofala Coast (Mozambique) in the 16th Century: Between the African Trade Routes and Indian Ocean Trade." In Walkier, I., Manuel, J. R. and Kaarsholm, P. (eds) *Fluid Networks and Hegmonic Powers in the Western Indian Ocean*. Centro de Estudos Internacionais.

Roque, R. (2021) "Transnational Isolates: Portuguese Colonial Race Science and the Foreign World." *Perspectives on Science*, 30: 108–136.

SAHO (2011/2019) "The Fight against Colonialism and Imperialism in Africa." *South African History Online*. https://www.sahistory.org.za/article/fight-against-colonialism-and-imperialism-africa

Samatar, A. (1988) *Socialist Somalia: Rhetoric and Reality*. Zed Books.

Samson, W. (2021) "In the Angolan Civil War, Angola Had an Unlikely Ally in Cuba." *War History Online*. https://www.warhistoryonline.com/cold-war/angolan-civil-war-cuba.html

Sherwood, M. (2015) "An Information 'Black Hole:' World War I in Africa." In Karvalics, L.Z. (ed) *Information History of the First World War*. Harmattan Publishing. https://www.voicesofwarandpeace.org/wp-content/uploads/2016/10/UNESCO_sherwood-m.pdf

Sommerville, D.M. (2004) *Rape and Race in the Nineteenth-Century South*. University of North Carolina Press.

Spencer-Wood, S. (2016) "Feminist Theorizing of Patriarchal Colonialism, Power Dynamics, and Social Agency Materialized in Colonial Institutions." *International Journal of Historical Archaeology*, 20(3): 477–491.

Stavisky, L.P. (1949) "Negro Craftsmanship in Early America." *The American Historical Review*, 54(2): 315–325. https://doi.org/10.2307/1845390

Sunseri, T. (2003) "Reinterpreting a Colonial Rebellion: Forestry and Social Control in German East Africa, 1874–1915." *Environmental History*, 8(3): 430–451. https://doi.org/10.2307/3986203

Tapalaga, A. (2023) "This Is How Slavery Fueled the Industrial Revolution." *History of Yesterday*. https://historyofyesterday.com/this-is-how-slavery-fueled-the-industrial-revolution/

Tetzlaff, R. (2022) "The Phase of Formal Colonization (1880–1960)." In Tetzlaff, R. (ed) *Africa* (pp 77–91). Springer. https://doi.org/10.1007/978-3-658-34982-0_4

Tillery, A.B., Jr. (2009) "Tocqueville as Critical Race Theorist: Whiteness as Property, Interest Convergence, and the Limits of Jacksonian Democracy." *Political Research Quarterly*, 62(4): 639–652. http://www.jstor.org/stable/25594436

Thompson, P.S. (2008) "Bhambatha and the Zulu Rebellion: 1906." *Journal of Natal and Zulu History*, 28: 32–59. https://researchspace.ukzn.ac.za/bitstream/handle/10413/8420/Thompson_Paul_2008.pdf

Trotter, J.W. Jr. (2019) *Workers on Arrival: Black Labor in the Making of America*. University of California Press.

Twitty, M.W. (2021) "How Rice Shaped the American South." *B.B.C.* https://www.bbc.com/travel/article/20210307-how-rice-shaped-the-american-south

Wheaton, T. (2001) "Colonial African American Plantation Villages." In Joseph, J.W. and Zierden, M.A. (eds) *Another's Country: Archaeological and Historical Perspectives on Cultural Interactions in the Southern Colonies* (pp 30–44). University of Alabama Press.

Williams, Y. (2020) "Why Thomas Jefferson's Anti-Slavery Passage was Removed from the Declaration of Independence: The Founding Fathers were Fighting for Freedom – Just Not for Everyone." *History.com*. https://www.history.com/news/declaration-of-independence-deleted-anti-slavery-clause-jefferson

Wilson, H.S. (1994) *African Decolonization*. E. Arnold. https://archive.org/details/africandecoloniz0000wils/page/n1/mode/2up

Woldeyes, Y.G. (2020) "The Battle of Adwa: An Ethiopian Victory that Ran Against the Current of Colonialism." *The Conversation*. https://theconversation.com/the-battle-of-adwa-an-ethiopian-victory-that-ran-against-the-current-of-colonialism-132360

Wolfe, P. (2006) "Settler Colonialism and the Elimination of the Native." *Journal of Genocide Research*, 8(4): 387–409.

Zabecki, D.T. (2006) "How North Africa Became a Battleground in World War II." *History Net*. https://www.historynet.com/how-north-africa-became-a-battleground-in-world-war-ii/

Zhang, A. (2023) "Harris Rejects DeSantis' Offer to Debate Florida's New Black History Standards." *Politico*. https://www.politico.com/news/2023/08/01/kamala-harris-ron-desantis-black-history-00109170

## Chapter 4

Alexander, O. (2022) "Haïtien immigration to the U.S. (1972–)." *Blackpast. org*. https://www.blackpast.org/african-american-history/haitien-immigration-to-the-u-s-1972/

Altman, I. (2007) "The Revolt of Enriquillo and the Historiography of Early Spanish America." *The Americas*, 63(4): 587–614. http://www.jstor.org/stable/4491300

Ballard, J.R. (1998) *Upholding Democracy: The United States Military Campaign in Haiti, 1994–1997*. Praeger.

Bishop, M. and Fernandez, T. (2017) "80 Years on, Dominicans and Haitians Revisit Painful Memories of Parsley Massacre." *NPR*. https://www.npr.org/sections/parallels/2017/10/07/555871670/80-years-on-dominicans-and-haitians-revisit-painful-memories-of-parsley-massacre

Blackburn, R. (2006) "Haiti, Slavery, and the Age of the Democratic Revolution." *The William and Mary Quarterly*, Third Series, 63(4): 643–674. https://www.jstor.org/stable/4491574

Blassingame, J.W. (1969) "The Press and American Intervention in Haiti and the Dominican Republic, 1904–1920." *Caribbean Studies*, 9(2): 27–43.

Bodenheimer, R. (2019) "The Haitian Revolution: Successful Revolt by an Enslaved People." *Thought Co*. https://www.thoughtco.com/haitian-revolution-4690762#:~:text=In%20October%201790%2C%20affranc his%20led%20their%20first%20armed,some%20rights%20to%20affranc his%2C%20which%20angered%20White%20colonists

Boisvert, J. (2001) "Colonial Hell and Female Slave Resistance in Saint-Domingue." *Journal of Haitian Studies*, 7(1): 73.

Bradshaw, J. (2023) "Saint-Domingue Revolution." *64 Parishes*. https://64 parishes.org/entry/saint-domingue-revolution

Burgard, J.-M. and Farole, T. (2011) "When Trade Preferences and Tax Breaks are No Longer Enough: The Challenge of Adjustment in the Dominican Republic's Free Zones." In Farole, T. (ed) *Special Economic Zones: Progress, Emerging Challenges, and Future Directions* (pp 159–182). The World Bank.

Charles, J. and Iglesias, J.A. (2020) "Ten Years After Haiti's Earthquake: A Decade of Aftershocks and Unkept Promises." *The Miami Herald*. https://pulitzercenter.org/stories/ten-years-after-haitis-earthquake-decade-aftershocks-and-unkept-promises

Danticat, E. (2015) "The Long Legacy of Occupation in Haiti." *The New Yorker*. https://www.newyorker.com/news/news-desk/haiti-us-occ upation-hundred-year-anniversary?utm_source=npr_newsletter&utm_ medium=email&utm_content=20211001&utm_term=5819359&utm_ campaign=money&utm_id=46765242&orgid=305&utm_att1=money

Dollar, J.E. (2008) "Haiti's Black Racial Essentialism and Unites States Involvement in the 2004 Removal of President Aristide." *St. Thomas Law Review*, 20(3): 642–669.

Doyle, K. (1994) "Hollow Diplomacy in Haiti." *World Policy Journal*, 11(1): 50–58.

Dubois, L. (2014) "How Will Haiti Reckon With the Duvalier Years." *The New Yorker*. https://www.newyorker.com/news/news-desk/will-haiti-reckon-duvalier-years

*Encyclopedia Britannica* (2022) "Charles Leclerc." *Encyclopedia Britannica*. https://www.britannica.com/biography/Charles-Leclerc

*Encyclopedia Britannica* (2023, November 9) "Haitian Revolution." *Encyclopedia Britannica*. https://www.britannica.com/topic/Haitian-Revolution

Farmer, P. (2006) *The Uses of Haiti*. Common Courage Press.

Fick, C.E. (2007) "The Haitian Revolution and the Limits of Freedom: Defining Citizenship in the Revolutionary Era." *Social History*, 32(4): 394–414. DOI: 10.1080/03071020701616696

Geggus, D. (2006) "The Arming of Slaves in the Haitian Revolution." In Brown, C.L. and Morgan, P.D. (eds) *Arming Slaves: From Classical Times to the Modern Age* (pp 14–39). Yale Scholarship Online. https://doi.org/10.12987/yale/9780300109009.003.0009

Hazard, S. (1873) *Santo Domingo, Past and Present: With a Glance at Hayti*. Harper.

Hidalgo, D. (1997) "Charles Sumner and the Annexation of the Dominican Republic." *Itinerario*, 21(2): 51–65.

Inter-American Dialogue (2022) "Haiti's Turnaround and its Impact on Remittances." https://www.thedialogue.org/blogs/2022/11/haitis-turn around-and-its-impact-on-remittances/

Johnson, J.W. (1920) "Self-Determining Haiti." *The Nation*. leflambeau-foundation.org

Jones, T.D. (1993) "The Haitian Refugee Crisis: A Quest for Human Rights." *Michigan Journal of International Law*, 15(1): 77. https://repository.law.umich.edu/mjil/vol15/iss1/2

Knight, F.W. (2000) "The Haitian Revolution." *The American Historical Review*, 105(1): 103–115. https://doi.org/10.2307/2652438

Lawless, R. and MacLeod, M.J. (2023, July 27) "History of Haiti." *Encyclopedia Britannica*. https://www.britannica.com/topic/history-of-Haiti

L'Ouverture, T. (1799) "Letter to the Minister of Marine, 13 April 1799." https://learninglink.oup.com/access/content/von-sivers-3e-dashboard-resources/document-speeches-and-letters-of-toussaint-louverture-on-the-haitian-revolution-1793-1800

Lowenthal, A.F. (1970) "The United States and the Dominican Republic to 1965: Background to Intervention." *Caribbean Studies*, 10(2): 30–55.

Lucien, C. (2023) "The Lost Haitian Generation and the 1826 'French Debt': The Case for Restitution to Haiti." *University of Miami Inter-American Law Review*, 55(1): 133–139.

Mullin, L. (2018) "How the United States Crippled Haiti's Rice Industry." *Haiti Action Committee*. https://haitisolidarity.net/in-the-news/how-the-united-states-crippled-haitis-domestic-rice-industry/

National Parks Service (n.d.) https://nps.gov/places/tolson-s-chapel.htm

Nicholls, D. (1986) "Haiti: The Rise and Fall of Duvalierism." *Third World Quarterly*, 8(48): 1239–1252. http://www.jstor.org/stable/3991713

Olsen-Medina, K. and Batalova, J. (2020) "Haitian Immigrants in the United States." *Migration Policy*. https://www.migrationpolicy.org/article/haitian-immigrants-united-states

Palsson, C. (2021) "The Medium-run Effects of a Foreign Election Intervention: Haiti's Presidential Elections, 2010–2015." *Contemporary Economic Policy*, 40(2): 369–390.

Park, M. (2016) "Disaster divided: Two countries, one island, life-and-death differences." CNN. https://cnn.com/2016/10/11/americas/haiti-dominican-republic-visual-explainer

Porter, C., Méheut, C., Apuzzo, M. and Gebrekidan, S. (2022) "The Root of Haiti's Misery: Reparations to Enslavers." *New York Times*. https://www.nytimes.com/2022/05/20/world/americas/haiti-history-colonized-france.html

Rosalsky, G. (2021) "The Greatest Heist in History: How Haiti was Forced to Pay Reparations for Freedom." *NPR*. https://www.npr.org/sections/money/2021/10/05/1042518732/-the-greatest-heist-in-history-how-haiti-was-forced-to-pay-reparations-for-freed#:~:text=Over%20the%20next%20century%2C%20Haiti%20paid%20French%20slaveholders,independent%20country%27s%20ability%20to%20prosper.%22%20Righting%20The%20Wrongs

Roth, R. (2011) "Haiti Before and After Aristide's Return." *Counterpunch*. https://www.counterpunch.org/2011/04/11/haiti-before-and-after-aristide-s-return/

San Miguel, P.L. (1997/2005) *The Imagined Island: History, Identity, and Utopia in Hispaniola*. University of North Carolina.

Scherr, A. (2011) "Jefferson's 'Cannibals' Revisited: A Closer Look at His Notorious Phrase." *The Journal of Southern History*, 77(2): 251–282. http://www.jstor.org/stable/41306196

Shaw, J. (2020) "In the Name of the Mother: The Story of Susannah Mingo, a Woman of Color in the Early English Atlantic." *The William and Mary Quarterly*, 77(2): 177–210.

Shilliam, R. (2008) "What the Haitian Revolution Might Tell Us about Development, Security, and the Politics of Race." *Comparative Studies in Society and History*, 50(3): 778–808. http://www.jstor.org/stable/27563698

Smith, G. (1995) "Haiti: From Intervention to Intervasion." *Current History*, 94(589): 54–58.

Stone, E.W. (2013) "America's First Slave Revolt: Indians and African Slaves in Española." *Ethnohistory*, 60(2): 195–217. https://doi.org/10.1215/00141801-2018927.

Whitney, K.M. (1996) "Sin, Fraph, and the CIA: U.S. Covert Action in Haiti." *Southwestern Journal of Law and Trade in the Americas*, 3(2): 321.

Willis, K. (2023) "How Toussaint L'ouverture Rose from Slavery to Lead the Haitian Revolution." *History.com*. https://www.history.com/news/toussaint-louverture-haiti-revolution

Wines, M. (2004) "Aristide Says He Was Duped by U.S. Into Leaving Haiti." *The New York Times*. https://www.nytimes.com/2004/03/14/world/aristide-says-he-was-duped-by-us-into-leaving-haiti.html

Wolf, R. (2021) "U.S. Policy Toward Haitian Immigrants Is Part of a Long, Troubled History." *Immigration Impact*. https://immigrationimpact.com/2021/09/24/haitian-immigrants-border-patrol-history/

## Chapter 5

Akala, A. (2020) "Cost of Racism: U.S. Economy Lost $16 Trillion Because of Discrimination, Bank Says." *NPR*. https://www.npr.org/sections/live-updates-protests-for-racial-justice/2020/09/23/916022472/cost-of-racism-u-s-economy-lost-16-trillion-because-of-discrimination-bank-says

Barcia, M. and Harris, J. (2020) "The Slave Trade Continued Long After it Was Illegal – with Lessons for Today." *History News Network*. https://historynewsnetwork.org/article/178405

Berry, D.R. and Parker, N.D. (2023) "How U.S. Westward Expansion Breathed New Life into Slavery." *History.com*. https://www.history.com/news/westward-expansion-slavery

Brown, D.L. (2020) 'It was a modern-day lynching': Violent deaths reflect a brutal American legacy." *National Geographic*. https://www.nationalgeographic.com/history/article/history-of-lunching-violent-deaths-reflect-brutal-american-legacy

Buman, N.A. (2012) "Historiographical Examinations of the 1811 Slave Insurrection." *Louisiana History: The Journal of the Louisiana Historical Association*, 53(3): 318–337. http://www.jstor.org/stable/23266745

Century Foundation (2020) "Education Funding Gaps." https://tcf.org/content/report/closing-americas-education-funding/?agreed=1

Cobb, James C. 2017. "The Other Side of Confederate Memorial Day." *Time*. https://time.com/4750347/confederate-memorial-day-history/

Coleman, C. (2023) "How Literacy Became a Powerful Weapon in the Fight to End Slavery." History.com. https:/www.historycom.news/nat-turner-rebellion-literacy-slavery

Cooperman, J. (2014) "The Story of Segregation in St. Louis." *St. Louis Magazine*. https://www.stlmag.com/news/the-color-line-race-in-st.-louis/

Darity, W., Mullen, A.K., and Slaughter, M. (2022) "The Cumulative Costs of Racism and the Bill for Black Reparations." *The Journal of Economic Perspectives*, 36(2): 99–122. https://www.jstor.org/stable/27123976

Egerton, D.R. (1993) *Gabriel's Rebellion: The Virginia Slave Conspiracies of 1800 and 1802*. University of Carolina Press.

Egerton, D.R. (1999) *He Shall Go Out Free: The Lives of Denmark Vesey*. Rowman & Littlefield.

GAO (2022) "K-12 Education: Student Population Has Significantly Diversified, but Many Schools Remain Divided Along Racial, Ethnic, and Economic Lines." *Government Accountability Office*. https://www.gao.gov/products/gao-22-104737

Ghandnoosh, N. and Barry, C. (2023) "One in Five: Disparities in Crime and Policing." *Sentencing Project*. https://www.sentencingproject.org/reports/one-in-five-disparities-in-crime-and-policing/

Horne, G. (2015) *Confronting Black Jacobins: The U.S., the Haitian Revolution, and the Origins of the Dominican Republic*. Monthly Review Press.

Jackson, R. (2022) "Redlining: How Discriminatory Practices Led to Urban Heat Islands." *Louisiana State University Journal of Energy Law and Resources*. https://jelr.law.lsu.edu/2022/03/03/redlining-how-discriminatory-practices-led-to-urban-heat-islands/#_ftn29

Jefferson, T. (1820) *Letter to John Homes*. https://rumbletalk-images-upload.s3.amazonaws.com/6b6fc8d4dcaad4069e2a03799cde7943/1519739804-Thomas%20Jefferson%20to%20John%20Holmes%20-%20Thomas%20Jefferson%20_%20Exhibitions%20-%20Library%20of%20Congress.pdf

Keys, A. (2017) "The East St. Louis Race Riot Left Dozens Dead, Devastating a Community on the Rise." *The Smithsonian Magazine*. https://www.smithsonianmag.com/smithsonian-institution/east-st-louis-race-riot-left-dozens-dead-devastating-community-on-the-rise-180963885/

Lipsitz, G. (2011) *How Racism Takes Place*. Temple University Press.

Lockwood, B. (2020) "The History of redlining." *ThoughtCo*. https://www.thoughtco.com/redlining-definition-4157858

McCullar, E. (2020) "How Leaders of the Texas Revolution Fought to Preserve Slavery." *Texas Monthly*. https://www.texasmonthly.com/being-texan/how-leaders-texas-revolution-fought-preserve-slavery/

Morgan, I. (2022) "Equal is Not Good Enough." *The Education Trust*. https://edtrust.org/resource/equal-is-not-good-enough/

NAACP (2023) "The History of Lynching in America." https://naacp.org/ find-resources/history-explained/history-lynching-america

National Park Service (nd) "Denmark Vesey." *The United States Department of Interior.* https://www.nps.gov/people/denmark-vesey.htm

Nicholls, M. (2020) "Gabriel's Conspiracy (1800)." *Encyclopedia Virginia.* https://encyclopediavirginia.org/entries/gabriels-conspiracy-1800/

Paquette, R.L. and Egerton, D.R. (2004) "Of Facts and Fables: New Light on the Denmark Vesey Affair." *The South Carolina Historical Magazine,* 105(1): 8–48. http://www.jstor.org/stable/27570665

PBS (2023) "The East St. Louis Riot." *American Experience.* https://www.pbs. org/wgbh/americanexperience/features/garvey-riot/#:~:text=The%20 riots%20raged%20for%20nearly%20a%20week%2C%20leaving, and%20p roperty%20damage%20estimated%20at%20close%20to%20% 24400%2C000

Schipper, J. (2022) *Denmark Vesey's Bible: The Thwarted Revolt That Put Slavery and Scripture on Trial.* Princeton University Press.

Sexton, J. (2011) *The Monroe Doctrine: Empire and Nation in Nineteenth-century America.* Hill & Wang.

Shaffer, D.R. (2011) "Specter of the Haitian Revolution." *Civil War Emancipation.* https://cwemancipation.wordpress.com/2011/09/06/ specter-of-the-haitian-revolution/

Sitton, T. (2007) "Freedmen's Settlements." *Texas State Historical Association.* https://tshaonline.org/handbook/entries/freedmens-settlements

Texas Constitution (1845) "Article VIII." *Constitution of Texas.*

Thompson, T.M. (1992) "National Newspaper and Legislative Reactions to Louisiana's Deslondes Slave Revolt of 1811." *Louisiana History: The Journal of the Louisiana Historical Association,* 33(1): 5–29. http://www.jstor.org/ stable/4232918

Urofsky, M.I. (2023, October 27) "Compromise of 1850." *Encyclopedia Britannica.* https://www.britannica.com/event/Compromise-of-1850

U.S. Senate (n.d.) "The Enforcement Acts of 1870 and 1871." https://www. senate.gov/artandhistory/history/common/generic/EnforcementActs.htm

Ward, L.F. (1903) *Pure Sociology.* Macmillan.

Waters, L.A. (2023) "Jan. 8, 2011: Louisiana's Heroic Slave Revolt." *Zinn Education Project.* https://www.zinnedproject.org/news/tdih/louisianas-slave-revolt/

## Chapter 6

Allen, K. and Turner, C. (2022) " 'She's a Friend of My Mind': A Reflection of Black Sisterhood in Academia." *Race, Ethnicity, and Education.* 10.1080/ 13613324.2022.2088724

Associated Press (2022) "Kyrgios Losses in U.S. Open Quarterfinals to Khachanov, Breaks Rackets on Court." *Sports Illustrated.* https://www. si.com/tennis/2022/09/07/kyrgios-loses-in-u-s-open-quarterfinals-to- khachanov-breaks-rackets-on-court

Bailey, M. (2021) *Misogynoir Transformed: Black Women's Digital Resistance.* New York University Press.

B.B.C. (2020) "Black Lives Matter Founders: We Fought to Change History and We Won." *B.B.C.* https://www.bbc.com/news/world-us-canada-55106268

Bernabe, A.J. (2022) "Texas A&M University Basketball Coach Fights Back After Facing Criticism for Her Outfits." *ABC News.* https://abcnews. go.com/GMA/Style/texas-university-basketball-coach-fights-back-fac ing-criticism/story?id=82974831

Cardi B (2017) "No Limits." On G-Eazy's album *The Beautiful & Damned.* R.C.A. Records.

Carten, A. (2016) "The Racist Roots of Welfare Reform." *The New Republic.* https://newrepublic.com/article136200/racist-roots-welfare-reform

C.D.C. (2023) "Working Together to Reduce Black Maternal Mortality." *Centers for Disease Control and Prevention.* https://www.cdc.gov/healthequity/ features/maternal-mortality/index.html

Chabane, A. (2020) "1866 to 2020: Black Women Have Always Led the Sexual Assault Awareness Movement." *Equal Rights Advocates.* https:// www.equalrights.org/viewpoints/1866-to-2020-black-women-sexual-assault-awareness/

Clarke, J.H. (1971) "The Black Woman: A Figure in World History." *Essence,* May: 42–43.

Clinton, C. (1995) *Tara Revisited: Woman, War, & the Plantation Legend.* Abbeville Press.

Coles, S.M. and Pasek, J. (2020) "Intersectional Invisibility Revisited: How Group Prototypes Lead to the Erasure and Exclusion of Black Women." *European Continental Ancestry Group ResearchGate.* University of Michigan.

Crenshaw, K.W., Ocen, P., and Nanda, J. (2015) "Black Girls Matter: Pushed Out, Overpoliced and Underprotected." *African American Policy Forum.* https://www.aapf.org/_files/ugd/62e126_4011b574b92145e383234513a 24ad15a.pdf

Crumpton, T. (2020) "Women in Hip-Hop cannot Thrive While Misogynoir Exists." *Harpers Bazaar.* https://www.harpersbazaar.com/ culture/art-books-music/a33471010/megan-thee-stallion-shooting-misogynoir/

Curtis, S. (2023) "Walker, Aida Overton (1880–1914)." *St. James Encyclopedia of Popular Culture.* https://www.encyclopedia.com/media/encyclopedias-almanacs-transcripts-and-maps/walker-aida-overton-1880-1914

Davis, T. (2003) "Nina Simone, 1933–2003." *The Village Voice.* https:// www.villagevoice.com/nina-simone-1933-2003/

Equal Justice Initiative (2016) "Sexual Exploitation of Black Women." *Equal Justice Initiative.* https://eji.org/news/history-racial-injustice-sexual-explo itation-black-women/

Frith, S. (2009) "Searching for Sara Baartman." *The Johns Hopkins Magazine*. https://pages.jh.edu/jhumag/0609web/sara.html.

G-Eazy (2017) "No Limit." RCA.

Goldenberg, S. (2008) "U.S. Election: 'Terrorist Fist Bump' Cartoon Misfires." *The Guardian*. https://www.theguardian.com/world/2008/jul/15/barackobama.usa.

Hill, L. (1998) *The Miseducation of Lauryn Hill*. Ruffhouse Records and Columbia Records.

Hill Collins, P. (1991) *Black Feminist Thought: Knowledge, Consciousness, and the Politics of Empowerment*. Routledge.

Hipskind, K.M. (2009) "Consuming Mammy: A Review Essay on the Manifestations of Mammy in Twentieth-Century America." *Black Diaspora Review*, 1(1).

Horwitz, T. (2013) "The Mammy Washington Almost Had." *The Atlantic*. https://www.theatlantic.com/national/archive/2013/05/the-mammy-washington-almost-had/276431/

Hurston, Z.N. (1938) *Their Eyes Were Watching God*. J.M. Dent and Sons.

Jones, J. (1982) "My Mother Was Much of a Woman: Work, and the Family under Slavery." *Feminist Studies*, 8(2): 235–269. https://www.jstor.org/stable/3177562

Kelley, B.L.M. (2014) "Here's Some History Behind That 'Angry Black Woman' Riff the N.Y. Times Tossed Around." *The Root*. https://www.theroot.com/here-s-some-history-behind-that-angry-black-woman-rif-1790877149

King, C.I. (2022) "Slavery Reckoning Requires Confronting Sexual Exploitation of Black Women." *Washington Post*. https://www.washingtonpost.com/opinions/2022/04/29/reckoning-slavery-accounting-sexual-exploitation-black-women/

Lewis, D. (2022) "How Josephine Baker Learned to Hate the Nazis Before Most America." *Lithub*. https://lithub.com/how-josephine-baker-learned-to-hate-the-nazis-before-most-of-america/

Lee, L. (2021) "How Former N.F.L. Star Warrick Dunn's Mother Inspired Him to Tackle Housing Inequity." *CNN*. https://www.cnn.com/2021/12/23/us/warrick-dunn-charities-affordable-housing-iyw-trnd/index.html

Linchong, V. (2024) "She was the Queen of the Cakewalk and the Most Famous Black Woman of the Gilded Age." *Messy Nessy*. https://www.messynessychic.com/2022/05/03/she-was-the-queen-of-the-cakewalk-and-the-most-famous-black-woman-of-the-gilded-age/#google_vignette

Little, B. (2024) " 'Unbought and Unbossed': Why Shirley Chisholm Ran for President." *History*. https://www.history.com/news/shirley-chisholm-presidential-campaign-george-wallace

LL Cool J (1996) "Doin' It." *Mr. Smith*. Def Jam Recordings.

Lorde, A. (2006) "The Uses of the Erotic: The Erotic as Power." In Lovaas, K.E. and Jinkins, M.M. (eds) *Sexualities and Communication in Everyday Life* (pp 87–91). SAGE. https://uk.sagepub.com/sites/default/files/upm-binaries/11881_Chapter_5.pdf

Manring, M.M. (1998) *Slave in a Box: The Strange Career of Aunt Jemima.* University of Virginia Press.

McKinsey & Company (2022) *Women in the Workplace.* https://wiw-report.s3.amazonaws.com/Women_in_the_Workplace_2022.pdf

Mock, J. (2014) "Sex Workers Matter: Sharing My Own Complicated Experience." *Janet Moc.com.* https://janetmock.com/2014/01/30/janet-mock-sex-work-experiences/

N.W.A. (1988) "F★★★ Tha Police." *Straight Outta Compton.* Ruthless Records.

Olson, A. and Ott, M. (2020) "Aunt Jemima Brand Due to Racial Stereotype." *A.P. News.* https://apnews.com/article/race-and-ethnicity-lifestyle-business-us-news-ap-top-news-e71abe3b6e25e05fb7c76c20b86f6b60

Pilgrim, D. (2008) "The Sapphire Caricature." *Jim Crow Museum*, Ferris State University. https://jimcrowmuseum.ferris.edu/antiblack/sapphire.htm

Prasad, R. (2018) "Serena Williams and the Trope of the 'Angry Black Woman'." *B.B.C.* https://www.bbc.com/news/world-us-canada-45476500

Public Enemy (1989) *Fight the Power.* Motown Records.

Queen Latifah (1993) "U.N.I.T.Y." *Black Reign.* Motown.

Rihanna (2015) "Bitch Better Have My Money." Westbury Road and Roc Nation.

Shakur, T. (1992) "Changes." *Greatest Hits.* Amaru Entertainment, Death Row Records, Interscope Records, and Jive Records.

Stowe, H.B. (1852) *Uncle Tom's Cabin; or, Life Among the Lowly.* John P. Jewett and Company.

Thompson, C. (2020) "Mammy and How Racist Stereotypes Impact Black Women." *Minnesota Spokesman-Recorder.* https://spokesman-recorder.com/2020/02/05/mammy-and-how-racist-stereotypes-impact-black-women/

Toohey, G. (2020) "Body Camera Video: 6-year-old Girl Cries, Screams for Help as Orlando Police Arrest Her at School." *Orlando Sentinel.* https://www.orlandosentinel.com/2020/02/24/body-camera-video-6-year-old-girl-cries-screams-for-help-as-orlando-police-arrest-her-at-school/

West, C.M. and Johnson, K. (2013) "Sexual Violence in the Lives of African American Women." *National Online Resource Center on Violence Against Women.* https://vawnet.org/sites/default/files/materials/files/2016-09/AR_SVAAWomenRevised.pdf

West, K. (2005) "Gold Digger." *Late Registration.* Roc-A-Fella, Def Jam.

Williams, H (2023) "Surviving Academia: An Interview with Lorgia García Peña Pt. 2." *Black Perspectives*. https://www.aaihs.org/surviving-academia-an-interview-with-lorgia-garcia-pena-pt-2/

Williams, H.A. (2012) *Help Me Find My People: The African Search for Family Lost in Slavery*. University of North Carolina Press.

## Chapter 7

Assari, S. and Caldwell, C.H. (2018) "High Risk of Depression in High-Income African American Boys." *Journal of Racial and Ethnic Health Disparities*, 5: 808–819. https://doi.org/10.1007/s40615-017-0426-1

Assari, S., Lankarani, M.M., and Caldwell, C.H. (2018) "Does Discrimination Explain High Risk of Depression among High-Income African American Men?" *Behavioural Sciences*, 8(4): 40. doi: 10.3390/bs8040040

Badger, E., Miller, C.C., Pearce, A., and Quealy, K. (2018) "Extensive Data Shows Punishing Reach of Racism for Black Boys." *The New York Times*. https://www.nytimes.com/interactive/2018/03/19/upshot/race-class-white-and-black-men.htmll

Baldwin, J. (1955/2012) *Notes of a Native Son*. Beacon Press.

Bates, K.G. (2005) "Race and 'King Kong'." *NPR*. https://www.npr.org/templates/story/story.php?storyId=5066156

Bates, K.G. (2019) "When Civility Is Used As a Cudgel Against People of Color." *NPR*. https://www.npr.org/sections/codeswitch/2019/03/14/700897826/when-civility-is-used-as-a-cudgel-against-people-of-color

Bell, R.J. (2013) "John Jea." *African American National Biography*. https://doi.org/10.1093/acref/9780195301731.013.35768

Berger, M. (2016) "Black Dandies, Style Rebels With a Cause." *New York Times*. https://archive.nytimes.com/lens.blogs.nytimes.com/2016/06/16/black-dandies-style-rebels-with-a-cause/

Booker, B. (2020) "Uncle Ben's Changing Name to Ben's Original After Criticism of Racial Stereotyping." *NPR*. https://www.npr.org/sections/live-updates-protests-for-racial-justice/2020/09/23/916012582/uncle-bens-changing-name-to-ben-s-original-after-criticism-of-racial-stereotypin

Boskin, J. (1986) *Sambo: The Rise and Demise of An American Jester*. Oxford University Press.

Brockell, G. (2022) "The Senate's First Woman Also Its Last Enslaver." *The Washinton Post*. https://www.washingtonpost.com/history/2022/01/10/rebecca-felton-last-enslaver/

Brooms. D.R. (2018) "Exploring Black Male Initiative Programs: Potential and Possibilities for Supporting Black Male Success in College." *The Journal of Negro Education*, 87(1): 59–72. https://doi.org/10.7709/jnegroeducation.87.1.0059

Brown-Nagin, T. (2022) "Constance Baker Motley Taught the Nation How to Win Justice." *Smithsonian Magazine*. https://www.smithsonianmag.com/history/constance-baker-motley-how-to-win-justice-180979527/

Callahan, A. (2020) "Why Black Male Teachers Matter." American Federation of Teachers.

Camera, L. (2020) "School Suspension Data Shows Glaring Disparities in Discipline by Race." *USNews*. https://www.usnews.com/news/education-news/articles/2020-10-13/school-suspension-data-shows-glaring-disparities-in-discipline-by-race

Clark, C. (2005) *Shuffling to Ignominy: The Tragedy of Sepin Fetchit*. IUniverse.

Coleman, C. (2023) "How Literacy Became a Powerful Weapon in the Fight to End Slavery." *History*. https://www.history.com/news/nat-turner-rebellion-literacy-slavery

*Django Unchained* (2012) The Weinstein Company and Columbia Pictures.

Edelman, A. (2023) "Tennessee Democrats expelled by GOP over protests win back their seats."NBC News. https://www.nbcnews.com/politics/elections/tennessee-democrats-expelled-gop-protests-special-election-rcna97374

Elliott, S. (2007) "Uncle Ben, Board Chairman." *The New York Times*. https://www.nytimes.com/2007/03/30/business/media/30adco.html

Equal Justice Initiative (2020) "Reconstruction in America." https://eji.org/report/reconstruction-in-america/

Eshun, E. (2016) "The Subversive Power of the Black Dandy." *The Guardian*. https://www.theguardian.com/artanddesign/2016/jul/04/the-subversive-power-of-the-black-dandy

Foley, M.B. (2020) "Lynching Preachers: How Black Pastors Resisted Jim Crow and White Pastors Incited Racial Violence." *The Conversation*. https://theconversation.com/lynching-preachers-how-black-pastors-resisted-jim-crow-and-white-pastors-incited-racial-violence-129963

Ford, L.K. (2011) *Deliver Us from Evil: The Slavery Question in the Old South*. Oxford University Press.

Gershenson, S., Hart, C., Hyman, J., Lindsay, C., and Papageorge, N.W. (2022) "The Long-Run Impacts of Same-Race Teachers." *American Economic Journal: Economic Policy*, 14(4): 300–342.

Griffith, D.W. (1915) *Birth of a Nation*. Produced by David W. Griffith Corporation and Epoch Production Corporation.

Gustkey, E. (1990) "80 Years Ago, the Truth Hurt: Johnson's Victory Over Jeffries Taught Lesson to White America." *Los Angeles Times*. https://www.latimes.com/archives/la-xpm-1990-07-08-sp-462-story.html

Hensley-Clancy, M. (2023) "NBA Star Ja Morant Accused in Police Reports of Punching Teen, Making Threats." *The Washington Post*. https://www.washingtonpost.com/sports/2023/03/01/ja-morant-punch-teen-laser/

Henson, J. (1848) *The Life of Josiah Henson, Formerly a Slave, Now an Inhabitant of Canada as Narrated by Himself.* Author D. Phelps. https://docsouth.unc.edu/neh/henson49/henson49.html

History.com Editors (2024) "Civil Rights Movement." History.com. https://www.history.com/topics/black-history/civil-rights-movement

Hoekstra, D. (2000) "The Happy Hustler." *Chicago Reader.* https://chicagoreader.com/news-politics/the-happy-hustler/

Holliday, D. (2018) "Georgia's readmission to the Union." *The Marshall News Messenger.* https://www.marshallnewsmessenger.com/opinion/columns/georgias-readmission-to-the-union/article_afb9fc3e-8865c-5b5d-ac2f-0e97f68b32e.html

James, F. (2010) "Can a President be an Angry Black Man?" *NPR.* https://www.npr.org/sections/thetwo-way/2010/06/could_america_handle_an_angry.html

James, S.A. (1994) "John Henryism and the Health of African-Americans." *Culture, Medicine, and Psychiatry*, 18(2): 163–182.

Johnk, Z. (2017) "National Anthem Protests by Black History Have a Long History." *The New York Times.* https://www.nytimes.com/2017/09/25/sports/national-anthem-protests-black-athletes.html?auth=login-google1tap&login=google1tap

Johnson, T.R. (2014) "Recall that Ice Cream Truck Song? We Have Unpleasant News For You." *NPR.* https://www.npr.org/sections/codeswitch/2014/05/11/310708342/recall-that-ice-cream-truck-song-we-have-unpleasant-news-for-youThis

Kimble, L. (2017) "Emmett Till's Accuser Recants Part of Her Story – 60 Years After His Beating Death Stoked Civil Rights Movement." *People.* https://people.com/crime/emmett-till-carolyn-bryant-interview/

King, G. (2011) "What Paul Robeson Said." *Smithsonian Magazine.* https://www.smithsonianmag.com/history/what-paul-robeson-said-77742433/

King, S. (2013) " 'The Mack' is Back after 40 Years." *Los Angeles Times.* https://www.latimes.com/entertainment/movies/la-xpm-2013-sep-25-la-et-mn-the-mack-lacma-20130925-story.html

Kornhaber, S. (2016) "Kid Cudi Sparks a Conversation on Depression, Race, and Rap." *The Atlantic.* https://www.theatlantic.com/entertainment/archive/2016/10/kid-cudi-depression-rehab-yougoodman-rap-mental-health/502973/

Lamarre, C., Mitchell, G., Murphy, K., Saponara, M., Thomas, D., Elbert, M., Dlep, E., Ketchum III, W.E., Mamo, H., and Rouhani, N. (2023) "50 Greatest Rappers of All Time." *Billboard.* https://www.billboard.com/lists/best-rappers-all-time/50-rick-ross/

Lamparski, R. (1982) *Whatever Became of ___? Eight Series: The Best (Updated) and Newest of the Famous Lamparski Profiles of Personalities of Yesteryear.* Crown Publishers. https://archive.org/details/whateverbecameof00001amp/mode/2up

Lemons, J.S. (1977) "Black Stereotypes as Reflected in Popular Culture, 1880–1920." *American Quarterly*, 29(1): 102–116. https://doi.org/10.2307/2712263

Lett, E., Asabor, E.N., Corbin, T., and Boatright, D. (2021) "Racial Inequity in Fatal US Police Shootings, 2015–2020." *Journal of Epidemiology and Community Health*, 75: 394–397.

Litsky, F. (2010) "Wayne Collett, Track Medalist Barred Because of a Protest, Dies at 60." *The New York Times.* https://nytimes.com/2010/03/18/18collett.html

M4BL (2021) "The Ongoing Persecution of Black Movement by the U.S. Government." https://m4bl.org/struggle-for-power/

Martin, M. (2008) "Why African-Americans Loathe 'Uncle Tom'." *NPR.* https://www.npr.org/templates/story/story.php?storyId=93059468

Miller, C. (1998) "The Representation of the Black Male in Film." *Journal of African American Men*, 3(3): 19–30. http://www.jstor.org/stable/41819338

Miller, J.R. (2019) "Deputy Tried to Arrest Black Mistaking Him for Fugitive." *New York Post.* https://nypost.com/2019/05/16/deputy-tried-to-arrest-black-man-after-mistaking-him-for-fugitive-video/

Miller, K. (2016). "Kid Cudi Checked Into A Mental Health Facility Because of Depression." Self.com. https://www.self.com/story/kid-cudi-ashamed-depressed-rehab#:~:text=Kid%20Cudi%20is%20opening%20up%20about%20his%20struggle,at%20peace%2C%E2%80%9D%20he%20wrote%20in%20the%20candid%20post

Morris, W. (2008) "Monkey Business: So is that Vogue Cover Racist or Not?" *Slate.* https://slate.com/culture/2008/03/so-is-that-vogue-cover-racist-or-not.html

Novak, S. (2023) "Half of the 250 Kids Expelled from Preschool Each Day are Black Boys." *Scientific America.* https://www.scientificamerican.com/article/half-of-the-250-kids-expelled-from-preschool-each-day-are-black-boys/

Pilkington, E. (2009) "Harvard Scholar Henry Louis Gates Outraged at His Home." *The Guardian.* https://www.theguardian.com/world/2009/jul/22/henry-louis-gates-arrested-at-home

Raham, K. (2021) "Full List of Black People Killed by Police in 2021." *Newsweek.* https://www.newsweek.com/black-people-killed-police-2021-1661633

Renshaw, D. (2013). "Snoop Dogg claims he briefly operated as an actual pimp." *NME.* https://nme.com/news/music/snoop-dogg-72-1262899

Strong, A. (2018) "The Shocking 'Slave Bible': Here Are the Parts That Were Deleted to Manipulate Slaves." *CBN.* https://www2.cbn.com/news/us/shocking-slave-bible-here-are-parts-were-deleted-manipulate-slaves

Sullivan, E. (2018) "Laura Ingraham Told LeBron James to Shut Up and Dribble: He went to the Hoop." *NPR*. https://www.npr.org/sections/the two-way/2018/02/19/587097707/laura-ingraham-told-lebron-james-to-shutup-and-dribble-he-went-to-the-hoop

Traditional Tune Archive (2023) "Turkeys in the Straw." https://tunearch. org/wiki/Annotation:Turkey_in_the_Straw

U.S. Sentencing Commission (2017) "Demographic Differences in Sentencing: An Update to the 2012 Booker Report." https://www.ussc.gov/ sites/default/files/pdf/research-and-publications/research-publications/ 2017/20171114_Demographics.pdf

Vega, T. (2016) "For Affluent Blacks, Wealth Doesn't Stop Racial Profiling." *CNN*. https://money.cnn.com/2016/07/14/news/economy/wealthy-blacks-racial-profiling/index.html

Ward, G.C. (2004) "Unforgivable Blackness: The Rise and Fall of Jack Johnson." *PBS*. https://www.pbs.org/kenburns/unforgivable-blackness

White, D.G, Bay, M., and Martin Jr., W.E. (2020) *Freedom on My Mind: A History of African Americans with Documents*. St. Martin's Press.

White, S. and White, G. (1998) *Stylin': African-American Expressive Culture, from Its Beginnings to the Zoot Suit*. Cornell University Press. http://www. jstor.org/stable/10.7591/j.ctv75d14w

Wilcox, W.B., Wang, W., and Mincy, R. (2018) "Black Men Making It in America: the Engines of Economic Success for Black Men in America." *American Enterprise Institute*. https://www.aei.org/wp-content/uploads/ 2018/06/BlackMenMakingItInAmerica-Final_062218.pdf

Yatt, J. (2002) "Wraiths and Race." *The Guardian*. https://www.theguard ian.com/books/2002/dec/02/jrrtolkien.lordoftherings

Zanuck, L.F. and Zanuck, R.D. (Producers), and Beresford, B. (Director). (1989) *Driving Miss Daisy* [Motion picture]. United States: The Zanuck Company.

## Chapter 8

Bradford, S.H. (2012) *Harriet, the Moses of Her People*. A DocSouth book, distributed for the University of North Carolina at Chapel Hill Library.

Brown, J., The James Brown Orchestra and Pee Wee Ellis (1968) "Say It Loud: I'm Black and I'm Proud." *Say it Loud: I'm Black and I'm Proud*. Produced by James Brown. Lyrics at: https://genius.com/James-brown-say-it-loud-im-black-and-im-proud-lyrics

Burke, M. (2024) "In History: Nina Simone on how racial injustice fuelled her songs". BBC. https://www.bbc.com/culture/article/20240215-in-history-nina-simone-how-racial-injustice-fuelled-her-songs

Cartwright, S.A. (1851) "Diseases and Peculiarities of the Negro Race." *De Bow's Review, Southern and Western States*, vol XI. A.M.S. Press, Inc. https://www.pbs.org/wgbh/aia/part4/4h3106t.html

Hawn, C.M. (2018) "History of Hymns: 'O Freedom' and 'Freedom Is Coming'." https://www.tandfonline.com/doi/pdf/10.1080/00064246.1970.11430682?casa_token=tiqTFUPKmpUAAAAA:hfwX1jzYSIMA0leWHrlMGNtUZZElkAqMEeFGzhVdrK_dnvaPgvDxO6D0hDkHgyYarp6wFbi_BCLG

Hernandez, J.C. (2018) " 'Frost Boy' in China Warms Up the Internet, and Stirs Poverty Debate." *The New York Times*. https://www.nytimes.com/2018/01/13/world/asia/frozen-boy-china-poverty.html

King, M. (1963) "I Have a Dream." https://www.npr.org/2010/01/18/122701268/i-have-a-dream-speech-in-its-entirety

Lee, S. (1989) *Do the Right Thing*. 40 Acres and a Mule Filmworks. Universal Pictures. https://en.wikipedia.org/wiki/Do_the_Right_Thing

Margolick, D. (2000) *Strange Fruit: Billie Holiday, Café Society, and an Early Cry for Civil Rights*. Running Press.

Metcalfe Jr., R.H. (1970) "The Western African Roots of Afro-American Music." *Journal of Black Studies and Research/The Black Scholar*, 1(8): 16–25.

Park, R.E. (1919) "The Conflict and Fusion of Cultures with Special Reference to the Negro." *The Journal of Negro History*. https://www.journals.uchicago.edu/doi/pdf/10.2307/2713533

PBS (2016) "From Drug Dealer to College Graduate: A Second Chance." https://www.pbs.org/wnet/dream-on/2016/08/15/drug-dealer-college-graduate-second-chance/

Shriver, J. and Jones, S. (2015) "Blues Icon B.B. King Dies at 89." *USA Today*. usatoday.com/story/life/music/2015/05/15/bb-king-obit/25381783/

Simone, N. (1964) "Mississippi Goddam." *Nina Simone in Concert*. Produced by Hal Mooney. First performed and recorded at Carnegie Hall. Lyrics at: https://genius.com/Nina-simone-mississippi-goddam-lyrics

Tindley, C.A. (1900) "I'll Overcome Some Day." Tune: "This World is One Great Battlefield." Published in nine hymnals.

Tindley, C.A. [attributed] (1901) "We Shall Overcome." Thought to be lyrically descended from "I'll Overcome Some Day."

Wonder, S. (1996) "Hold on to Your Dreams." *Song Review: A Greatest Hits Collection*. Motown.

Work, J.W. (1915) *Folk Song of the American Negro*. Press of Fisk University.

# Index